Contending for American Nationhood

Contending for American Nationhood

Joseph Story and the Debate Over a Federal Common Law

Benjamin Clark

LEXINGTON BOOKS
Lanham • Boulder • New York • London

Published by Lexington Books
An imprint of The Rowman & Littlefield Publishing Group, Inc.
4501 Forbes Boulevard, Suite 200, Lanham, Maryland 20706
www.rowman.com

86-90 Paul Street, London EC2A 4NE

British Library Cataloguing in Publication Information Available

Library of Congress Cataloging-in-Publication Data

Names: Clark, Benjamin (Writer on Contending for American nationhood), author.
Title: Contending for American nationhood : Joseph Story and the debate over a federal common law / Benjamin Clark.
Description: Lanham : Lexington, 2024. | Includes bibliographical references and index. | Summary: "The irreconcilable claims of Compact Theory and Nationalist Theory underlay countless constitutional debates, including recognition of a federal common law. The push for federal common law jurisdiction and the assertion that American nationhood preceded the states come together in the thoughts of Supreme Court Justice Joseph Story" — Provided by publisher.
Identifiers: LCCN 2024028519 (print) | LCCN 2024028520 (ebook) | ISBN 9781666965841 (cloth) | ISBN 9781666965858 (epub)
Subjects: LCSH: Story, Joseph, 1779–1845—Social and political views. | Common law—United States—History. | Jurisprudence—United States—History. | United States. Supreme Court.
Classification: LCC KF394 .C53 2024 (print) | LCC KF394 (ebook) | DDC 349.73—dc23/eng/20240722
LC record available at https://lccn.loc.gov/2024028519
LC ebook record available at https://lccn.loc.gov/2024028520

For Caryl

Acknowledgments

This book began as my doctoral dissertation, so first thanks for the final product go to my dissertation director, Dr. Dennis Coyle, whose encouragement of the initial topic and wise advice at various stages along the way proved immensely helpful. Thanks also go to my other committee members, Dr. Claes Ryn and Dr. Steven Schneck, whose insightful questions during my dissertation defense were helpful in turning it into what it is now. Countless friends and grad school peers made the dissertation-writing process and graduate school generally, endurable.

A book manuscript that goes through a few fits and starts before getting published, as this one did, owes a debt of gratitude to even more individuals than one that gets published right away. Particularly, much credit should go to the peer reviewers whose job is often a thankless one. Many thanks go to the anonymous reviewers for Lexington Press, whose corrections and suggestions for further reading on the nature of the common law strengthened what was the weakest part of the manuscript. Thanks also to reviewers at other university presses where earlier iterations of the book were under consideration: Dr. Kate Brown at Western Kentucky University, along with four anonymous reviewers, all of whom offered very helpful critiques that substantially improved the work from what it once was. If I could thank them individually by name, I would.

My editor at Lexington Press, Mr. Joseph Parry, along with his assistants Anna Debiec and Violet Lane-Ruckman have been wonderful to work with, and I would heartily recommend the press to a colleague or peer looking to publish any book manuscript. Writing and publishing a book is never easy from the author's perspective, but they have made it as seamless as possible. Mr. Arun Rajakumar and everyone at Deanta Publishing were very helpful at the production stage.

My students, mostly unknowingly, bore some of the cost of this manuscript in the form of delayed return dates for graded assignments and occasionally being greeted by a puzzled countenance when visiting office hours. Their relevant questions and comments in class have no doubt shaped my understanding of these issues more than I realize. Most of all, they have made a career in academia feel worthwhile during those inevitable seasons along the way when the "life of the mind" loses its luster. For years, this manuscript sat on the shelf while they kept me engaged with these issues and questions.

Finally, my family has been incredibly supportive throughout the repetitive process of researching, writing, editing, and waiting. My mother Barbara Clark and my in-laws Stuart and Cheryl Skelton deserve special mention for believing in this book manuscript long before anyone else did. My children have borne the cost of my prolonged hours in the office more times than I care to recount, and every day has given me a reason to look forward to coming home. Some days classes go better than others; some days the labor of research and writing is slow or tedious or doesn't happen at all. But every day when I walk in the front door I am greeted by joyous acclamation; I confess I don't look forward to losing that as they get older, although I am sure new joys will take its place. They have also given me reason to write another book, so I can have one to dedicate to them.

As always, though, my greatest debt of gratitude—for this book, as in so many other things—goes to the one who daily labors alongside me in the work of raising these "immortal beings" we've been blessed with, who daily gives of herself in acts of selfless love, who reminds me in everything she does of the importance of beauty and hope, and who every day gives me reason to thank Providence for leading her to me. On top of all that, she also painted the cover art. I appreciatively dedicate this book to my loving wife.

Contents

Introduction

The Question of Nationhood

> Four score and seven years ago our fathers brought forth on this continent, a new nation, conceived in Liberty, and dedicated to the proposition that all men are created equal.
>
> —Abraham Lincoln, Gettysburg Address, November 19, 1863

Lincoln's opening words to his most famous speech are today as much a part of American political rhetoric as anything written by the founding generation. Often taken as a definitive statement of what America is and what it aspires to be, it is rivaled, at most, by only a handful of other nearly sacred texts—the opening argument of the Declaration of Independence, the Preamble of the Constitution, and some isolated clauses from the Bill of Rights and the 14th Amendment. Yet with its ubiquity comes the risk of an over-familiarity that hides the provocative nature of Lincoln's core claim. In its own time, by contrast, Lincoln's words carried not so much the ring of Holy Writ as they did a starkly partisan, hotly contested assertion. To claim that the "fathers" of 1776 ("four score and seven years" prior to Lincoln's delivery of these lines in 1863) had created a "new nation" of any sort was to take a side in an 87-year-old debate that had, throughout the lifespan of American independence, been fought and refought, typically along partisan lines.

The tension between two irreconcilable conceptions of the union—Compact Theory and Nationalist Theory—forms a consistent backdrop throughout antebellum American political thought. Although almost forgotten today, this debate lay just under the surface of many of the political and constitutional conflicts of the early republic. The attention paid to it by the leading political and legal figures of this period signifies it as one of the most important debates of the era, perhaps rivaled only by the problem of slavery for its foundational connection to virtually all of the issues of the day. Consequently, this forgotten debate over the nature of the American union is one of the most indispensable tools for getting at the knot of many of antebellum America's most pressing political and legal questions.

In the interest of clarity, it may be worth pausing to examine what, precisely, was being disputed. This book uses the term nationhood to encapsulate the debate; however, nationhood is an abstract concept, difficult to define and admitting of many possible interpretations. In the context of the debate over the nature of the American Union, what lay at the core of the debate was a disagreement over the chronology of the American founding: whether the states existed as distinct political communities before or after the national political community was formed. Relatedly, the participants in this debate differed on the question of where ultimate sovereignty in the American federal system lay: whether with the separate people of each state or with the American people as an aggregated national whole. The answers to these two questions were closely related, for whichever political community was formed later would then logically be the creature of the preexisting community which had formed it, and thus would have been answerable to it; meanwhile, the older political community would necessarily hold ultimate power and sovereignty under the Constitution, enjoying the right to hold their delegated agents accountable, and would be presumed to have the final right of constitutional interpretation in the case of a disagreement. The debate was thus far from academic, as it held significance for practical political questions, such as the relative power of the state and federal governments. By 1863, both sides of this debate over American nationhood could claim their share of intellectual and political luminaries, both had worked out a variety of highly developed arguments—philosophical and constitutional, as well as historical—to justify their position, and both had enough of a discernible political tradition that both could claim they were the true carriers of the American spirit.

On one side of this debate, with Lincoln, stood the proponents of American nationhood, who claimed that America was every bit the sovereign, unified nation-state that England or France was, and this conviction led them to embrace a variety of interrelated constitutional positions. These nationalist thinkers were led by the internal logic of their position to say that as a full-fledged nation the federal government was entitled to certain "inherent powers" common to all nations, whether or not those powers had been specifically enumerated in the Constitution. Crucially, they also held that the "American people," taken collectively, were sovereign, omnipotent, and—in a term that would gain ground shortly after Lincoln's time—indivisible. This understanding of the union can be traced back to the very beginning of American independence, but only received a full articulation and defense over time, eventually receiving its most definitive expression in Supreme Court Justice Joseph Story's comprehensive *Commentaries on the Constitution*. The

Nationalist Theory of the Union, as it has come to be known, would later be summarized by Lincoln's assertion that "The Union is older than any of the States, and, in fact, it created them as States."[1] Although Story was neither the first nor the last to assert the core premise of the Nationalist Theory—that the union was the direct creation of a national American people—his role in systematizing the theory and further developing a reading of American history to bolster it has long led to his recognition as a central figure in the development of American nationalist thought.

On the other side of the debate stood the opponents of American nationhood who argued that the United States of America was largely unique among the world powers it had begun to rival in influence, and that the union of American states was best conceived not as a single conglomerated nation but as a voluntary confederation of distinct political units, each retaining its full sovereignty. At most, it could be considered what Thomas Jefferson deemed "a nation, but for special purposes only,"[2] those purposes being chiefly concerned with matters between separate states and with foreign powers. Directly counter to the Nationalist Theory's claims of a conglomerated national American people, the opponents of American nationhood held that it was the people of each separate state who had created the American union: first by giving their delegates in the Continental Congress the authority to issue a joint declaration of independence, next through ratifying the Articles of Confederation through their delegates in the Continental Congress, then by drafting the Constitution through their delegates to the Constitutional Convention, and lastly by voting to ratify the Constitution through separate conventions within their distinct states. It was thus the people of each separate state who retained ultimate sovereignty and, indeed, every power that they had not expressly given away to the federal government. This theory of autonomous states creating the federal government and delegating a select portion of their powers to it has been dubbed the Compact Theory of the Union by future generations and would eventually find its most complete articulation in the constitutional writings of John C. Calhoun, although just as with the Nationalist Theory, the core claims of this view can be traced back to the earliest days of American independence.

It may be worth pointing out that the "compact" that these theorists saw as forming the union was not philosophically connected to the "social contract" theory that dominated much of early modern political theory. "Social contract" thought suggested that the origins of political society lay in the voluntary choice of atomistic individuals in a pre-political "state of nature"; the Compact Theory of the Union, on the other hand, suggested that the American Union was a voluntary confederation signed onto not by unsocialized individuals, but by pre-existing political communities. Adherence to these two theories was not necessarily mutually exclusive: many adherents of the Compact Theory, such as Jefferson, did express belief in a foundational social contract—as most leading political figures of his generation probably did also—but others, such as Calhoun, explicitly shunned modern notions of a voluntary, individual choice underlying society in favor of the Aristotelian view that all political communities grew organically out of preexisting social bonds.[3] What held such philosophically different thinkers together in the same constitutional theory was that they both viewed the union as a compact or agreement between the sovereign people of each state, even if they disagreed on how those original states had come into being.

Both sides of this debate felt assured that they were the true defenders of the spirit of the American Revolution, and moreover, that their opponents were radical innovators who were actively rewriting the history of the founding in order to thrust their own partisan agenda upon the Constitution. In truth, the historical record of the founding was much more ambiguous than either side acknowledged. For instance, both sides claimed that the Declaration of Independence supported their unique claims in its climactic declaration, "That these united Colonies are, and of Right ought to be Free and Independent States,"[4] although they did so by emphasizing different portions of the sentence. The advocates of American nationhood emphasized that the signatories spoke as "the Representatives of the united States of America" and that they claimed independence only for "these united Colonies." The opponents of American nationhood, on the other hand, could very easily point out that the Declaration included no announcement that it was creating a single nation and, in fact, seemed to say the direct opposite by declaring the former colonies to be "Free and Independent States." Moreover, the history surrounding the passage of the Declaration seemed to indicate that the delegates to the Second Continental Congress voted more as representatives of their own states instead of as representatives of a single national entity—with, for instance, Richard Henry Lee's resolution for independence being introduced at the instruction of the Virginia Convention[5] and delegates from New York abstaining from voting on the Declaration in the absence of direct authorization from their colonial legislature[6]—while the general importance that the delegates apparently placed on acting in unison still left sufficient room for Nationalist theorists to hold to their own interpretation.

Interestingly, this divergence of opinion over what exactly the Declaration of Independence had accomplished—whether it had created a "new nation" instantaneously, as the adherents of the Nationalist Theory claimed, or had merely secured the separate independences of thirteen distinct political communities—appears to date back all the way to the Declaration's passage. The recorded debates over the proposed Articles of Confederation in late July and early August 1776 seem to indicate that some delegates believed they were representing a new American nation, while others that they were representing only their own distinct state.[7] In arguing for equal representation for all states in the new Confederation government, Roger Sherman of Connecticut asserted that "We [delegates of the Continental Congress] are representatives of States, not individuals" before Benjamin Rush rejoined that "I would not have it understood that I am pleading the cause of Pennsylvania; when I entered that door, I considered myself a citizen of America."[8] These two distinct strands of American political thought thus both trace their origins back to the very starting point of the American Union, and the debate that could not be solved on the floor of the Pennsylvania State House was carried over onto the floor of the United States Capitol and eventually onto the battlefields of the Civil War.

Along the way, the debate over American nationhood was sometimes carried on openly, with historians, jurists, and politicians consciously taking sides either for or against American nationhood in speeches from the floor, philosophical discourses, public orations, and history textbooks. Other times, the question of American nationhood was waged indirectly, through a series of intimately connected proxy debates, ranging from the issues of state nullification and secession to questions of the interpretation of the "General Welfare" or "Necessary and Proper" clauses to questions of the Supreme Court's appellate power over state court decisions to assertions of federal "implied powers." In each of these debates, the arguments of some or all participants demonstrated a sensitivity to the importance of the nationhood question. Indeed, virtually every question of American constitutional interpretation in this period can be seen as either directly or indirectly dealing with the question of the fundamental nature of the union: was the United States of America a mere voluntary confederation of sovereign political communities or did it have its own claim to sovereignty, bestowed on it directly by the "American people"?

To fully illustrate the manifold ways in which each of these early constitutional debates was—and is—at its core a dispute on the underlying question of American nationhood would require many volumes. However, it is hoped that by emphasizing the centrality of this question to one particularly contentious debate from the early years of the republic, the far-reaching ramifications of the two competing positions will be made clear enough to draw analogies to other constitutional debates, including many modern ones. Consequently, this book focuses on the debate surrounding the assertion of a federal common law jurisdiction for federal courts, focusing particular attention on one of the doctrine's most forceful and effective advocates: Supreme Court Justice Joseph Story. It is hoped that this book will thus draw appropriate attention to the fundamental question of American nationhood by illustrating the indispensable connection between Story's career-long push in a long string of legal decisions seeking to recognize a federally adopted common law distinct from the common law as it was practiced in the state judiciaries and the Nationalist Theory of American nationhood that he advanced through his historical narrative.

Ultimately, the connection of the federal common law debate to the much larger debate on American nationhood is much deeper than their intersection in Story's thought: virtually all arguments for a common law jurisdiction for the federal courts necessarily assumed the starting premise of the Nationalist Theory, and most critics of the federal common law doctrine made their case against it by explicitly relying on their Compact Theory presumptions of the nature of the union. This book will thus examine not only Story's argument for recognizing a federal common law but also the Jeffersonian Republican arguments against the existence of a federal common law, as opposed to the common law tradition as it had been adopted and then adapted in each state. In particular, it will be argued that opposition to the federal common law doctrine by Jefferson, James Madison, St. George Tucker, and other members of the Republican Party was premised on their acceptance of the Compact Theory.[9]

Joseph Story's attempts to recognize a federal common law were, in a certain sense, unsuccessful: in 1938, the Supreme Court overturned the federal common law established by Joseph Story in *Swift v. Tyson* (1842). From this fact, it is not to be presumed that the Compact theorists arguing against the doctrine eventually won their overarching political and constitutional struggle against Story and the Nationalists, at least not in the grand scheme of American political development. On the whole, subsequent political developments have proved comparatively favorable to Story's expansive view of federal power, while moving American constitutional practice steadily further from the more constrained views of Jefferson and Tucker. To a large degree, the steady growth in federal power relative to the states over time can be tracked by examining the popular and legal acceptance of the idea of American nationhood: as Story's historical narrative written to bolster the Nationalist Theory has gained popular acceptance, so has the federal government gained more of the full power of a modern nation-state that Story and other early proponents of American nationalism sought to secure.

This book, nevertheless, attempts to restore to a place of prominence a seemingly arcane debate that might otherwise be confined to the legal archives: for the real issue at stake in the debate over a federal common law is one that continues to be a factor in constitutional interpretation in the twenty-first century, albeit without the same level of intensity as two centuries ago and possibly even without the recognition by many of its modern participants of what is truly being argued. By focusing on the underlying assumptions of participants on both sides of this debate, it is hoped that this book will thus demonstrate the indispensable connection between the federal common law debate and the debate over American nationhood. Moreover, it is hoped that the far-reaching ramifications of the two competing positions will be made clear enough to draw analogies to other constitutional debates, including many modern ones. Just as the original ambiguity over the nature of the union led to rival incompatible frameworks of constitutional interpretation in Story's day, the continued ambiguity surrounding these same questions—Who, ultimately, is sovereign under the Constitution? What level of government should have the final say? How loosely should the Constitution be interpreted and how much are we to weigh the broad language of the Preamble against the specific power grants of Articles I through III?—underscores some of the most interminable constitutional debates in contemporary America. Perhaps, in examining what caused the participants in the federal common law debate to speak past, and not to, each other we shall examine what causes participants in contemporary constitutional debates to do much the same thing.

As the book focuses on the intersection of constitutional theory with judicial politics, appropriate attention will be given to judicial opinions and the outcomes of legal cases. Despite some overlap in material, however, this examination of case history—and the attention to judicial precedent that must necessarily attend it—does not play the same role that it would for students and practitioners of the law, both of whom study the case record in order to ascertain the current state of the law and then dutifully apply it to additional cases by analogy from old cases to new. Rather, as the focus of this book is on the relationship of legal opinions to the constitutional theories that they presuppose, cases will be examined with an eye toward uncovering their underlying presumptions about the nature of the Constitution and of the union. Overall, this treatment of legal decisions and doctrines as expressions of political and constitutional theory can also provide unique insights, inasmuch as the process of applying the law to individual cases closely resembles the process of applying the general precepts of political philosophy to the practical, concrete circumstances of political reality. Judicial opinions, like the legal doctrines they embody, are thus an under-recognized resource in the study of political thought, and this book is written as an attempt to unpack the unavoidable presumptions about the nature of the union that directly or indirectly, knowingly or unknowingly, guide jurists in writing decisions.

Before looking at Story, however, it is first necessary to examine the origins of the federal common law debate. Story joined the Supreme Court at a time when the most heated argument over the federal common law doctrine had already taken place; Story himself was thus trying to resurrect what many of his contemporaries considered to be a settled question that they were eager to move on from. Thus, to understand Story's push to recognize a federal common law, it is important to first look at where the debate stood when Story first joined the Supreme Court. Chapter 1 will provide the necessary historical setting for the examination of the federal common law question, including a detailed examination of the debate over the asserted jurisdiction of the federal courts over common law crimes, leading up to Joseph Story's appointment to the Supreme Court in 1811. Chapter 2 will proceed by tracking Justice Story's career-long drive to recognize a federal common law, paying particular attention to his understanding of how and when this federal common law came to be adopted by the United States and to his arguments in two key legal decisions: his failed attempt to establish jurisdiction for the federal courts over common law crimes in *United States v. Coolidge* and his successful recognition of a federal common law in a certain category of civil cases in *Swift v. Tyson.* Chapter 3 will examine the Nationalist Theory, tracing the doctrine of American nationhood through its earliest intimations through Story's defense of the doctrine in his *Commentaries on the Constitution.* Chapter 4 will address the Republican opponents of an asserted common law jurisdiction for the federal courts, focusing on what they perceived as the doctrine's incompatibility with the nature of the union. Chapter 5 will demonstrate the indispensability of the Nationalist Theory in maintaining any argument for a federal common law and the irreconcilability of any asserted federal common law with the Compact Theory. Chapter 6 will examine the "Swift Doctrine" and the role that the recognition of a limited federal common law had on the functions of the Supreme Court. Particular attention will be paid to why the creation of a federal body of common law jurisprudence failed to have the significant impact that both Story and his opponents had expected it would and to how different categories of critics all coalesced around their shared opposition to Story's precedent in Swift. The conclusion will address the enduring impact of the debate over American nationhood, looking in particular at the relevance of this dispute for analyzing current constitutional debates.

THE COMMON LAW AT THE FOUNDING

As a final note of introduction, it may be worthwhile to give some preliminary comments on the common law as it was understood at the time of the American founding in order to set the stage for the discussion of a federal common law jurisdiction in the subsequent chapters. Such an introduction is particularly necessary in the case of the common law, given that a substantial shift has taken place in how the common law is conceived. Standing between contemporary readers and the members of the founding generation is the figure of Oliver Wendell Holmes Jr., whose famous lectures entitled "The Common Law" redefined the term for subsequent generations in a way that obscures certain assumptions about the common law in the late eighteenth and early nineteenth centuries that the participants on both sides of the federal common law debate would have shared. For starters, the contemporary way of discussing common law as "judge-made law" must be understood as a modern development, as traditional English notions of the common law held it to be "found, not made"[10] by judges, with the task of the common law judge thought of as articulating and discovering existing law, rather than "making" or creating the common law themselves.[11]

Robert Lowry Clinton, in his book *God and Man in the Law: The Foundations of Anglo-American Constitutionalism,* describes the intimate relationship of the common law (as it was understood at this time) to classical and medieval conceptions of a universal "natural law," with the common law conceived of as a "blend of nature, custom, and reason."[12] While the modern reader may see in such a description an invitation for a judge to use their own individual reason to decide cases, Clinton emphasizes that common law "reason," at least at this time, was understood not in the sense used by modern "enlightenment rationalism," but in a much older tradition: "the reason of the common law is classical, taking its cues from Aristotle and Aquinas, not from Hobbes and Voltaire."[13] Thus, Clinton, drawing on James Stoner's *Common Law and Liberal Theory*, describes the "reason of the common law" as tied to classical and medieval "normative" conceptions of the common law[14]—a view of the common law "firmly rooted in the legal thought of the medieval era in which English common law was born"[15]—and thus not subject to invention by a legislator or judge. This historically grounded common law reasoning thus helped to ground American constitutionalism in the older tradition by "tempering the abstract reason of the Founders in accord with their experience of a living legal tradition."[16] The common law itself was thus conceived of as having an independent, objective existence outside of the judge, and the judge's job was thus to uncover and "declare" the principles of this law. As one recent jurist put it in attempting to explain the traditional view of the common law, "judges did not make law, but declared it"[17]—a view that has come to be known as the "declaratory theory."

This traditional view was challenged by two waves of criticism that became dominant in elite law schools in the late nineteenth and early twentieth centuries: legal positivism, and then later American Legal Realism. Legal positivism can be thought of as a rejection of the concept of natural law; whereas the older natural law tradition (as laid out by Cicero, Thomas Aquinas, and Blackstone, among many others) held that law could not violate certain overriding moral or religious standards without then ceasing to be law, legal positivism instead held that law was whatever was declared by the sovereign, disregarding its relationship to such a higher standard. As the British legal philosopher John Austin put the central premise of legal positivism: "the *existence* of a law is one thing: its *merits* or *demerits* are another thing.

Whether a law *be*, is one inquiry: whether it *ought* to be, or whether it agree with a given or assumed test, is another and a distinct inquiry."[18] Austin did not directly dispute that the moral question—what the law ought to be—could or should be answered; what he disputed was that a law's moral standing had a direct relevance to its standing as law.[19] For Austin, who endeavored to turn the study of law into an empirical "science of jurisprudence," the study of positive laws—what he deemed "laws strictly so called"—was to be carried out "without regard to their goodness or badness."[20] He also distinguished such "laws properly so called" from other so-called laws, which only earned the name analogically or metaphorically by sharing some characteristics of proper laws, but missing a crucial one: "Laws proper or properly so called," Austin informs his readers, "are commands."[21] Elsewhere in the work, he describes positive laws as necessarily being made by "the direct or circuitous command of a monarch or sovereign number in the character of political superior . . . to a person or persons in a state of subjection to its author."[22] This definition of the law—in its classic formulation, Austin's theory views law as the command of the sovereign, backed by sanction—comes to be known as the "command theory" or the "imperative theory" of the law and stands in sharp contrast to the "declaratory theory" of Blackstone and the American framers, which viewed law—and especially the common law—as inherently tied to a moral and religious framework.

To be sure, the positivist conception of law did not take shape overnight: Austin and others were drawing on earlier conceptions of law as stemming from "the command of the sovereign," and pushing back on the natural law tradition, which held that the content of law stemmed from a universal source and that the legislator (or the judge, in the case of the common law) was therefore not at liberty to declare the law to be whatever they wished. Clinton portrays the positivist impulse as expressed in ancient times—in the views voiced by Thrasymachus and Callicles and rhetorically defeated by Socrates in Plato's *Republic* and *Gorgias*, respectively—but suppressed in the Western philosophical tradition until gaining dominance in the modern world with Machiavelli and Thomas Hobbes.[23] Hobbes, in particular, comes indeed very close to Austin's theory of law. Law, to Hobbes as to Austin, was simply a command and in particular "a Command . . . of him, whose Command is addressed to one formerly obliged to obey him."[24] Comparisons can easily be made from Hobbes' seventeenth--century conception of law and the "command theory" as laid out by Austin nearly two centuries later. Austin drew upon Hobbes' theory, as well as that of his contemporary Jeremy Bentham, in developing a notion of law as something made, not found.

If the legal positivist critique of natural law theory can be seen as undermining the traditional notion of the common law as something "found, not made," then the same could also be said of the critique of American Legal

Realism against the tradition they called "Legal Formalism." Just as the traditional "declaratory theory" held that common law judges did not make law but rather announced preexisting legal principles, so Legal Formalism presented the task of the judge as applying general legal (as opposed to policy-driven or outcome-driven) rules to particular cases in order to determine the correct outcome of a case,[25] a description that easily accords with traditional common law notions of the judge merely discovering and announcing the rule as it existed, as discussed above. Against the "mechanical jurisprudence" described by Formalism, the Legal Realists held that the process of the judge deciding cases was quite different: law was "indeterminate" and thus general legal principles did not require a judge to rule one specific way, and thus the general legal rules could not, by themselves, explain the outcomes of cases.[26] At most, the legal rules that judges pointed to were "*post hoc* rationalizations for decisions reached on the basis of non-legal considerations," such as the facts of the particular case and the judge's own sense of fairness.[27]

Perhaps the most famous expression of this view comes from Oliver Wendell Holmes' 1897 essay "The Path of Law."[28] There, Holmes decried the "fallacy" and the "danger" that came from the Formalist view that there existed general legal principles guiding the judge that "can be worked out like mathematics from some general axioms of conduct" so that disagreement among judges "meant simply that one side or the other were not doing their sums right, and, if they would take more trouble, agreement inevitably would come."[29] In dismissing this view, Holmes thus saw different judges arriving at different outcomes as arising from something more than their mechanically doing their sums, and some of them doing so in a "right" way (and thus coming to the "right" outcomes) and others doing so in a haphazard way (and thus coming to the "wrong" outcomes). Instead of such logical Formalism, Holmes saw differing legal outcomes as resulting from disagreements over policy outcomes: judges based their decisions not upon such "general axioms" of law, but upon "a judgment as to the relative worth and importance of competing legislative grounds," upon "some belief as to the practice of the community or of a class, or because of some opinion as to policy"[30]—in short, upon the judge's own political preferences. The problem, according to Holmes, was that since judges were blind to the fact that they were pursuing some legislative goals and avoiding others, valuing some political goods as higher than others, that the judge's judgment on these questions was frequently "inarticulate and unconscious";[31] the problem was not that the judge was allowing too much of their own preferences for policy outcomes to bleed into their judicial decision-making, the problem was that they were not conscious that this is what they were doing, and instead believed that they were merely applying neutral legal principles. Instead of the "inarticulate and unconscious" shaping of society through judicial decision-making, Holmes proposed that judges should recognize their social duty and decide cases accordingly:

> I think that the judges themselves have failed adequately to recognize their duty of weighing considerations of social advantage. The duty is inevitable, and the result of the often proclaimed judicial aversion to deal with such considerations is simply to leave the very ground and foundation of judges inarticulate, and often unconscious . . . .[32]

Here in Holmes, we finally see the culmination of the legal positivist turn. Embedded in the "command theory" of Hobbes, Bentham, and Austin was the notion that the sovereign had the power to declare whatever they wanted to be the law, and that their decision was not bound by earlier legal decisions, nor by any universal natural or divine law above them. Holmes takes this realization a step further to hold that judicial decision-making is nothing more than the expression of the judge's social and political preferences; the common law thus becomes, under the influence of Holmes, a system of "judge-made law," as it is often referred to today.

Of course, there are certain aspects of the older conception of law as something "found, not made" that are perhaps not completely foreign today and thus may appear at least somewhat familiar to modern readers. For instance, the ideal of the constrained judge merely applying a law that has its own content independent of the judge's personal preferencesthat view, or at least an echo of it, may still find expression in the theories of textualism and originalism (though critics of these schools make the Legal Realist argument that textualists and originalists end up pursuing their own preferences anyways), as well as in ideals of "judicial restraint" and judicial deference to elected branches of government. But such notions are, at a minimum, in competition with more "judicial activist" models that emphasize with Holmes the social duty of judges to self-consciously shape society in positive ways. And there are likely limits to how much modern originalists and self-identified judicial restraintists are willing to push back on this fundamental transformation; Stoner, for instance, points out that Antonin Scalia appears to view it as "either impossible or undesirable to revive the traditional understanding of common law as something discovered, not invented."[33] Like many fundamental transformations, the revolution wrought by the legal positivists has been so sweeping that it is hard even for its critics to see their way back to the original understanding.

Now, these later shifts in legal theory are, in a sense, mostly beyond the scope of the present study; the purpose of the foregoing overview was to demonstrate some of the differences between the ways law—and particularly the common law—was viewed in the early nineteenth century and today, and the difficulties that accompany the modern reader attempting to enter into debates between two sides which shared certain assumptions that the modern reader lacks. This transformation is not completely separate from the later phases of the debate over a federal common law, and this shift caused by the advent of legal positivism and American legal realism will be discussed again in chapter 6, in examining the role that these debates over the nature of law had in the overturning of Story's establishment of a federal common law for certain categories of cases in the 1938 case *Erie Railroad Co. v. Tompkins*.

It can generally be said, then, that the "declaratory theory" of law was one shared by participants on both sides of the federal common law debate. This is not to say that there was nobody in this period who held the view that the common law was "judge-made," but merely that such views can be thought of as outliers. Micah Quigley, in a 2022 article detailing the older conception of the common law judge, points to Thomas Hobbes and Jeremy Bentham as holding an early version of the "command theory" of the law, which viewed law as the command of the sovereign.[34] Similarly, James Stoner notes in his book *Common-Law Liberty: Rethinking American Constitutionalism* that the contemporary view of the common law—"that it is 'judge-made law,' devised in cases, extended by precedent, and limited only by the consensus of the bench and bar or by legislative intervention"—was a view that was "not entirely unknown to the Founders, but it was the cynic's perspective, to which no self-respecting lawyer or judge, much less republican citizen, could admit."[35] Against the modern Holmesian view of the judge creating common law however they see fit, members of the founding generation saw the practice of common law adjudication as a much more constrained exercise, in which judges were "bound by past precedents, and the dictates of reason, natural law, and tradition"[36] along with "tradition and custom" or communal consensus;[37] the common law was seen—rightly or wrongly—as having an independent existence that the judge was tasked with declaring.

A second feature of the common law is also worth touching on at the outset is that there was widespread agreement among participants on both sides of this debate that the common law not only had been the basis of the legal system in each of the colonies; but moreover after the Revolution, there appears to have been very little desire to effect a widespread overhaul of the common law as it existed in the state. There was, in other words, widespread agreement among both Federalist proponents of the federal common law and Republican critics of the federal common law that the common law was the basis of the legal system in each state; the disagreement came with the question of how the ratification of the federal Constitution changed—or, perhaps, had the potential to change—the common law as it existed in each state. A necessary consequence of this point—and one that is argued at length in chapter 4—is that Republican opposition to the federal common law arose not out of antipathy that the Republicans received from common law inheritance, but out of a desire to protect it in its current form, as it had been modified and adapted in each separate state.

The common law provided the backdrop for all American legal culture and for the Constitution itself. But lawyers and jurists on both sides of the federal common law debate were careful to point out that the common law as it was practiced in America was not exactly the same as the common law of England—or, at least, not the common law of England in its entirety. Tied as the common law was to considerations of local custom, the long-standing recognition within each of the colonies was that the colonists brought over only those portions of the common law as fit their new circumstances; this transplanted common law, moreover, was subject—just as in England—to modification or repeal by the legislative body. As Story would describe it, the common law of the American states was

> that portion of the common law of England, (as modified and ameliorated by English statutes,) which was in force at the time of the emigration of our ancestors, and was applicable to the situation of the colony, and has since been recognized and acted upon, during the successive progresses of our Colonial, Provincial, and State Governments, with this additional qualification, that it has not been altered, repealed, or modified by any of our subsequent legislation now in force.[38]

That process of determining which portions of the common law were applicable and which were not led to variations in how the common law was practiced in each state. By the time of the Revolution, the common law indeed was not exactly the same in any two colonies, and in none of them was it practiced exactly as it was in England; and when, after the Revolution, the states came to pass statutory or constitutional measures formalizing the adoption of such parts of the common law of England as were then in practice, this adoption included clear indications that they adopted the common law as it had been adapted and modified and as it had grown in each particular state.[39]

And yet, even if not the exact same as the common law of England in every respect, it would be a mistake to not think of the American colonists as sharing in a single tradition, a single body of law—virtually all American lawyers were educated on Sir Edward Coke's *Institutes of the Lawes of England* and William Blackstone's *Commentaries on the Laws of England*. It is worth noting, though, that the American lawyers did not thereby accept every part of Coke or Blackstone as applicable to their situation—Blackstone's views on parliamentary sovereignty, for instance, were roundly rejected by the American colonists.[40] And as much as some aspects of the common law—such as its attentiveness to differences in local custom and its being subject to modification by the colonial and state legislatures—led naturally to divergences in the common law practices between the states, still, there was another sense in which certain aspects of the traditional understanding of the common law—for instance, its compatibility with the universal natural law and its being common or shared throughout the several states and the British realm—pointed to its transcending political boundaries. Americans already shared a common legal inheritance, and it was only natural that when the Constitution—and particularly the federal Bill of Rights—was ratified, all of the various terms and concepts taken from that shared common law tradition would be understood with reference to that of shared tradition.[41] The big question was what effect the Constitution would have on the common law as it then existed at the state level—that was a question that led to one of the most controversial legal and political debates of the early Republic.

NOTES

1. Abraham Lincoln, "Special Session Message to Congress, July 4, 1861." From online *Modern History Sourcebook, Abraham Lincoln (1809–1865)*, ed. Paul Halsall. Available through Fordham University, http://sourcebooks.fordham.edu/mod/1861lincoln-special.asp.

2. Thomas Jefferson to Edmund Randolph, August 18, 1799, in *Founders Online*, National Archives, http://founders.archives.gov/documents/Jefferson/01-31-02–0142.

3. Aristotle, *The Politics*, trans. T.A. Sinclair (London: Penguin Books, 1992), 59.

4. Thomas Jefferson, *Declaration of Independence* (1776).

5. Pauline Maier, *American Scripture: Making the Declaration of Independence* (New York: Vintage Books, 1997), 41.

6. Ibid., 45.

7. See the interchange between John Witherspoon of New Jersey and Benjamin Franklin, Benjamin Rush, John Adams, and James Wilson in Jefferson's notes on the debates in the Continental Congress on August 1, 1776. *Journals of the Continental Congress, 1774–1789*, ed. Worthington C. Ford et al. (Washington, DC: Government Printing Office, 1904–1937), 6:1102–1106. John Adams" notes on the exchange on pp. 1081–1082 are also enlightening on this point.

8. John Adams" notes of debates, *Journals of the Continental Congress*, 6:1081.

9. For Madison in particular, no attempt is made in this book to square his apparent compatibility with the Compact Theory in the episode focused on here—the argument he levels against the federal common law doctrine in his *Report of 1800*—with his apparent attempts to distance himself from that same theory at other points in his career. For purposes of an examination of the federal common law debate and the constitutional and historical arguments on both sides, Madison may here safely be treated as an adherent to the basic premise of the Compact Theory on the basis of his

Report, even if a full examination of the wider scope of his constitutional writings makes such a generalization problematic, to say the least.

10. Micah S. Quigley, "Article III Lawmaking." *George Mason Law Review* 30, issue 1 (April, 2022), 279–348, 287.

11. It is worth noting in passing that some have argued that the notion of the judge as a law "maker" did gain some acceptance in the years following the ratification of the Constitution, including in the period discussed here. While there is disagreement on the timing of that shift, it is possible that some of the participants in the federal common law debate had come to accept the conception of common law as something "made" by judges, not merely discovered by them. At most, however, this means that the participants in the debate may have held a variety of views on the role of the common law judge, as the traditional view seems to have at least continued to be the dominant view in America throughout the time period discussed here. For further discussion, see Quigley, 296–299.

12. Robert Lowry Clinton, *God and Man in the Law: The Foundations of Anglo-American Constitutionalism* (Lawrence: University Press of Kansas, 1997), 102.

13. Ibid., 99.

14. Ibid., 101.

15. Ibid., 103.

16. Ibid., 101.

17. Diarmuid F. O'Scannlain, "Rediscovering the Common Law." *Notre Dame Law Review* 79, issue 2 (February, 2004), 755–763, 759.

18. John Austin, *The Province of Jurisprudence Determined* (London: John Murray, 1832), 278.

19. Samuel Enoch Stumpf, "Austin's Theory of the Separation of Law and Morals." *Vanderbilt Law Review* 14, issue 1 (December, 1960), 117–149, 117–118.

20. Austin, 132.

21. Ibid., vii.

22. Ibid., 129.

23. Clinton, 145.

24. Thomas Hobbes, *Leviathan*, Ch. XXVI (London: Penguin Classics, 2017), 217.

25. Brian Leiter, "American Legal Realism," Ch. 3 in *The Blackwell Guide to the Philosophy of Law and Legal Theory*, ed. Martin P. Golding and William A. Edmundson (Malden, MA: Blackwell, 2005), 50–66, 50.

26. Ibid., 51.

27. Ibid., 50.

28. Oliver Wendell Holmes, "The Path of the Law." *Harvard Law Review* 10, no. 8 (March, 1897), 457–478.

29. Ibid., 465.

30. Ibid., 466.

31. Ibid.

32. Ibid., 467.

33. James R. Stoner, *Common Law Liberty: Rethinking American Constitutionalism* (Lawrence: University Press of Kansas, 2003), 2–3.

34. Quigley, 291.

35. Stoner, *Common-Law Liberty*, 10–11.
36. O'Scannlain, 757.
37. Ibid., 762.
38. Story, "Codification of the Common Law," in *The Miscellaneous Writings of Joseph Story*, ed. William W. Story (Boston: Charles C. Little & James Brown, 1852), 701. Quoted in Stoner, *Common-Law Liberty*, 14.
39. O'Scannlain, 757.
40. Stoner, *Common-Law Liberty*, 13.
41. James R. Stoner, *Common Law and Liberal Theory* (Lawrence: University Press of Kansas, 1992), 7

Chapter 1

Origins of the Debate

In 1799, a circuit court case out of Hartford, Connecticut, electrified political opposition when Chief Justice of the United States Oliver Ellsworth[1] pronounced a decision against the defendant Isaac Williams.[2] Williams, a Connecticut mariner, had been indicted in the federal courts for having accepted a commission to serve as an officer in the French navy with instructions to commit acts of hostility against Great Britain, thereby violating the Jay Treaty and jeopardizing the fragile American neutrality in the ongoing conflict between Great Britain and France. In his defense, Williams argued that he had renounced his American citizenship and been naturalized, according to the laws of France, as a French citizen, thus effectively expatriating himself and rendering himself no longer subject to indictment by United States courts nor in violation of his birth country's proclamation of neutrality.[3] In his circuit court opinion, Ellsworth rejected this argument, asserting on the contrary that "the common law of this country remains the same as it was before the Revolution" and that, according to that common law, Williams was unable to expatriate himself without the consent of the United States government.[4] None doubted at this time that the common law of England disallowed individuals from renouncing their own citizenship, but the application of that common law principle to a federal court case—on the grounds that it was a part of "the common law of this country"—was much more controversial.

That the common law was the basis of the legal system in every state—as modified by the state legislature—was beyond dispute. Ellsworth's decision, though, rested on a further contention: that in addition to the common law as it was practiced in each state, the federal courts themselves had recourse to a distinct body of common law that federal judges had recourse to in deciding cases. Consequently, Ellsworth's claim of a federal common law had enormous legal and political ramifications that went far beyond the immediate issue of expatriation. If such a common law existed, it would presumably be as much a part of federal law as any statute passed by Congress and thus any rule or precedent included in it became, by that very fact, a matter of federal law open to use and elaboration by federal judges. Since any federal common law was obviously drawn from the common law of England, it could reasonably be expected to encompass the same incredible range of subject matters as that law, and thus could be used to grant the federal courts access to innumerable issues that were outside the original scope of the federal courts' jurisdiction as outlined in the explicit language of Article III. Since in England, the legislative authority of Parliament had historically been understood to extend at least as far as the common law did, a federal common law jurisdiction for the federal courts was bound to have dramatic ramifications for the power of Congress as well. Moreover, it left open the possibility that federal judges presiding over criminal cases might think themselves competent to declare certain acts to be unlawful which, while prohibited by the common law, had not been outlawed by congressional statute.

Ellsworth's opinion in *Williams' Case* thus was hailed by opponents as an attempt by Federalist-appointed jurists to expand the reach of the federal government far beyond its constitutionally prescribed limits. Members of the nascent Republican Party that was forming around Thomas Jefferson echoed this common concern in their responses to the ruling. In October of 1799, Jefferson himself wrote a letter to Charles Pinckney describing the federal common law doctrine as effecting the "compleat [sic] consolidation" of the federal system, in comparison to which all of the previous Federalist invasions of state power were "mere retail stuff."[5] More detailed in his examination of the doctrine was former Attorney General Edmund Randolph, who wrote, but apparently did not publish, a series of reflections illustrating the effect that Ellsworth's common law doctrine would have on federal power, summarizing that "the principle is broad enough to let in the common law as the law of the U.S. in all civil cases. If this be the consequence Congressional power is all but unlimited,"[6] as congressional power would have to be coterminous with the common law in order to amend or correct it when necessary—just as the state legislatures had power to make changes to the growing common law tradition in each of the states. In short, the recognition of a federal common law promised to vastly expand the scope of federal power.

Randolph also raised the thorny question of how this newly discovered federal common law would relate to the common law as it was accepted and practiced in each state. Following its formal adoption, the governments of each state had made such alterations to the common law of England as to leave a unique body of law in each.[7] On the one hand, if Congress did not have the authority to override state variations in the adoption of the common law, how could it be said to be a national body of law at all? On the other hand, if all of the state modifications to the common law were subject to this federally adopted common law, then all of the state alterations were immediately wiped away and the American people were subject to the whole law of England until this federal common law was amended by Congress. This suggestion hinted at another unsettling possibility: what were federal judges to make of those elements of the common law that were archaic, or that dealt with royal and ecclesiastical powers and were obviously inapplicable to the American situation? Randolph pointed out that heresy and witchcraft were offenses at common law.[8] Were these too a part of "the common law of this country" that Ellsworth had ambiguously alluded to? If not, were the federal judges to be placed in the enviable position of determining—at least in the absence of congressional direction—what parts of the common law of England *were* and *were not* also a part of the common law of America?

Randolph's *Notes on the Common Law* help explain Jefferson's reaction to the pronouncement of a federal common law. Randolph, like Jefferson, feared that such a federal common law would vastly expand federal power and would threaten the common law as it already existed in Virginia and the other states. Most of all, opposition to the federal common law focused on what they saw as a threat to constitutional authority. Randolph noted that the sovereignty of the federal government, though considerable, was still "dependent for its powers on the Constitution."[9] Inasmuch as the federal common law promised to give Congress and the courts a broader justification for their actions than the text of the Constitution allowed for, it undermined the central authority of the Constitution by creating a rival source of congressional and judicial power.

To the Jeffersonian Republicans, the existence of a federal common law essentially negated the previously accepted doctrine that Congress and the other branches of the federal government drew their authority from the language of the Constitution; Ellsworth's opinion had expanded the horizons of federal power by making their only constraint a vast, unwritten body of law. Republicans opposed this transformation not just because they hesitated over vastly expanding federal power; their opposition to assertions of a federal common law stemmed from the fact that they saw the doctrine as wholly incompatible with the principles of constitutionalism and limited government. Of course, Ellsworth and other Federalist advocates of the federal common law did not see this advocacy as a rejection of the Constitution: they simply felt they were reading the Constitution in light of the common law tradition that it seemed throughout the document to presuppose. It is important to note, then, that underlying the federal common law debate was a divergence of opinion over what the Constitution meant, what kind of government it was written for, and how it should be interpreted.

Pinpointing the exact nature of this divergence quickly becomes crucial to understanding this debate.

STATE AND FEDERAL COMMON LAW

Viewing the federal common law debate in this way—as the secondary effect of a deeper divergence—helps to explain one of the curious elements of Republican opposition to the federal common law doctrine. That curious element is that even while adamantly opposing the doctrine of a federal common law, Jefferson, Randolph, and every other Republican opponent of the federal common law readily accepted that, when the English immigrants first came to settle the American colonies, they brought their common law inheritance—or at least a great portion of it—with them. In other words, none of these opponents of a federal common law doubted that the common law provided the foundation for the legal system of every state. On this point, the most illuminating of the federal common law opponents is the Virginia jurist St. George Tucker, whose essay *Of the Unwritten, or Common Law of England*[10] was included as an appendix to his Americanized edition of Blackstone and stands as the most thorough of the Republican arguments against the federal common law doctrine, particularly in examining the adoption of the common law in each of the colonies. Once again, each of the colonies had adopted the common law and brought it over from England; nevertheless, despite this common foundation in the common law of England, it must be noted that the common law as it was practiced in the several states—though obviously drawn from the common law of England—did not exist in the exact same form in any two states.

Tucker noted that the colonists only brought with them such parts of the British common law as fit their new circumstances.[11] This attention to the demands of local circumstances meant that there were some parts of the common law of England that were considered "inapplicable" to any of the colonies' situations and thus never took root in any of the American colonies, and others that were accepted by some colonies and apparently rejected by others.[12] The diversity of factors leading emigrants to settle in the various colonies would encourage deviations between the common law adoptions of each.[13] Furthermore, absent any common governing institutions over them—save the British monarch—this process of adaptation and modification—of determining what parts were "applicable" to the circumstances of the colonies—was of course carried on by the political institutions of each colony. Variations from one colony to the next on which parts of the common law had been transplanted and which jettisoned are thus hardly surprising. Moreover, as each new colony was founded, the settlers brought with them the common law as it then stood in England, meaning that later colonies would inevitably bring with them certain developments that were then alien to the common law practice in certain earlier colonies.[14] Lastly, even after their formal adoption, the common law, as defined and expanded by both British and American courts, was subject to alteration or amendment by the colonial—then by the state—legislatures,[15] just as it was to Parliament in England. Indeed, so great was the alteration of the common law in each colony-turned-state that by 1803, Tucker could comment that "it would be altogether a hopeless attempt, to endeavor to extract from such discordant materials, an uniform system of national jurisprudence, were there any grounds in the American constitutions to warrant such an undertaking."[16] In short, Tucker argued that while the common law of England undoubtedly provided the foundation for the legal system of every state, trying to ascertain the exact parameters of a *national* common law that was fully accepted in each became extremely problematic.

The result of this colony-by-colony—or, after the revolution, state-by-state—process of adoption, modification, and partial repeal was a curious mix within the legal system of each state of elements that were genuinely *common* to all Americans and others that were modified from the British original, or else were based upon some older element of the common law that had long been amended by parliamentary statute, but nevertheless enjoyed continued application in Virginia or other early colonies.[17] While these differences are, of course, of enormous significance to the question of federal common law, it should not be forgotten that the law as adjudicated by each state court system was built upon the shared foundation of the common law and that this foundation remained intact throughout the revolutionary and Founding period. Even among the often-emphasized post-revolutionary democratic fervor of the Articles of Confederation period, there is little indication that there was any major movement away from the continued application of the common law in every state judicial system. Gordon Wood, in discussing the revolutionary period, noted that most of the original state constitutions from the period explicitly adopted "as much of the English statute and common law as was applicable to the local circumstance, until it should be altered by future legislative acts."[18] This should not be surprising, inasmuch as the people of each state had long before taken the common law of England, dispatched with such parts as no longer fit their needs and circumstances, and honed and developed the remainder as they saw fit. In short, the colonists had made the common law their own long before they ever dreamed of removing themselves from underneath the British crown.

With universal agreement, then, on the adoption of the common law at the state level, the debate over the federal common law centered on whether the common law had been adopted *solely* by each separate state or whether it had been adopted and enacted at a national level as well. What is significant also is that writers on both sides of the issue tended to agree on the basic narrative of common law adoption within the colonies: the settlers brought with them such parts of the common law of England as were "applicable to their situation" and then continued to develop and alter that common law through their own judicial and legislative bodies.[19] To be sure, there were differences in how the two sides viewed this adoption, and much will be said later on the limits of this general acceptance, but overall there seems to have been a common understanding on all sides that the first settlers of each colony brought with them the common law—or at least such parts of the common law as were applicable to them—as their legal inheritance as British subjects.

In summary, it is worth reiterating that participants on both sides of the debate saw the common law as stemming from a universal body of law—tied to natural law and discoverable, in part, through reason—that transcended national boundaries and was, of course, shared throughout the Anglo-American legal world. Each of the states brought over much of the English common law, but with modifications—"the common law," however, always referred to the body of law that they were continually drawing from, even once they had made it their own. Thus, despite the language of the debate (on both sides) over whether there was a "federal common law," it would be misleading to conceive of the debate as whether, in addition to each colony having *its own* common law tradition, the federal government was to have a completely distinct body of law all *its own*. Such a conception probably would owe more to the Hobbesian notion of the law as the creation of some sovereign than the notion still prevalent at this time of law as having an independent and objective—and to some degree universal—existence all its own. The common law was, to some degree, "*the*" common law and was, again to some degree, "common" to all Americans at the time.

However, participants on both sides of the debate also recognized that the common law had been adapted and changed in each colony-turned-state that it did not exist and was not practiced in exactly the same form in any two, nor was the common law in any state exactly identical to the common law of England. They could, and did, think and speak of them all together as part of "the common law" inheritance they received as one-time British subjects, but they also recognized that a single federal common law—if one existed—could not be exactly identical to the common law practice in every state: a fact that could potentially have wide-reaching ramifications under the Supremacy Clause for the ongoing practice of developing the common law in each of the states. The common law accorded high value to precedent but was not viewed as static—thus, while recognizing a federal common law would certainly open up to the federal courts a body of precedents they could use in resolving cases, it also would grant them the power to shape and contribute to that national "American" system of common law. And they also recognized that, just as the common law in each state was subject to modification by the state legislature, recognizing a general federal common law in all its breadth would require a similarly broad jurisdiction for Congress—a fact that would call into question the supposedly limited jurisdiction of the federal government under the constitution.

FEDERAL POWER OVER CRIMES AGAINST THE UNITED STATES

Ellsworth was not the first to suggest that there existed a uniquely federal common law distinct from the common law as it existed in the states, but ascertaining exactly how widespread the acceptance of the proposition was in the years leading up to *Williams' Case* is a much more vexatious question. Given how pervasive the influence of the common law was at the state level, it is perhaps telling that historical evidence surrounding the earliest attempts at recognizing a federal common law is somewhat scarce. There were some scattered judicial efforts at uncovering a national body of non-statutory law, but this handful of isolated incidents does not have the look of some orchestrated plan by the Federalists, nor does it seem to signify a broad-based acceptance of a federal common law across the legal and political landscapes of the early republic. Indeed, it appears that some judges and writers of this period would advance this project when they happened to come across it in the course of their usual duties and others would discourage it.

The historical evidence surrounding these early claims of a federal common law is somewhat scattered and inconclusive. A handful of commentators have portrayed the idea of a federal common law as widely accepted—at least by the members of the federal judiciary themselves—and consistently applied in an unbroken string of cases throughout the Washington and Adams administrations. For instance, Phillip Blumberg, in his book *Repressive Jurisprudence in the Early American Republic,* claimed that "In 1800 there could be no question [on the acceptance of a federal common law] to the legal observer of the time."[20] According to Blumberg, the federal circuit courts, then dominated by Federalist appointees, were "routinely" trying criminal cases based on an understanding of a federal common law; outside the federal judiciary, however, the doctrine did not enjoy this universal acceptance.[21]

Most commentators, on the other hand, are careful not to draw generalized claims that such isolated assertions of a general federal common law could in any way be seen as comprising the operative legal "doctrine" of the period.[22] To the extent that a generalized statement on the accepted limits of federal criminal jurisdiction can be drawn, it would perhaps be safest to portray these various isolated references to a federal common law as *exceptions* to the general rule; that rule being that the federal courts usually restricted themselves only to answering those cases which could be resolved through recourse to congressional statutes and the text of the Constitution. To be sure, that general rule was not one that was always easy to follow, given the bare-bones nature of American statutory law at this point, and this lack of statutory direction was nowhere more evident than in the field of criminal law. In all areas of law, but especially in criminal prosecutions, the federal courts in this period seemed to operate within a certain tension: constantly reliant on statutory and constitutional justifications for their exercise of power, but painfully aware of the difficulties caused by this reliance.

When Congress passed the Crimes Act of 1790, they established the first federal criminal code and thus gave the federal courts jurisdiction over certain crimes defined in the statute. The list of crimes that the courts had authority to punish, however, was quite limited. In addition to some serious felonies committed on federal reservations or on navigable waters and the high seas, the act outlawed treason, counterfeiting, forgery, perjury in federal courts, and bribery of federal officials, along with various other crimes—all of which relate to impeding the federal government in its constitutionally prescribed roles. The limited scope of the act was, in a certain sense, the unavoidable result of the built-in structural limits that still hem in the federal judiciary: since the federal government, unlike the state governments, enjoys only enumerated, delegated powers, the scope of federal authority cannot extend beyond the powers granted by the Constitution. Consequently, the federal judicial power reaches no further than the jurisdiction given to the courts in Article III. There, in addition to granting the federal courts jurisdiction in a number of highly specific categories of cases—cases affecting ambassadors, cases between citizens of different states or involving land claims in different states, cases involving admiralty or maritime jurisdiction, etc.—the federal courts are given a comparatively broad jurisdiction over "all cases, in law and equity, arising under this Constitution, the laws of the United States, and treaties made, or which shall be made, under their authority." Since the Constitution had given only limited lawmaking powers to Congress, the number of policy areas "arising under" the laws and the Constitution was inherently limited.

The actions outlawed in the Crimes Act were thus intentionally restricted to those pertaining to the enumerated powers of the federal government in Article I, Section 8, and other parts of the Constitution, such as the general vesting of the "judicial power of the United States" in the Supreme Court and inferior courts in Article III, Section 1. This limited scope posed problems for federal criminal prosecutions: even where the Constitution apparently gave the federal courts jurisdiction in a case, the narrow range of crimes identified in the act prevented the adequate exercise of this jurisdiction. Without the enactment of a more comprehensive federal criminal code, federal judges were left in an untenable position: expected to punish crimes occurring on federal reservations or otherwise within the jurisdiction of the United States, yet without recourse to congressional definition of such crimes. Federal District Court judge Richard Peters dramatically made this case in a letter to Nathaniel Williams in 1813, complaining that he could not, "Unless some legislative authority be given to define crimes . . . the whole (or nearly) of our criminal code may be expunged."[23] Without a more comprehensive statutory body of definitions and prescribed penalties, Peters argued, heinous crimes such as rape and murder could be "committed with impunity in places under the exclusive jurisdiction of the United States."[24] Although Peters' letter was written significantly after the passage of the Crimes Act, it helps to illustrate the problematic position that federal judges found themselves in, absent a federal common law.

True, the vast majority of criminal cases were left in the hands of the state court systems at this time, including cases involving questions of federal law. This fact, however, provided little relief for Federalists. For one thing, state jurisdiction had its limits as well, and even if the state courts were admitted to have concurrent jurisdiction over questions of federal law—as envisioned by Alexander Hamilton in *Federalist 82*—they were still not capable of prosecuting crimes in those areas of *exclusive* federal jurisdiction discussed by Peters. Moreover, as Professor Anton-Hermann Chroust noted in his two-volume *The Rise of the Legal Profession in America*,[25] the judicial and legal fields of knowledge at the time were undeveloped,[26] with the state court systems in particular being frequently filled with inexperienced or amateur judges.[27] There was, moreover, the broader constitutional question of whether the state court systems were even competent to interpret the federal constitution and answer questions of federal law.

In short, in order to prosecute crimes against the federal government, federal judges needed a legal framework that was, at least on the national level, conspicuously absent in the early republic. That Federalist judges in this position should seek out a non-statutory basis for prosecuting crimes is not entirely surprising. Even while it was the standard practice of the federal courts to rely on a statutory foundation for their cases whenever one was available, it is also clear from the historical record that there was no general consensus on what, other than enactments by Congress, counted as "federal law."[28] The general ambiguity of Article III only aggravated the confusion on this matter. The question of a federal common law was thus perhaps inevitable, inasmuch as the appointees to federal judgeships had been steeped in the common law within their home states, and inasmuch as the meager body of American statutory law failed to provide much direction to federal judges.

EARLY INTIMATIONS OF THE FEDERAL COMMON LAW

Against this backdrop, it is perhaps telling that the first mention of a federal common law is a complaint about its absence. During the ratification debates, George Mason, a leader of the Anti-Federalist faction in Virginia, wrote a letter to George Washington that enclosed a list of his objections to the proposed Constitution. The list of objections had seemingly already been published as a folio broadside. Foremost among these objections was his complaint that the proposed Constitution contained no "declaration of rights"—a criticism that would largely lead to the federal Bill of Rights as a concession to Anti-Federalist fears. "Nor," Mason argued, "are the people secured even in the enjoyment of the common law."[29] Mason's fear seems to have been that the federal government might ignore fundamental common law rights and procedures in prosecuting crimes in federal court. This critique on the absence of recognition of the common law in the Constitution came as a surprise to at least two of Mason's contemporaries who in turn wrote responses to the critique: fellow Virginian James Madison and North Carolinian James Iredell.[30]

In a published response, Iredell argued that the Constitution did nothing to change the status of the common law as it had been previously adopted, added to, and modified by the several states. "So far as the people are now entitled to the benefit of the common law," wrote Iredell, "they certainly will have a right to enjoy it under the new Constitution until altered by the general legislature, which even in this point has some cardinal limits assigned to it."[31] The common law as it was practiced by the people of each state would stay absolutely the same, save for Congress' authority over those particular areas of policy which the Constitution explicitly granted authority to the federal government; in no other area of the common law would Congress have the authority to alter it.[32] In other words, Iredell agreed with Mason that the plan put forth by the 1787 Convention had not included a general, national adoption of the British common law system; he disagreed, however, with Mason's assertion that this lack of a national common law adoption would pose a threat to the liberties of Americans. To the contrary, Iredell maintained that Americans under the proposed Constitution would still maintain whatever elements of the common law they had previously enjoyed within their individual states. Iredell also believed in the principle that Congress could only alter the varying acceptances of the common law tradition within the several states on those few enumerated subject matters that the Constitution gave Congress power to legislate in—such as those areas detailed in the Crimes Act. The question of what constituted "federal law" was, for him, settled within the four corners of the Constitution itself, along with whatever statutes Congress should pass, provided such statutes were within Congress' constitutional jurisdiction.[33]

Iredell's more restrictive views on federal law were not shared by all justices at the time. Due to the limited nature of American statutory law as well as differing opinions on the legitimate sources of law, throughout the Washington and Adams administrations, many federal judges were less satisfied to limit themselves solely to deciding cases based on congressional enactment. While Iredell, writing in 1792, described the federal criminal code as "derived from the Legislatures alone,"[34] two of his fellow justices on the court—Associate Justice James Wilson and Chief Justice John Jay—held separately that the "law of nations" could be used as an additional guide for trying crimes against the United States,[35] and Jay instructed Grand Juries in 1790 that "the laws of nations make part of the laws of this and every other civilized nation."[36] By 1796, even Iredell had come to see the law of nations as an appropriate basis for charging individuals with crimes, even in the absence of a congressional enactment adopting the "law of nations" as such.

Still, the prevailing preference of the court then, as now, was to rely on explicit legislative enactments whenever possible. The jury charges based on the law of nations or any other non-statutory standard of criminal behavior are worth noting but were more the exception than the rule.[37] This can be seen clearly by the eventual passage of the Sedition Act in July 1798. Prior to the passage of this act, some federal judges had already asserted that a statutory enactment was not necessary in order to indict and try individuals for undermining or attacking the sovereignty of the United States government. In fact, from 1795 until the passage of the act, Federalist judges presided over no fewer than five indictments for the common law crime of seditious libel.[38] This belief in a non-statutory justification for sedition prosecutions is further evidenced by the aforementioned references to the law of nations, as well as Supreme Court Justice William Paterson's undated charge instructing a grand jury of the grave dangers to society posed by actions "of a treasonable and seditious nature."[39] Similarly, in September 1798, Pennsylvania jurist Alexander Addison gave a grand jury charge that defended the Sedition Act while arguing that its passage was not entirely necessary for the prosecution of such crimes.[40] Thus, many Federalists held, in principle, that the federal courts could prosecute individual actions designed to undermine the security and sovereignty of the American federal government, *even without statutory authorization*. In spite of this, the Sedition Act was introduced and passed by a Federalist Congress, suggesting that non-statutory bases for sedition prosecutions were not universally accepted, or at least not uniformly applied, and that Congress at the very least found it prudent to give federal judges a statutory basis for punishing crimes against the federal government. Even given the foregoing examples, it is worth reemphasizing that the federal courts, as a general rule, were reluctant to prosecute any individual without explicit statutory authorization.[41]

Given this general reticence to punish actions in the absence of a legislative statute, it is not surprising that federal judicial decisions expressly based solely on the common law were quite rare in this period, and consequently, it is difficult to establish from the checkered case record just how much acceptance the doctrine enjoyed. This difficulty is compounded by the fact that many of these early judicial opinions were not consistently gathered and reported as later cases would be. There is a familiar string of cases that are cited by all authors on this issue—the chief ones being *Henfield's Case* (1793),[42] *United States v. Ravara* (1794),[43] *Commonwealth v. Schaffer* (1797),[44] and *United States v. Smith* (1797)[45]—but although these cases demonstrate that the issue of federal common law was at least a subject of interest and discussion, all of these decisions are open to interpretation, and none provide an unambiguous assertion of a federal common law.[46] Most of these cases dealt with criminal prosecutions for actions that had not been outlawed by congressional statute but were nevertheless considered offenses against the United States government. Such prosecutions naturally drew their justification from the fact that these were offenses at common law, even if they had not been addressed by Congress. Nevertheless, despite the attempts of some later commentators to present the federal common law as well-established in this period,[47] in none of these cases did the Supreme Court ever expressly affirm or deny the existence of a federal common law.

This ambiguity was ultimately broken by a 1798 circuit court decision that finally addressed the issue head-on. *United States v. Worrall*[48] dealt with a federal prosecution for the common law crime of bribery; there, the two judges hearing the case—Supreme Court Justice Samuel Chase and Judge Richard Peters—were split on how to answer the question.[49] Chase did not deny that Congress had the authority to outlaw bribery if it so chose, but until it did, the courts could not "supply the silence of the constitution, and statutes, of the union" by deciding the case according to the common law.[50] Chase's argument against a general common law jurisdiction for the federal courts rested on the fact that there was no single, federal set of common law principles adopted by the United States; each individual state having made variations on the original British common law since adopting it, resulting in great differences in the accepted common law from one state to the next.[51]

Judge Peters, on the other hand, argued that the courts had the authority to articulate a federal common law jurisdiction, even in the absence of a formal adoption of the common law by Congress.[52] Every government had the inherent authority to defend itself; the fact that this inherent power of all governments to define and try offenses was to be exercised, in this particular case, by the judiciary and not by Congress did not defeat the underlying principle.[53]

Therefore, to deny the institutions of the federal government, including the judiciary, the ability to prosecute actions designed to undermine the safety and integrity of that government—such as bribery of a federal official—was to put that government on such unsafe ground that "it could no longer be called an independent government."[54] It is perhaps worth pointing out that the heart of Peters' opinion rested not on an outright affirmation of a federal common law jurisdiction *as such*. Although he recognized the power to punish misdemeanors as "strictly a common law power," he argued that this particular component of the federal common law—the power to punish misdemeanors—was within the jurisdiction of the courts because of the inherent power of the United States government to defend itself against crimes. Consequently, Peters cannot fairly be said to be claiming here the existence of a general federal common law, or that such a general common law was thus open to discovery and application by the federal courts, only that this particular "common law power" was one inherent to all governments.

Worrall thus represented the first direct judicial answer to the federal common law question; but while the two conflicting opinions may have been enough to dismiss the case, they did little to definitively answer the question. Indeed, Tucker, who included the text of both Chase's and Peter's opinions in a postscript to his essay on the federal common law question summarized the case by saying only, "here then are two opposite opinions on this great question."[55] Similarly, the great Federalist legal commentator Chancellor James Kent wrote that the case "settled nothing, as the Court were divided; but it contained some of the principal arguments on each side of this nice and interesting constitutional question."[56] *Worrall* perhaps can be seen as an indication of both sides' willingness to definitively settle the federal common law question; the inconclusive outcome of the case may only have served to amplify the intensity of conviction with which both sides approached the issue, and when another federal circuit court handed down the decision in *Williams' Case* the following year, Republican critics of the federal common law doctrine responded with vigor.

Taken as a whole, then, the federal case history from 1793 to 1799 thus reveals an undeniable lack of consensus on the question of a common law jurisdiction for the federal courts. Of the twelve Supreme Court justices to serve on the federal circuit bench during the decade of 1789 to 1799, only four—Wilson, Jay, Iredell, and Ellsworth—are known to have embraced the doctrine, with some indications that William Paterson and Bushrod Washington had adopted the position as well, although the evidence for either of these two justices is less conclusive; Chase is the only definite Supreme Court justice to come out against the doctrine over the same period.[57] *Worrall* and *Williams* seemed to be moving toward a direct judicial answer to this question but, as all of the aforementioned cases were heard by federal circuit courts and not by the entire Court, these could not be considered to be fully binding on all other federal courts one way or another.[58]

The lack of a widely accepted position on the federal common law should not be surprising. These cases can perhaps best be seen as emblematic of not one, but several major ambiguities surrounding the federal judiciary. The most immediate was the particular question of a federal common law: some Supreme Court justices in the Washington and Adams years held that the American people had, in their national capacity, adopted the British common law, while at least one held that it had not. Second was the more general ambiguity surrounding the scope of federal law itself; for although Article III had granted the federal courts jurisdiction over all cases arising under the laws or Constitution, there existed at this time considerable debate over what should be considered the "laws of the United States." On a more practical note, the lack of consensus among members of the Court on this question was likely exacerbated by the fact that circuit court decisions in these days were not generally reported,[59] meaning that even if members of the Court had wanted to go along with the decisions of their colleagues in prior circuit court cases, there was no composite collection of decisions for them to have recourse to.

To the modern reader who is accustomed to the Supreme Court settling controversial matters of constitutional interpretation, it may seem surprising that on a constitutional matter of such legal importance the Court did not immediately step in to settle the issue. That the Supreme Court played a much lesser role in this period than even the lower federal courts can be seen by the conspicuous absence of the Supreme Court throughout the foregoing discussion. The reader may here be reminded of the ambiguity surrounding the role of the Supreme Court prior to two momentous shifts that occurred in 1801: the removal of circuit-riding responsibilities for Supreme Court justices in the Judiciary Act and the beginning of John Marshall's tenure as Chief Justice. Second, while it is true that the modern Court does perform this role of final interpreter, the limited number of cases it hears, as well as the structure of the federal court system ensure that it generally does not do so quickly or consistently, but only after a significant legal question lingers for some time. Even today, as in the earliest days of the federal judiciary, much of the fighting over legal battles is waged at the circuit court level.

This large-scale uncertainty over the federal common law question, however, did not prove lasting. As discussed earlier, reactions to *Williams' Case* by Republican leaders were fierce and helped to create a narrative of an out-of-control Federalist judiciary that recognized no constitutional limits on its jurisdiction. This narrative played well politically: popular opposition to Federalist prosecutions under the Sedition Act was one of the driving forces behind the ascendancy of the Republican Party in the election of 1800. And with Jefferson's election in the "Revolution of 1800," the stage was set for the next claim of a federal common law jurisdiction. Here, the push for a federal common law jurisdiction would come from a surprising source: the Republicans.

THE REVOLUTION OF 1800

For as long as American political historians have focused attention on the Election of 1800 as a transformative moment in the development of the American Union, little attention has been paid to the central role that questions of federal judicial power played in that transformation. When Jefferson's party swept into power, they did so upon the promise that they would reverse all of the perceived unconstitutional and un-republican policies of the previous administration; at the forefront of the asserted abuses and excesses of the Adams administration was the expansive use of the federal judiciary. This attention to the Federalist judicial policy proved to be a salient issue, as the federal prosecution of Republican newspaper editors under the Sedition Act was still fresh in the nation's mind. Moreover, the Jeffersonians saw their rejection of the federal common law doctrine as an application of their larger understanding of the Constitution as creating a very limited scope for the Federal government;[60] by contrast, what they saw in Federalist decisions like Ellsworth's in *Williams' Case* was the wholesale replacement of the carefully limited scope of Article III with an essentially unlimited jurisdiction for the federal judiciary.[61] This contrast fit nicely with the political narrative that Republicans were trying to create as it set up the election as a contest between Republican limited, constitutional government, on the one hand, and Federalist crypto-monarchism, on the other.

After the election, the results were quickly given symbolic significance by both parties. For Republicans, the victory was interpreted as a reclaiming of the original revolutionary spirit that had guided the American struggle for independence. In the year leading up to the election, Jefferson himself wrote a famous letter to Thomas Lomax of Monticello: "The spirit of 1776 is not dead. It has only been slumbering. The body of the American people is substantially republican. But their virtuous feelings have been played on by some fact with more fiction; they have been the dupes of artful manoeuvres . . . "[62] The winter of 1800 found many Republicans adopting the same posture as their president-elect and devoting themselves to the pressing task of reversing many of the Federalist policies that they saw as running contrary to the intentions of the Constitution's ratifiers and to the principles of the American Revolution. For these Jeffersonians, reclaiming the federal judiciary held special meaning: it represented not only the last remnant of the defeated

Federalist establishment but also the most dangerous branch of the federal government to the liberties of the states and the people. The "Revolution of 1800" would never be truly realized until the power of the Federalist-dominated, Federalist-appointed judiciary was brought into check.

High on their list of judicial priorities was dealing with the threat of the asserted federal common law. Leading Republicans continued to call for a complete denunciation of the doctrine. Madison, in his 1799 report to the Virginia House of Delegates, had described the effect the doctrine had on the committee charged with writing the Virginia Resolutions, claiming that it had "filled them with equal astonishment and apprehension."[63] Jefferson himself wrote to Edmund Randolph in 1799 of the need "to portray at full length the consequences of this new doctrine, that the common law is the law of the US" ending the letter by exclaiming, "But, great heavens! Who could have conceived in 1789 that within ten years we should have to combat such windmills."[64] In his brief essay *The Danger Not Over*,[65] published in October 1801, Edmund Pendleton joined in the Republican celebration over the results of the recent election but then promptly called on his fellow Republicans to introduce constitutional amendments to clarify the original meaning of the Constitution, including "to declare that the common law of England or of any other foreign country in criminal cases shall not be considered as a law of the United States."[66] In short, the gradual escalation of the Federalist drive for a common law jurisdiction for the federal courts had prompted a very strong response from many leading Republicans who apparently saw the very idea of a federal common law as a complete novelty, and thus implicitly a betrayal of founding constitutional principles. By the turn of the century, the doctrine of a federal common law had come to symbolize the height of Federalist constitutional heresy.

Whatever constitutional objections they had to the doctrine, Republicans considered the question to have been sufficiently answered by Justice Chase's opinion in *Worrall*.[67] Still, even *Worrall* was not exactly the indisputable refutation of the doctrine the Republicans were looking for. The decision had not been heard by the whole Court and was not binding in any other districts of the circuit court. Furthermore, the decision had been evenly split, with Peters and Chase offering diametrically contrasting answers to the important question—while this had been enough to ensure that Worrall was not convicted at common law, it did little to settle the issue from either a political or a legal standpoint. Third, the answer given by Chase in *Worrall* had arguably been superseded by Ellsworth's opinion in *Williams' Case*. At the very least, it is easy to see how some Republicans would have seen answering the question as an increasingly pressing task. Most importantly, the doctrine still had its enthusiastic proponents in the Federalist camp[68] and thus was bound to continue generating controversy.

Given the starkly political nature of sedition prosecutions under the Adams administration, it is not at all surprising that the Republican majority in Congress allowed the Sedition Act to expire in 1801. Neither is it surprising that Jefferson stopped the common law prosecution against Republican newspaper editor William Duane[69] and indeed virtually all common law prosecutions during the Jefferson administration ceased to involve the assertion of a federal common law. Some Federalist newspaper editors were prosecuted for the common law crime of seditious libel, but these prosecutions were carried out in the state courts, with Jefferson's apparent approval.[70] In 1802, Jefferson's Attorney General Levi Lincoln ordered the prosecution of William Hardin in Kentucky,[71] but it is clear from Jefferson's written memorandum on the case that he supported the prosecution because it was allowable under the accepted common law in Kentucky and not under a federal common law, which Jefferson still disavowed.[72] Jefferson may have, as the critical historian Leonard Levy has argued, "accepted without question the dominant view of his generation that government could be criminally assaulted merely by the expression of critical opinions that allegedly tended to subvert it by lowering it in the public's esteem,"[73] yet he generally maintained that the state courts were the proper constitutional form for prosecuting crimes against the general government.[74] Even in the Jefferson administration's vigorous attempts to indict Aaron Burr for treason, the prosecution still did not claim a federal common law.[75]

Given this, it is quite ironic that the major federal common law case to arise under the Jefferson administration dealt with a libel case initiated by a Republican judge against Federalist newspaper editors. In 1806, the Federalist-controlled state government in Connecticut brought seditious libel charges against the editors of a Republican newspaper. Seemingly in retaliation, Pierpont Edwards, Jefferson's recent appointment to the position of District Judge in Connecticut, sought a grand jury indictment against the editors of the Federalist newspaper, the *Connecticut Courant*.[76] The ensuing case, *United States v. Hudson and Goodwin*,[77] would ultimately prove to be the very first case on the federal common law question to be heard by the Supreme Court when the case finally came before them in 1812. The editors, Barzillai Hudson and George Goodwin, were charged with seditious libel against the president and, since the Sedition Act had been allowed to lapse, the case rested on the existence of a common law jurisdiction for the federal courts.[78]

It is perhaps worth noting that there is no evidence that Jefferson himself directed the prosecution or even supported it.[79] In fact, there are several indications that he opposed the proceedings and even sent his Postmaster General, Gideon Granger to Connecticut to convey his opposition to such prosecutions.[80] In a letter to Jefferson two years afterward, Granger complained that he had been "denounced and charged with siding with federalism, for the part

I took in silencing the Common-law sedition prosecutions in Connecticut" and went on to note that he had "silenced those prosecutions in conformity to your written request."[81] Whatever other ideological inconsistencies may have arisen from his tenure as president, it seems that Jefferson's opposition to the doctrine of a federal common law remained relatively constant.

By the time *United States v. Hudson and Goodwin was* finally decided by the Supreme Court in March 1812, the Court was already operating with its first Republican majority—the result of twelve years of Republican rule in the White House and the recent addition of two Republican appointments by Madison: Gabriel Duvall and Joseph Story.[82] The latter, although a Republican by identification, was firmly nationalist in his sentiments, and his appointment by Madison had come in spite of Jefferson's fervent advice to the contrary.[83] No counsel appeared either for the government or for the defendants, and the Court at this point did not require written briefs to be submitted, thus leaving the Court to decide the case without any argument by either side.[84] Still, the Court moved nevertheless to issue a long-delayed decision in the case.[85] The longest-serving Jeffersonian appointee on the Court, William Johnson, penned the opinion of the court. On the question of the federal common law, Johnson wrote that "although this question is brought up now for the first time to be decided by this Court, we consider it as having been long settled in public opinion."[86] Johnson side-stepped the disagreement among federal judges and the checkered case record at the circuit court level and instead rested his decision, somewhat dubiously, on what he perceived to be "the general acquiescence of legal men" against the idea of a federal common law jurisdiction.[87]

In addition to claiming an essential agreement within the legal community, Johnson also provided a constitutional argument that stayed faithful to the Jeffersonian theory of delegated federal powers. First, Johnson argued that the powers of the general government had been delegated by the states.[88] However, while the jurisdiction of the Supreme Court is outlined in the Constitution, the jurisdiction of the other federal courts is granted by Congress.[89] Consequently, the question of whether the lower federal courts had a common law jurisdiction must be answered by looking to whether Congress had granted them one. In particular, Johnson questioned the propriety of a federal court assuming to itself jurisdiction over the common law—a jurisdiction "in its nature very indefinite" and "applicable to a great variety of subjects—varying in every state of the Union."[90]

Johnson avoided some of the broader questions that would have gone beyond the immediate scope of the case: he found it "not necessary to inquire" whether Congress had the constitutional authority to grant a common law jurisdiction, noting only that they had chosen not to do so, even if they had the authority.[91] On the matter of implied governmental powers, he demurred on "examining how far this consideration is applicable to the peculiar character of our Constitution."[92] The "peculiar character" of the Constitution seemingly referred to the unique nature of American federalism and the distinctly limited view of federal authority that corresponds to Johnson's view that all powers of the federal government are "concessions from the several states."[93] More will be said later on the relationship of this delegated view of federal authority to the denial of a general common law jurisdiction for federal courts. Johnson did not limit himself solely to the narrow facts at issue in *Hudson and Goodwin*: although this case dealt only with a common law indictment for libel, Johnson wrote that the Court's denial of a federal common law jurisdiction would "apply to every case in which jurisdiction is not vested in those courts [i.e., federal circuit courts] by statute."[94] In other words, Johnson extended the opinion to all claims of a federal common law.[95]

Whatever the merits of Johnson's constitutional argument, his claim of a "general acquiescence of legal men" is made somewhat suspect by the fact that the vote in the decision was not unanimous.[96] Since no written dissent was filed, it is impossible to know for certain which justices voted with Johnson in the majority and which justices did not. Johnson himself, in an unreported circuit court opinion the following year, stated that the decision in *Hudson and Goodwin* had been "almost unanimous" with Bushrod Washington being the only dissenter.[97] It seems much more likely that the recent Madison appointee Joseph Story joined Washington in the minority, making the vote in the case 5–2 against a federal common law. Additionally, William Winslow Crosskey suggested that the majority was even narrower than this, with John Marshall dissenting alongside Story and Washington.[98] Marshall's inclusion, however, is more problematic as it would seemingly contradict Marshall's stated opposition to a federal common law in *Livingston v. Jefferson* the previous year.[99] At any rate, with or without the vote of the chief justice, the new Republican majority on the Court had succeeded in defeating the much-debated federal common law of crimes. The Supreme Court had finally given a direct answer on the question and denied the existence of a general common law jurisdiction for the federal courts. Jefferson, who had tried to squash the prosecution years earlier, was pleased with the result and wrote to John M. Goodenow in 1822, noting that he was glad the Supreme Court eventually rejected the federal common law basis for Hudson and Goodwin's convictions, although he supposed they could have been indicted under the common law as adopted by Connecticut.[100] Johnson had attempted to lay the whole issue to rest, but any sense of victory against the idea was not lasting, as Story, perhaps the federal common law doctrine's most capable and vigorous adherent, had just begun his tenure on the Supreme Court.

Throughout his long subsequent tenure on the Court, Story would find the Court's decision in *Hudson and Goodwin* difficult to accept and would work tirelessly to establish a common law jurisdiction for the federal courts. Story's career-long pursuit of such a jurisdiction would include early unsuccessful attempts to resurrect the rejected federal common law of crimes in *United States v. Coolidge* and would eventually result in the creation of a federal common law in civil cases in the 1842 case *Swift v. Tyson*, a precedent that would stand for nearly a century.

NOTES

1. It was, at this time, the practice for Supreme Court and District Court judges to sit together to hear cases for the Circuit Court of Appeals.
2. *Williams' Case*, 29 Fed. Cas. 1330 (1799), also with the majority opinion reprinted in part on pp. 367–369 of St. George Tucker's essay "Of the unwritten, or Common Law of England," found in Views of the Constitution of the United States, with Selected Writings (Indianapolis: Liberty Fund, 1999), 313–370.
3. Ibid., 1330.
4. Ibid., 1331.
5. Thomas Jefferson to Charles Pinckney, October 29, 1799, in Founders Online, National Archives, https://founders.archives.gov/documents/Jefferson/01-31-02–0193.
6. Edmund Randolph, "Edmund Randolph's Notes on the Common Law," [ca. September] 1799, in *Founders Online*, National Archives, https://founders.archives.gov/documents/Madison/01-17-02–0170.
7. Ibid.
8. Ibid.
9. Ibid.
10. St. George Tucker. "Of the unwritten, or Common Law of England," found in Views of the Constitution of the United States, with Selected Writings, (Indianapolis: Liberty Fund, 1999), 313–370.
11. Ibid., 318–344.
12. Ibid., 324–325.
13. Ibid., 323–324.
14. Ibid., 326.
15. Ibid., 344.
16. Ibid., 345.
17. Ibid., 326.
18. Gordon Wood, *The Creation of the American Republic* (Chapel Hill: University of North Carolina Press, 1998), 299–300.
19. Joseph Story's account of common law adoption in his *Commentaries on the Constitution* is relatively compatible with the general thrust of Tucker's argument. Joseph Story, *Commentaries on the Constitution*, Fourth edition (Boston: Little, Brown and Company, 1873), Sec. 156, 1:105
20. Phillip I. Blumberg, *Repressive Jurisprudence in the Early American Republic: The First Amendment and the Legacy of English Law* (Cambridge: Cambridge University Press, 2010), 166–167.

21. Ibid.

22. Kathryn Preyer is emblematic of this caution: "In their efforts to determine contemporary views regarding federal common law jurisdiction over crimes, scholars have used pretty much the same evidence, a few charges to grand juries made by some of the federal judges and a handful of cases decided in the federal circuit courts. It is hazardous, however, to fashion this type of evidence too tightly into abstract doctrinal logic for the evidence itself takes on appropriate meaning only from its historical context." "Jurisdiction to Punish: Authority, Federalism and the Common Law of Crimes in the Early Republic." *Law and History Review* 4, no. 2 (Autumn, 1986), 223–265, 227.

23. Richard Peters to Nathaniel Williams, May 27, 1813, quoted in James McClellan, *Joseph Story and the American Constitution* (Norman, OK: University of Oklahoma Press, 1990), 177n55.

24. Ibid.

25. Anton-Hermann Chroust, *The Rise of the Legal Profession in America* (Norman, OK: University of Oklahoma Press, 1965).

26. Ibid., 47–49.

27. Ibid., 41–43.

28. Ibid., 227.

29. Mason to Washington, October 7, 1787. Reprinted in *Pamphlets on the Constitution of the United States, published during its Discussion by the People, 1787–1788*, ed. Paul Leicester Ford (Union, NJ: The Law Book Exchange, Ltd., 2000), 329–332.

30. Madison's views on the common law—which appear to be close to Iredell's, at least at this period—will be discussed in more detail in Chapter 4.

31. James Iredell, "Marcus," "Answers to Mr. Mason's Objections to the New Constitution, Recommended by the Late Convention." Reprinted at Ford, *Pamphlets on the Constitution*, 333–370, 336.

32. Ibid.

33. One can see a parallel here to Justice Iredell's most famous opinion in *Calder v. Bull*, where he argued that the Supreme Court could only overturn an action of the legislature when it violated the text of the Constitution and not, as Justice Samuel Chase argued in a separate seriatim opinion in that case, when it violated the Court's own views of natural law: "If any act of Congress, or of the Legislature of a state, violates those constitutional provisions, it is unquestionably void. . . . If, on the other hand, the Legislature of the Union, or the Legislature of any member of the Union, shall pass a law, within the general scope of their constitutional power, the Court cannot pronounce it to be void, merely because it is, in their judgment, contrary to the principles of natural justice . . ." *Calder v. Bull*, 3 U.S. 386, 398.

34. Griffith J. McRee, ed., *The Life and Correspondence of James Iredell* (New York: D. Appleton and Company, 1949), ii:369. Quoted in Preyer, 228.

35. Preyer, 228.

36. April 4, 1790; Henry P. Johnston, ed., *The Correspondence and Public Papers of John Jay*, 4 vols. (New York: G.P. Putnam's Sons, 1890–93), iii:393. Quoted in Preyer, 227.

37. Preyer, 227.

38. Derek L. Mogck, "Connecticut Federalists in President Jefferson's (Republican) Court: *United States v. Hudson and Goodwin*." *Connecticut History* 41, no. 2 (September 2002), 144–172, 149. It should be noted that none of these indictments resulted in a conviction and also that there is some ambiguity over whether the defendants were indicted under the common law of their particular state or of an asserted federal common law. See also Bruce A. Ragsdale, *The Sedition Act Trials* (Washington: The Federal Judicial Center, 2005), 18–21.

39. Preyer, 227–228. Although, as Preyer noted, the charge is undated, the absence of any reference to the Sedition Act and its constitutionality (which Paterson affirmed in later, also undated, jury charges) indicates that this charge was prior to that Act.

40. Addison argued in "A charge to the grand juries of the County Courts of the Fifth Circuit, of the state of Pennsylvania" that the Sedition Act was merely a prudent clarification and affirmation of the judiciary's preexisting power to punish acts against the government, not an effective grant of additional jurisdiction. Federal courts had the authority to punish such acts, even without a statute declaring such actions to be illegal. Addison: "The judicial power of the United States extends to all cases arising under the constitution, the laws, and treaties of the United States. Hence results a jurisdiction to try and punish, as misdemeanors, all acts tending to violate or weaken the authority of the constitution, or of any act or measure of the government of the United States. For it cannot be supposed, that such misdemeanors should pass unpunished, or that the government of the United States should be obliged to beg protection from the individual states. The doubt however existing, it might be thought proper to remove it." Reprinted in Mark deWolfe Howe, *Readings in American Legal History* (Cambridge: Harvard University Press, 1949), 349–353. Quoted by McClellan, 172n38.

41. See, for instance, Preyer's assessment that "It seems to have been commonly assumed that federal authority over crimes and punishments was to be limited and limited solely to that which was specified by statute." Preyer, 227.

42. *Henfield's Case*, 11 Fed. Cas. 1099, No. 6,360 (1793).

43. *United States v. Ravara*, 27 Fed. Cas. 713, Nos. 16,122, 16,122a (1794).

44. *Commonwealth v. Schaffer*, 4 Dallas Appendix xxv (1797). This is the only one of these four cases to not be a federal case. Here the defense attorney, Alexander Dallas, attempted to have the case thrown out of state court on the grounds that the offense arose under federal common law and thus could only be heard in federal court. Dallas noted that the issue of federal common law jurisdiction for criminal cases had not been sufficiently decided by the federal courts. It is also interesting to note that Dallas seems to have distanced himself from the argument for a federal common law. The record noted "Dallas observed . . . it was his duty, as counsel for the defendant (without declaring his own opinion)." 4 Dallas Appendix xxv. Dallas would later make essentially the opposite argument in the case *United States v. Worrall*.

45. *United States v. Smith*, 27 Fed. Cas. 1147, No. 16,323 (1797). The date for this case is often inaccurately presented as 1792. See Preyer, 229n23.

46. Henfield's Case dealt with a breach of George Washington's 1793 neutrality proclamation, and thus the prosecution could have been based on the violation of a treaty instead of a federal common law jurisdiction. Preyer, 230. Similarly, commentators have disagreed on whether Ravara is an example of a common law indictment. Francis Wharton recorded that "the court found the defendant guilty, the offense being held indictable at common law." See Wharton, *State Trials of the United States during the Administrations of Washington and Adams* (Philadelphia: Carey and Hart, 1849), 85n. On the other hand, Julius Goebel noted that this offense was covered by Section 27 of the Crimes Act, and thus the Court could have held the offense to be indictable, even without reference to a federal common law. See Julius Goebel Jr., *History of the Supreme Court of the United States, Antecedents and Beginnings* (New York and London: Cambridge University Press, 1971), 627. In Schaffer, the court could have dismissed the defendant's arguments for removal on the grounds that state courts had concurrent jurisdiction over questions of federal law, which was then not an uncommon position. *United States v. Smith* also appears to have been decided with an eye toward statutory law, with the court there asserting that Congress' creation of the Bank of the United States was a constitutional act, and therefore the case arose "under the laws of the United States." Smith, 1147, 1148. Thus, Preyer argued that, far from establishing a federal common law jurisdiction for crimes against the United States, this case relied on congressional statute and the text of the Constitution. Preyer, 230. On the other hand, a parenthetical comment at the end of the case—presumably added by the reporter or else by Nathan Dane in Volume VI of his *A General Abridgement and Digest of American Law* (Boston: Cummings, Hilliard & Co., 1824)—stated simply "see Seventh Amendment of the Federal Constitution as to Common Law," vi:719. The judges deciding Smith observed that the same offense could have been punished at common law in the state courts, the implication being that the appropriate penalty would be assigned based on the common law as adopted by Massachusetts and not according to some national standard. Smith, 27 Fed. Cas. 1147, 1148.

47. McClellan, for instance, cited Smith, along with Henfield's Case and Ravara, in favor of his assertion that the federal courts had embraced the concept of a federal common law in "a number of decisions." McClellan, 174n42. He argued that these cases presented a "chain of precedent" that was broken by subsequent denials of a criminal common law jurisdiction in *United States v. Worrall*, discussed below, and by Justice Story's opinion in *United States v. Coolidge*, 14 U.S. 415 (1816), discussed in chapter 2.

48. *United States v. Worrall*, 28 Fed. Cas. 744 (1798).

49. The opinions of Justices Chase and Peters in *United States v. Worrall* are reprinted in the postscript of St. George Tucker's essay "Of the Unwritten, or Common Law of England," found in Tucker, 364–367.

50. *Worrall* in Tucker, 365.

51. Ibid., 366.

52. Ibid., 367.

53. Ibid.

54. Ibid.

55. Tucker, 367.

56. James Kent, *Commentaries on American Law*, 2nd ed. (New York: O. Halstead, 1832), i:333. Quoted in McClellan, 174n43.

57. Preyer, 231n32. Preyer also approvingly cited Julius Goebel, who maintained that there seems to have been considerable uncertainty on the point not only among later scholars but even among the justices themselves.

58. Kent Newmyer, *Supreme Court Justice Joseph Story, Statesman of the Old Republic* (Chapel Hill: University of North Carolina Press, 1985), 101.

59. Ibid., 101n96.

60. Stephen B. Presser, "The Supra-Constitution, the Courts, and the Federal Common Law of Crimes: Some Comments on Palmer and Preyer." *Law and History Review* 4, no. 2 (Autumn 1986), 325–335, 329.

61. Stewart Jay, "Origins of the Federal Common Law: Part Two." *University of Pennsylvania Law Review* 133, no. 6 (July, 1985), 1231–1333, 1242.

62. Thomas Jefferson to Thomas Lomax, March 12, 1799, in *Founders Online*, National Archives, https://founders.archives.gov/documents/Jefferson/01-31-02–0056.

63. James Madison, "The Report of 1800," January 7, 1800. From *Founders Online*, National Archives, https://founders.archives.gov/documents/Madison/01-17-02–0202.

64. Jefferson to E. Randolph.

65. Edmund Pendleton, "The Danger Not Over." Published in the Richmond Enquirer, October 1801. Accessed online from the Mises Institute, https://mises.org/library/danger-not-over. The essay can be found reprinted in *Liberty and Order: The First American Party Struggle*, ed. Lance Banning (Indianapolis: Liberty Fund Press, 2004).

66. Ibid.

67. Preyer, 329.

68. One of the most outspoken of which being Judge Peters, who later wrote to Senator Timothy Pickering: "When I meet with Occasions, in my Place, I always act as if no Dispute existed about that Matter [the availability of the Common Law to the federal courts]; & am careless about Consequences, where my Mind is made up . . .. As to Admiralty Jurisdiction as to Place, & the Common Law Jurisdiction over Offences, I think more liberally (tho' not extravagantly) than some tight laced or time serving People. . . . In Cases of the lower Offences-Assaults & Batteries, etc. I take Jurisdiction & punish under Indictments at Common Law, if committed below Low Water Mark, & out of any State Jurisdiction." Richard Peters to Timothy Pickering, December 5, 1807. Pickering Papers, 28:99, Massachusetts Historical Society. Quoted in Preyer, 242.

69. Preyer, 238.

70. Ibid., 239.

71. Blumbery, 153.

72. Thomas Jefferson, "Observations on the Common Law and Hardin's Case," November 11, 1802. Memorandum. From *Founders Online*, National Archives, http://founders.archives.gov/documents/Jefferson/01-38-02-0592–0002. Reprinted in

Barbara B. Oberg, ed., *The Papers of Thomas Jefferson*, vol. 38, July 1–November 12, 1802 (Princeton: Princeton University Press, 2011), 668–672.

73. Leonard W. Levy, *Jefferson and Civil Liberties: The Darker Side* (New York: The New York Times Book Company, 1963), 46. Cited in Mogck, 152.

74. Mogck, 152.

75. Preyer, 243n65. It may also be noted that in the ensuing case *United States v. Burr*, (25 Fed. Cas. 55, No. 14,693), then-Chief Justice John Marshall held that the charge of treason could only be applied on common law grounds. In the apparent absence of a federal common law jurisdiction, Burr was acquitted. Marshall would later explicitly go against the doctrine of the federal common law in the 1811 case *Livingston v. Jefferson*, arguing, "I am decidedly of the opinion that the jurisdiction of the courts of the United States depends, exclusively, on the Constitution and laws of the United States." *Livingston v. Jefferson*, 15 Fed. Cas. 660, No. 8,411 (1811). Quoted in McClellan, 174.

76. Preyer, 242.

77. *United States v. Hudson and Goodwin*, 11 U.S. 32 (1812).

78. By this point, as stated before, a number of Supreme Court justices had accepted the claim of a federal common law for crimes against the government. In his charge to the grand jury, Edwards reminded them that a majority of Supreme Court justices approved of the federal common law: "Whatever may be my own opinion upon the question, are there any common law offences recognizable by the courts of the United States? I deem it my duty to declare to you the law, as pronounced by those judges." The Witness (Litchfield, CT), April 30, 1806. Quote in Preyer, 242–243.

79. Preyer, 243.

80. Mogck, 154.

81. Gideon Granger. Gideon Granger to Thomas Jefferson, February 22, 1814. Letter. From *Founders Online*, National Archives, https://founders.archives.gov/documents/Jefferson/03-07-02–0131.

82. Preyer, 247.

83. Jefferson considered Story not only to be "too young" at 32, but also a "pseudo-republican" and a "tory." Newmyer, 70. By contrast, Jefferson had hoped Madison would pick a justice who would be firm enough in his Republican principles to provide a counterweight to Marshall's influence on the Judiciary, writing to Albert Gallatin, "It will be difficult to find a character of firmness enough to preserve his independence on the same Bench with Marshall." Thomas Jefferson to Albert Gallatin, September 27, 1810. From *Founders Online*, National Archives, https://founders.archives.gov/documents/Jefferson/03-03-02–0077. Quoted in McClellan, 39n137.

84. Mogck, 155. Why counsel for both sides declined to argue a case of such political and legal importance is an interesting question. Defense attorney Samuel Dana may have done so as a form of protesting the assertion of common law jurisdiction by the Court. Attorney General William Pinkney, however, was then reputed to be an advocate for a federal common law jurisdiction and in 1812 forwarded to President Madison a letter from Story asking for a congressional grant of criminal common law jurisdiction to the federal courts. It is possible that Pinkney merely surmised that the doctrine would not be approved by the Court. Gary D. Rowe, "Jeffersonian

Ascendancy and the Abolition of Federal Common Law Crimes." *The Yale Law Journal*, Vol. 101, no. 4 (January 1992), 919–948, 926.

85. Preyer, 247.
86. *Hudson and Goodwin*, 32 .
87. Ibid.
88. Mogck, 155.
89. *Hudson and Goodwin*, 33.
90. Ibid.
91. Ibid.
92. Ibid., 34.
93. Ibid., 33.
94. Ibid., 32.
95. Ibid.
96. Preyer, 248.
97. Ibid., 248n86.
98. Ibid.
99. *Livingston v. Jefferson*.
100. Thomas Jefferson. Thomas Jefferson to John M. Goodenow, June 13, 1822. Letter. From *Founders Online*, National Archives, https://founders.archives.gov/documents/Jefferson/98-01-02–2876.

Chapter 2

Story and the Federal Common Law

Judge Story would not be easily reconciled to Johnson's decision. It was unthinkable to him that the common law should be everywhere with the federal courts—including embedded in the language of the Constitution itself—and the federal courts nevertheless be prohibited from having recourse to it in cases where it would help federal judges interpret the Constitution. Writing to an ally in Congress in 1816, Story asked, "If then, State Courts may apply the common law to State constitutions, why may not United States Courts apply it to the Constitution of the United States?"[1] Since, in Story's constitutional theory, the American people had created both the federal and state governments to fulfill certain specified objects, the federal government was equally entitled to use the great common law tradition that was the shared inheritance of all Americans. To Story, the Constitution and laws of the United States had been written against the backdrop of this shared common law tradition and made no sense without it. Given the obvious extent to which judges were reliant on the common law in order to interpret both state and federal law, the Republican rejection of a common law jurisdiction for the federal courts seemed nothing more than an overtly partisan attempt to encumber the federal courts with unnecessary additional barriers to their already-difficult task of interpreting and applying the new system of national law.

Moreover, to deny the widespread American acceptance and use of the British common law inheritance was to contradict the legal practices of every state judicial system, and therefore of the entire American people. This shared common law foundation at the state level fueled Story's desire to have the same foundation available to the federal courts. Story, in his seminal work *Commentaries on the Constitution*, later noted that "It would be a most extraordinary state of things" if the common law were held to be the "basis of jurisprudence" within every state of the original Union, and yet the federal courts, despite being "engrafted upon" the existing legal system, "should have no jurisprudence at all."[2] Such a result, argued Story, would have disastrous consequences for federal jurisprudence, as federal judges would then have "no guide, and no rule . . . in the exercise of any of the powers confided to them except so far as Congress has laid, or shall lay down a rule."[3] Like Peters, Story thus wondered how federal judges would go about punishing crimes without the firm basis of a general common law jurisdiction.

Here, it can be seen that Story's argument for a uniquely federal common law, distinct from the common law as it was practiced in each of the states, rested on both a practical argument—that there was a palpable need for a more comprehensive set of guides and rules than the undeveloped corpus of congressional statutory law would allow for—as well as a theoretical argument—that there must logically be a nationally existing federal common law, given the acceptance of the common law in every state. The practical need for a non-statutory basis for deciding cases has already been discussed, but it is this latter argument—that the existence of a federal common law was inferred by the very creation of the federal government itself—that gives the most insight into Story's theory of a federal common law, as well as his understanding of the nature of the union.

Following the Court's decision in *Hudson and Goodwin*, Story took the lead in pushing for a re-examination of the doctrine considered so essential by Federalist judges. There were almost immediate indications that Story was not willing to let the issue simply drop. Just three months after the Court's opinion in *Hudson and Goodwin*, Story decided the Massachusetts circuit court case *United States v. Wonson*.[4] The case dealt with the appellate review of findings by a jury at the trial court level, and Story's decision hinged, in part, on a reference to the common law in the Seventh Amendment. According to Story, when the amendment stipulated that facts tried by a jury shall only be re-examined "according to the rules of the common law," this could only refer to the common law of England, and not of any particular state. "Beyond all question," Story wrote, "the common law here alluded to is not the common law of any individual state, (for it probably differs in all), but it is the common law of England, the grand reservoir of all our jurisprudence."[5] Using the common law of England then, Story concluded that the "invariable usage settled by the decisions of the ages" was that appellate courts had jurisdiction only over errors of law and not over factual matters settled by the jury.[6]

On its face, this interpretation seems innocuous enough. As a matter of inferring the intention of the authors of the Seventh Amendment, Story might well have been correct in interpreting "the common law" to mean the common law of England and not of any individual state in the Union. Admittedly, the amendment could also be read to refer to the extant common law practice in whatever state the case was tried. This alternate interpretation, however, would lead to two potentially uncomfortable outcomes. First, it would mean that a federal constitutional amendment guaranteed different rights in different states—an outcome that, to Federalists, made a farce of the nominal supremacy of national law and defeated the purpose of the federal Bill of Rights altogether. Second, this deference to the accepted common law custom of each state still begged the question of what rule to follow in the District of Columbia, on the high seas, or in federal enclaves not under the jurisdiction of the states, such as military bases. Still, allowing the courts to create a federal common law rule in those rare cases where no state law is applicable was a much less radical concession from the states than declaring as a general principle, as Story did, that some version of the British common law was in force nationally, regardless of state law on the matter. *Hudson and Goodwin* may have held that the whole of the common law of England had not been adopted nationally, but in *Wonson*, Story held that at least one component of British common law procedure—the re-examination of facts established by jury—had been adopted nationally, by the ratifiers of the Seventh Amendment, if by no one else.

What Story achieved through his interpretation of the Seventh Amendment in *Wonson* was quite radical. He had established a new rule of practice for federal judicial proceedings that completely bypassed the common law establishments of the separate states and instead found its authority in what he reverently referred to as "the invariable usage settled by the decisions of ages."[7] While still a long way from his ultimate goal—as we shall see, Story desired to recognize a federal common law that could increase the jurisdiction of the federal courts and provide a historically rooted foundation for federal jurisprudence—he had at least established a precedent that he could rely on in future cases. The underlying assumption in *Wonson* was based on a principle that Story would assert more directly in the coming years: that the wording of the Constitution itself assumed the existence of a uniquely federal common law, distinct from the common law as it was practiced in the states. For the time being, perhaps because the case hinged on the common law rules of practice instead of common law jurisdiction—and thus avoided the politically charged issue of the federal prosecution of non-statutory offenses—*Wonson* does not seem to have aroused considerable controversy or attention.

Story followed up his decision in *Wonson* with another circuit court case the same year: the equity case *Van Reimsdyk v. Kane*,[8] which dealt with the issue of conflict of laws. Section 34 of the Judiciary Act of 1789 had bound federal courts to the "laws of the several states" in all cases,[9] but this created the question of whether the laws of a particular state should be applied in diversity-of-citizenship cases, where the parties were citizens of different states.[10] Story held that despite the stipulations of Section 34, there was an implicit "limitation" on the general applicability of state law, arguing that while a state statute might apply in cases between citizens of the same state, or in controversies over property ownership, other situations might call for the application of a neutral law: "in controversies affecting citizens of other states, and in no degree arising from local regulations as for instance, foreign contracts of a commercial nature," wrote Story, "I think it can hardly be maintained, that the laws of the state, to which they have no reference, however narrow, injudicious and inconvenient they may be, are to be the exclusive guides for judicial decision."[11] To follow state law in such cases would, according to Story, defeat the purposes of the Constitution's framers in creating a national court system.[12]

Since state law could provide no rules of procedure for diversity-of-citizenship cases, it stands to reason that federal courts would need to follow—and, if necessary, develop—federal procedural rules for all diversity-of-citizenship cases. Such rules could be based on inherited British common law rules or on private international law. Furthermore, rather than leaving each federal district to develop these rules for itself, standard rules of federal procedure could be established and a national body of procedural law attained. This standardization of federal judicial procedures had, in fact, already been put into place by Story himself not in diversity-of-citizenship cases, but in another area of law that was left to the federal courts: prize law.[13] By August of 1812, Story had crafted a set of procedural rules governing federal prize cases and then distributed them among the district judges in his circuit;[14] he would do the same in equity cases following his decision in *Van Reimsdyk*. These comprehensive rules seem to have been received quite happily by his fellow federal judges,[15] who no doubt appreciated any guidance or clarity Story's erudition could provide in dealing with such cases.

In *Van Reimsdyk*, Story had thus carved out another narrow area of law where the federal judges were encouraged to bypass state law and rely instead on foreign sources in order to form a uniform rule that they could apply equally in all states. As R. Kent Newmyer describes Story's ruling in *Van Reimsdyk*, "By permitting federal courts to consult private international law in such cases, Story left the door open for a broad exercise of judicial discretion in the area of commercial law."[16] Ever the pragmatist, Story was willing to make whatever little steps he could toward establishing a comprehensive body of law that was uniquely federal in nature. If he was, for the moment, unable to secure an express recognition of a federal common law by a majority of his fellow justices on the Supreme Court, he would advance the doctrine himself in the circuit courts with whatever opportunities he happened to come across.

Still, Story was not willing to restrict himself to achieving these peripheral gains. His rulings in *Wonson* and *Van Reimsdyk* were merely on the fringes of what he saw as the underlying issue: "whether," Story wrote in 1816, "the Courts of the United States have from their very organization a general common law jurisdiction, or the United States a general common law authority."[17] On this matter, he felt a conviction, he wrote, "on which I feel no doubt."[18] This firm conviction of Story's seems to have stemmed directly from the irreplaceable utility of the common law in interpreting the federal Constitution: Story saw a federal common law as indispensable in order for the federal courts to do the tasks assigned to them by the Constitution. Story assumed, as a first rule of constitutional interpretation, that the American people, in creating the federal government, had intended to give it all the powers necessary to fulfill its constitutional directive. There could be no doubt that the American people in their full sovereign capacity were competent to grant the federal courts the kind of "general common law jurisdiction" that Story believed so fervently in, and there was little reason to doubt that they had actually chosen to do so, given the use of common law language in the Constitution itself and the ubiquity of common law precedents and principles in the legal culture that everywhere surrounded the framers. Consequently, Story sought out an occasion to reconsider the Court's position in *Hudson and Goodwin* and establish that the federal courts did, indeed, have a common law jurisdiction over offenses against the United States government.

STORY'S CASE FOR A COMMON LAW OF CRIMES: *UNITED STATES V. COOLIDGE*

Despite his own firm convictions on the issue, Story knew that calling into question so recent a decision, especially a decision in such a high-profile case, would be difficult. In order to even have a chance at a rehearing of the issue, he would have to pick the right case. In the 1813 circuit court case *United States v. Clark*,[19] he followed, somewhat begrudgingly,[20] a slightly tailored rendition of Johnson's central holding in *Hudson and Goodwin*: common-law indictments, he said, could not stand unless supported by a congressional act.[21] But though he was obligated to temporarily defer to the position held by the whole Court, he continued to look for an opportunity to reopen the question.

Story did not have to wait long for such an opportunity: the renewed hostilities with Great Britain provided him with a perfect opportunity in the 1813 Massachusetts circuit court case *United States v. Coolidge*.[22] That case involved the issue of forcible rescue of a prize ship: American privateers had taken possession of a vessel and were *en route* to the port of Salem to have their monetary reward adjudicated when along the way the vessel was forcibly rescued.[23] The rescuers were now brought to trial, even though forcible rescue of a prize had not been addressed by a congressional statute.[24] Although the question in the case as formulated by Story—"whether the Circuit Court of the United States had jurisdiction to punish offenses against the United States, which have not been previously defined, and a specific punishment affixed by some statute of the United States"[25]—was very similar to the one at stake in *Hudson and Goodwin*, there were a few key differentiating factors in the facts of the two cases. First, while the prosecution of Hudson and Goodwin had been overtly political in nature, *Coolidge* dealt with a case of forcible rescue on the high seas—an issue that was, by comparison, politically neutral.[26] Second, the issue at stake in *Hudson and Goodwin* had been the common law jurisdiction of the courts: since there was no constitutional or statutory foundation for prosecuting sedition under federal law, a general federal common law jurisdiction was the only way the federal courts could even entertain such cases. The facts in *Coolidge*, on the other hand, dealt with admiralty and maritime law and thus made this case indisputably within the purview of the federal courts: Article III had explicitly extended the judicial power of the federal courts "to all cases of admiralty and maritime jurisdiction." Since federal courts had a direct constitutional authority to hear this case by the explicit language of Article III, the case itself could not be simply dismissed for a lack of jurisdiction. Or rather, it could not be simply dismissed for a lack of admiralty or maritime jurisdiction, had Story chosen to hear the case on such grounds.

Instead, however, Story chose to decide the case as a common law case, which achieved his objective in bringing the issue again before the Court, albeit at the cost of putting his ruling in the case immediately at hand in a much more tenuous legal position. The fact that Story chose to present what would otherwise have been a clear-cut case for federal jurisdiction in such a questionable light suggests how acutely Story wanted to reopen the question that had ostensibly been answered in *Hudson and Goodwin*. In stating the legal issue in the case as the highly contentious question of crimes against the United States at common law instead of basing jurisdiction on the unassailable grounds of it being a maritime case, Story demonstrated perhaps an over-eagerness to present his own views on the federal common law question. In an 1824 valedictory address, the nineteenth-century legal scholar Peter Stephen Du Ponceau brought attention this decision by Story and opined that "it is much to be regretted that he thought it necessary to travel out of his straight path, and to abandon an impregnable fortress to seek battle in the open field."[27] Du Ponceau went on to suggest that the only reason Story would have based jurisdiction in the case on such grounds was an underlying belief that the federal common law question was too important for the Court to dismiss it without hearing arguments for either side, as it had done in *Hudson and Goodwin*.[28] Because it had been decided without the aid of arguments by counsel for either side and with only the support of a bare majority of the Court, Johnson's decision in *Hudson and Goodwin* was not as conclusive an answer as the momentous question of a federal common law jurisdiction deserved, given its far-reaching consequences. The unusual circumstances surrounding the decision thus, in his mind, made the Court's opinion in *Hudson and Goodwin* less final, and Story appeared to be looking for a case that would provide an opportunity for a re-hearing of the question.

Story obviously felt strongly about the issue and considered its re-examination to be of paramount importance. Still, for all his personal assuredness on the question, he approached the precedent with studied humility: Justice Johnson's opinion was "entitled to the most respectful consideration," but given that the case had been decided without argument and without unanimity on the Court, he held the question as still open until it should receive "a more solemn decision."[29] Story pushed the issue further, noting that the constitutional jurisdiction of the federal courts was at stake in the question of the federal common law and pointedly adding that the federal courts themselves "cannot lawfully enlarge or diminish" their constitutionally-granted jurisdiction,[30] hinting at the possibility that a general common law jurisdiction for the federal courts had been granted by the Constitution itself. Moreover, Story highlighted the different subject matter of this case: *Hudson and Goodwin* may have declared a majority of the Court's opinion on the general question of federal prosecutions of non-statutory offenses, but it had not, "however broad in its language . . . settled the question now before the court, so far as it respects offenses of admiralty and maritime jurisdiction."[31] Story thus attempted to bring up the federal common law question with the issue of jurisdiction safely off the table. And yet, despite making a passing reference to admiralty and maritime jurisdiction, it is evident that Story was using the case to argue a much larger point.

Still, Story's argument regarding the federal courts' admiralty and maritime jurisdiction required at least one rather large assumption. No one could dispute that the federal courts had the constitutional authority to hear admiralty or maritime cases, given a prosecutable offence; yet it was indeed debatable whether the courts could find such an offence without statutory authorization. Indeed, the most straightforward reading of Johnson's decision in *Hudson and Goodwin* was that the federal courts could not prosecute individuals for common law offenses even if it fit one of the categories of cases that the courts were permitted to hear. Story's assumption was that a constitutional grant of jurisdiction to the federal courts meant that the federal courts were free to prosecute any offense that fell within that category. This assumption was consistent with his general method of constitutional interpretation which in turn stemmed from his conception of the union, to be discussed later.

Conversely, if the Constitution's grant of admiralty and maritime jurisdiction to the federal courts was seen as merely granting Congress permission to establish the basis for answering admiralty and maritime cases, then it was up to Congress to decide either to identify specific common law offenses to be outlawed or to pass a general adoption of the common law rules in admiralty and maritime cases, or to come up with some alternate basis for such prosecutions that completely disregarded the larger common law tradition they had been a part of in England. Either way, Johnson's opinion had indicated that it was Congress' prerogative to decide what actions should be punished, even if the courts had been given a general jurisdiction over cases of the same sort. Consequently, the issue at stake in *Coolidge* was the same one that had been dealt with before, and the fact that it was a maritime case did not change the fact that it had already been answered by the thrust of Johnson's opinion: no common law jurisdiction—maritime case or no—had yet been granted to the federal courts by Congress or by the Constitution, and it was not the place of the federal courts to provide such a jurisdiction for themselves.

Given the intensely political nature of the underlying question, Story proceeded with a caution that would often mark his judicial opinions. Although in both his public writings and private letters, Story appears to have been zealously certain that the entirety of the British common law—though modified to fit the American situation—was a part of the laws of the United States,[32] Story began his opinion in *Coolidge* by limiting the scope of his argument. "I do not think it necessary," he wrote, "to consider the more broad question, whether the United States, as a sovereign power, have entirely adopted the common law. This might lead to very elaborate inquiries, and the present question may well be decided without entering upon the discussion."[33] Story thus narrowed the question to whether the Court might hear questions of offenses against the United States—defined by Story as "all offences against the sovereignty, the public rights, the public justice, the public peace, the public trade and the public police of the United States"[34]—that had not been explicitly outlawed by a specific congressional statute. Story appeared, therefore, to be proceeding with incremental recognition of a partial common law jurisdiction, just as he had done in *Wonson* and *Van Reimsdyk*. Such piecemeal discoveries surely hinted at a larger, comprehensive body of law that all were drawing from but still managed to avoid the more trying task of ascertaining what the limits of this body of law were or in determining when and how it had been adopted.

Furthermore, Story's argument was limited because, due to the facts of the case, he did not need to resort to the common law to establish the case as a federal one. All he needed the common law for was to provide guidance and a rule of decision in a case that the courts undeniably had the authority to hear. This fact essentially mooted one of the most powerful Republican critiques against the federal common law doctrine: that, given the wide-ranging nature of common law concerns, such a doctrine would grant the federal courts virtually unlimited jurisdiction and totally obliterate the carefully laid out parameters of federal jurisdiction in Article III, section 2. As the federal common law critics in the Virginia House of Delegates put it in 1800, the doctrine of a federal common law "assumes a range of jurisdiction for the federal courts, which defies limitation or definition."[35] And yet, in the present case at least, Story claimed no such unlimited or ill-defined jurisdiction and, on the contrary, held that a common law jurisdiction could be had in this case without expanding beyond the strict constitutional limits on the federal judiciary's authority over certain types of cases. "I admit in the most explicit terms," he wrote in *Coolidge*, "that the courts of the United States are courts of limited jurisdiction, and cannot exercise any authorities, which are not confided to them by the constitution and laws made in pursuance thereof."[36] Story went on to say, however, that once the Constitution had given jurisdiction to the federal courts over an area of law, "the nature and extent of that authority, and the mode in which it shall be exercised, must be regulated by the rules of the common law."[37] Thus, Story was able to avoid the thorny question over whether the federal courts had jurisdiction over *every* area of law touched upon by the common law; all that he was asserting here was that, once the federal courts had jurisdiction over a case—by the unmistakable language of Article III in this case—they should have recourse to the common law to determine the course of action in that case.

Indeed, argued Story, what other law should they base it upon? If the American people had adopted the common law as their standard, then it stands as the obvious reference point for understanding the constitutional grants of jurisdiction in Article III. If the common law provides the foundation for jurisprudence in every state, then its status as a valid tool for interpreting the Constitution can be assumed. And if this were the case, then the constitutional grant of jurisdiction in a certain category of cases conveyed with it the bulk of common law precedents within that category—an impressive body of settled doctrines, but one still limited by the language of the Constitution itself. All that remained was for Story to demonstrate the last component of this assertion: that it *must* be the common law that guides the Court's decision and that federal judges were obligated to follow British common law precedents. This he would attempt to prove at length throughout the greater part of his opinion.

Despite these careful attempts to limit the scope of his claims, however, Story's opinion did little to ease Republican concerns over the federal common law doctrine. Whatever mediating value these distinctions held as a rhetorical device, *legally* speaking, they made hardly any difference at all. First of all, while Story attempted to distinguish his claim of a power to prosecute offenses against the sovereignty and public power of the United States government from the argument that the United States had adopted the *entire* British common law, there was little constitutional difference between claiming a common law jurisdiction for "offenses against the United States" and claiming a blanket common law jurisdiction in all cases, criminal and civil. In the entire debate over the federal common law, the most important issue at stake was the underlying question of whether the federal government was constitutionally competent to adopt the common law in the first place. If Story were to prevail in *Coolidge* and a common law for "offenses against the United States" be recognized by the Court, the most important outcome of the case would have been the explicit recognition that the common law—or at least some portion of it—had, in fact, been adopted nationally. The unavoidable implication would be that the United States was competent to adopt a comprehensive national common law system, all without explicit action by Congress or authorization in the constitutional text. On the other hand, to deny the principle that the United States was even capable of adopting the common law—as Jefferson and the Republicans did—was, of course, to make the question of its application in one case or another completely void.

Second, Story's distinction between using the common law as a guide in a case and using it as a source of jurisdiction also proves to be rather insignificant in practice. As stated above, the dispute in this debate lay over whether some version of the British common law tradition *had been*, or even *could be*, adopted by the United States in a national or federal capacity. If the federal courts had recourse to the common law to determine their ruling in a case—any case—it would thus be established that the common law had, in fact, been adopted. If this were the case, there would then be very little reason to not allow the jurisdiction of the federal courts to expand alongside their access to common law rulings and procedures. Richard Dana of Massachusetts understood the relationship between what Story argued for in *Coolidge* and an expanded jurisdiction of the federal courts. Nearly thirty years later, when arguing the case *Swift v. Tyson* before the Court, Dana asserted that Story's opinion in *Coolidge* "involved the general question [of] whether the common law had been adopted; for if it could be referred to at all, it was equally a source of jurisdiction as it would be the rule of decision."[38] Dana thus argued that the distinction Story had tried to hold in *Coolidge*—between allowing the courts to use the common law to answer cases and providing them with jurisdiction over every area of law that the common law had touched upon—was false. Once it was established, in principle, that a federal common law had been adopted, there was no reason to disallow federal justices from claiming it as the basis of their jurisdiction.

There was also a separation-of-powers principle at stake in Story's claim of a federal common law jurisdiction for trying "offenses against the United States." The situation in *Coolidge* provided an excellent case in point: the Constitution had given the federal courts jurisdiction over controversies arising on the high seas, but what was particularly at stake in this case was whether the federal courts could prosecute a crime which fell into that general category of cases, but which had not been, in Story's words, "previously defined, and a specific punishment affixed, by some statute of the United States."[39] As previously stated, the Constitution undeniably granted the federal courts jurisdiction over the general category of cases like the one at hand. Indeed, the constitutional architects must surely have envisioned fact patterns very similar to the one in *Coolidge* when drafting the jurisdictional authority of the federal courts. But the framers of the Constitution had also imbued Congress with the authority to effectuate such definition and punishment through the passage of legislation "to define and punish piracies and felonies committed on the high seas, and offences against the law of nations" as well as to "make rules concerning captures on land and water."[40] Article I, section 8 had gone on to grant Congress the power "to make all laws which shall be necessary and proper for carrying into execution the foregoing powers, and all other powers vested in this Constitution in the government of the United States, or in any department or officer thereof."[41] Consequently, according to the Jeffersonian reading of Article I, it was solely Congress' job to "make all laws" which would allow for all of the powers of the federal government to be carried out. That the Constitution granted the Supreme Court jurisdiction over cases of this type did nothing to change the fact that it was Congress' responsibility to pass legislation to carry that power into execution. That Congress had neglected to do so with the particular offence at hand may have been misguided, and very likely was an oversight, but this did not change the fact that the Constitution had given Congress the authority to pass such laws as would be necessary for the courts to punish these offenses. Without Congress first passing a law to outlaw an action, argued the Jeffersonians, the courts could not hear the case, maritime case or no.

There was an additional complication that belied Story's careful framing of the case. If Story were to succeed in recognizing a distinctly federal common law, it was bound to have serious ramifications for the relative power of the federal courts over the state courts and, more broadly, of the federal government over the state governments. Since, according to the language of Article III, federal courts had jurisdiction over all questions touching on "federal law," the only limitation on jurisdiction by the courts was the evasive line between what constituted "federal law" and what constituted "state law." If "federal law" was found to include the broader British common law tradition—even in truncated or modified form—it would give federal courts access to an innumerable number of questions, issues, and doctrines that the Constitution was silent on. As the distinction between "federal law" and "state law" began to fade, the federal courts—and thereby the federal government—could conceivably claim authority over any area of law touched on by the British common law, which is to say virtually every aspect of life and public policy. Thus, the Virginia General Assembly argued that proponents of a federal common law "would, themselves, be lost in an attempt to apply it to the existing institutions of federal and state courts, by separating with precision their judiciary rights, and thus preventing the constant and mischievous interference of rival jurisdictions."[42] The federal common law, according to the General Assembly, would demolish all of the careful constitutional distinctions between the rightful jurisdiction of the federal judiciary and that of the state courts. Thus, according to Republican critics of the federal common law doctrine, acknowledging the existence of the federal common law would lead to a virtually unlimited jurisdiction for the federal courts, effectively annulling the carefully-set-out parameters of federal jurisdiction in Article III. Story's attempts to limit the scope of his argument may thus have saved him from engaging in the unenviable task of demonstrating conclusively how and when and to what extent the British common law had been adopted by the United States, but it did not go very far in assuaging the fears of the opponents of a federal common law.

Even so, Story proceeded in *Coolidge* by attempting to frame the contentious issue in the most unobjectionable light possible. As discussed earlier, this was clearly a case that the federal courts were charged with answering; any concerns about the merging of state and federal jurisdictions were, for the moment, mere conjecture. Not only did this case deal with crimes that occurred on the high seas, but it also involved what Story described as attacks or offenses against the United States government, making the question whether the federal government would be allowed to even defend itself against such attacks. If ever the courts were to be allowed to prosecute nonstatutory offenses, this would be the case.

Since the federal courts, according to Story's interpretation of Article III, had to take the case, there were only two questions left to answer: Did it matter that Congress had not statutorily identified the crime of forcible prize rescue, and if not, what tools would the federal courts use in solving the case? To Story, the key to answering both of these questions lay in his belief that a distinct federal body of common law provided the groundwork for the Constitution. Answering these questions provided Story with the framework he needed to advance, in a more full exposition than he had in previous cases, his belief in a federal common law jurisdiction for crimes against the United States.

In a certain sense, given his argument for the existence of a federal common law, Story did not need to establish a congressional authorization for the courts. If indeed there was a single set of federally adopted common law principles underlying and supplementing the Constitution and laws of the United States, then it would not be necessary for Congress to statutorily define and affix punishments for every conceivable offense; the courts merely had to look to the wellspring of British legal custom. Story apparently believed very firmly that there was such a national common law, but chose in *Coolidge* to hedge his bets by citing congressional authorization anyway. Congress, he argued, had indeed authorized the federal courts' prosecution of non-statutory offenses through section 11 of the Judiciary Act of 1789, which provided that the circuit courts "shall have exclusive cognizance of all crimes and offences cognizable under the authority of the United States" unless otherwise directed by law.[43] The power of the federal courts to try common law offences thus hinged upon whether such offenses were "cognizable under the authority of the United States." This phrase, Story argued, could be rephrased as applying to "all crimes and offenses, to which by the constitution of the United States, the judicial power extends,"[44] but this phrase, like the one preceding, still was hopelessly ambiguous. It did not say what these offenses were, or if it included all offenses against the United States government.

What was needed was some outside source to give meaning and context to these words. This problem, of course, was one frequently encountered by federal judges in interpreting the laws and Constitution of the United States. Fortunately, Story asserted, there was one true source that federal judges must turn to in order to understand the language of the Constitution: the common law. Story supported this claim by demonstrating the many ways that the Constitution presupposed a familiarity with common law language, doctrines, and principles. Nor was Story bothered by the question of how far this national common law extended or of "Whether the common law of England, in its broadest sense, including equity and admiralty, as well as legal doctrines, be the common law of the United States or not."[45] Regardless of the answer to this broader—and more controversial—question, argued Story, "it can hardly be doubted, that the constitution and laws of the United States are predicated upon the existence of the common law."[46] In defense of this assertion, Story listed off numerous constitutional clauses and provisions that made reference to the common law: the requirement of trial by jury, the extension of the judicial power to "all cases, in law and equity," and the protection of the writ of habeas corpus, etc.[47] Such provisions not only assumed they were to be applied in a judicial system built upon the common law, but were, in fact, utterly incomprehensible without such a common law foundation giving them meaning and context. Based on these and other clauses, Story concluded that the text of the Constitution itself indicated that judges should make reference to the common law in interpreting federal powers.[48] In the particular context of criminal prosecutions, Story allowed that when a crime was addressed by an act of Congress, that act superseded the general common law interpretation, but summarized that absent such a statute, "the interpretation and exercise of the vested jurisdiction of the courts of the United States must ... be governed exclusively by the common law."[49] Given this rule of interpretation, the common law thus was also the obvious reference point for understanding what crimes and offenses were "cognizable under the authority of the United States."

Story's argument was pregnant with serious ramifications for the federal courts; for while it technically still followed the contours of the Constitution in determining federal power, it still allowed for a considerable broadening of federal jurisdiction. Instead of viewing Article III's grants of jurisdiction as establishing the outer limits of the federal courts' reach—still subject to Congress' power to declare what actions should be crimes—each grant of jurisdiction included with it the mandate that the federal courts exercise the jurisdiction according to common law principles and precedents. Such was obviously the intention of the American people in granting the federal courts the jurisdiction they had, according to Story, and the American people could everywhere be found abiding by the common law and incorporating it into every level of law and government. Needless to say, this interpretation also granted considerably more latitude in prosecuting common law offences, for all that would have to be shown was that the American people had, in ratifying the Constitution, granted jurisdiction over some area of the common law to the federal courts; this being shown, it did not matter at all whether Congress had outlawed the action by statute. Congress could no more override the will of the American people than the justices of the federal court could, and Story took the occasion in *Coolidge* to remind his fellow justices of their lack of authority to "enlarge or diminish" the jurisdiction granted to them by the American people in the Constitution.[50]

Relying on the Constitution's grant of jurisdiction to the federal courts to provide the parameters of the federal common law also allowed Story to avoid the difficult—and politically charged—question of whether the bulk of the British common law tradition was part of the "laws of the United States" in a general sense. Without validating Republican fears of a limitless federal jurisdiction unrestrained by the Constitution, he was still able to substantially free up the federal courts to pursue common law prosecutions and to use the common law as a guide in reaching decisions and assigning penalties. His critics might still hypothesize that Story's logic strongly implied the existence of a more comprehensive national common law adoption from which the federal courts were drawing, but such conjectures were muted by Story's argument that the common law foundation that gave meaning to the Constitution was only applicable in cases where the courts had already been given jurisdiction by the Constitution or by congressional enactment. Ostensibly, when framing the Constitution, the American people had access to the national body of common law in its entirety, but they had apparently chosen only to grant certain aspects or parts of it to the federal government. The "laws of the United States" alluded to in the Supremacy Clause thus didn't include the whole federal common law, but rather only those parts of it that corresponded to the powers granted by the people of the United States to the federal government. Story readily acknowledged that the United States government was one of specified, enumerated powers, and that the federal courts were reliant on the text of the Constitution for their authority to hear any case; to prohibit the federal courts from hearing a case under the jurisdiction granted to them by the American people, however, was to place additional restrictions on the federal judicial power that the American people had never instituted. Story hinted that Johnson's opinion in *Hudson and Goodwin* had done just that.

His interpretive framework being thus established, Story applied the general principle to the case at hand. Since the Judiciary Act granted the federal courts jurisdiction for crimes and offenses "cognizable under the authority of the United States," it was necessary to look to the common law to understand what kind of cases are included in this grant of jurisdiction, keeping also in mind the inherently limited nature of federal jurisdiction. Without attempting to provide an exhaustive list of offenses against the United States, Story suggested a general starting point for understanding the general scope of such crimes: "all offences against the sovereignty, the public rights, the public justice, the public peace, the public trade, and the public police of the United States, are crimes and offences against the United States."[51] Given the limited nature of the United States' sovereignty, many of these offenses would also be cognizable by the states; but, argued Story, "whenever the offense is directed against the sovereignty or powers confided to the United States, it is cognizable under its authority."[52] From this, Story reasoned that any offenses within the general scope of admiralty jurisdiction, which was the exclusive purview of the federal courts, were offenses directed against the sovereignty and constitutionally conferred powers of the United States government.

Thus, to put it most broadly, any crime at common law could be prosecuted by the federal courts, provided that it was deemed to be an attack on the sovereignty of the United States government or to touch on one of those areas of policy that the federal government had been given authority over. Whatever differentiating factors the two cases may have had in their fact patterns, Story's opinion in *Coolidge* was thus still a direct frontal attack on the central holding in *Hudson and Goodwin*. Story could only hope that the rest of the Court considered the issue as unresolved as he did, and that the passage of time and the chance to have full hearings on the case might lead his brethren on the Court to be swayed on the issue.

Unfortunately for Story, both of these hopes went unresolved when the Court overturned Story's opinion and again upheld the previous ruling in *Hudson and Goodwin*.[53] Once again, the counsel for both parties declined to appear to argue the case in person.[54] Prefacing the recorded opinion was a brief statement from Madison's attorney general at the time, Richard Rush, saying that he had considered the case at hand, as well as the precedent in *Hudson and Goodwin*, and that "considering the point as decided in that case [i.e. *Hudson and Goodwin*], whether with, or without, argument . . . he desired respectfully to state, without saying more, that it was not his intention to argue it now."[55] Story stated simply that he did not consider the question to be settled by *Hudson and Goodwin*; Johnson stated simply that he did consider the issue settled there.[56] Two other justices, Bushrod Washington and Henry Brockholst Livingston, were apparently open to considering the question if they were given the opportunity to hear arguments from counsel in the future, with Livingston adding, "but until the question is re-argued, the case of *United States v. Hudson and Goodwin* must be taken as law."[57] Johnson, having previously claimed a "general acquiescence of legal men" on the subject, here acknowledged that "a difference of opinion has existed, and still exists, among the members of the court," and suggested that the Court would have been willing to reconsider the question "upon solemn argument," had legal counsel for either side appeared to argue the case.[58] Since they did not, however, the Court decided simply to reaffirm to the circuit court their previous decision in *Hudson and Goodwin*.[59]

Thus, Story's colleagues on the Court half-heartedly admitted that he was right: given the import of the question, it should have been argued before the Court. But no one else on the Court seemed willing to revive the issue or bring it again for debate. Perhaps this reluctance was partially due to the Madison administration's apparent reluctance to argue the case before the Court, thus preventing the Court from having the full-fledged rehearing that Story desired. Whatever the reason for his colleagues' reluctance to re-examine the question, Story recognized after *Coolidge* that the matter had been decided, however wrongly, and opted not to further press the issue of a common law jurisdiction for crimes against the United States government.

Even so, he still could not bring himself to accept what he saw as the essential premise of the Court's position: that the principles of the common law were not applicable to the federal government. Those principles were too time-tested and firmly established, as well as too interwoven into the fabric of the young nation's legal system, to be placed out of reach of the federal courts' attempts to interpret the federal Constitution and laws that in so many ways presupposed them. To Story, it seemed completely arbitrary to put a barrier between the American people and their legal heritage or to presuppose a break with the common law when none was hinted at by the language of the Constitution. Story obviously understood Johnson's essential premise that the federal government had been granted certain powers and not others, but for the American people to grant the federal government certain powers and then have Supreme Court justices pretend that these powers were in no way related to the common law system that was everywhere about them was absurd.

Moreover, Story believed that such a divorce of federal jurisprudence from its common law roots was frankly dangerous. Such a separation would necessarily untether the federal judiciary from these ancient and venerable precepts and instead give federal judges free reign to invent their own interpretations: without the common law guiding their interpretations, Story had argued in his circuit court opinion in *Coolidge*, "the judicial power of the United States would be left, in its exercise, to the mere arbitrary pleasure of the judges, to an uncontrollable and undefined discretion."[60] Whatever his opponents may have feared from the common law, he argued, "such a despotic power could hardly be deemed more desirable."[61] He would elaborate further on this fear in his *Commentaries on the Constitution*, published in 1833: "Take an Act of Congress—How is it to be interpreted? Are the rules of the common law to furnish the proper guide, or is every court and department to give it any interpretation it may please, according to its own will?"[62] The question of a federal common law jurisdiction was thus a question of whether the courts would be bound by the venerable common law tradition or else be left completely at the whim of unelected federal judges. This was the "despotic" judicial power that the Republican rejection of the federal common law inadvertently led them to.

In truth, just as Story's argument for a federal common law jurisdiction was perhaps more nuanced than Republican critics acknowledged—in its recognition of constitutional limits to federal jurisdiction, for instance—so was Republican opposition to the federal common law more thoughtful than Story appeared to recognize. This argument in particular was one that Story's opponents could easily rebut and had already done so. During House debates to repeal the Judiciary Act of 1801, John Randolph of Roanoke argued against the Federalist claims of a federal common law, even while readily acknowledging the indispensability of a knowledge of the common law for interpreting the Constitution: "That the common law is to settle the meaning of common law phrases, few will feel disposed to deny," argued Randolph, noting the utility of the common law to understanding such basic notions as "court" or "jury."[63] He then went on to argue, however, that "because the common law is to be resorted to for an explanation of these and similar terms, does it follow that that indefinite and undefinable body of law is the irrepealable law of the land?"[64] In other words, just because a British common law rule provided the standard for interpretation of a particular word or clause in the Constitution did not make the common law as a whole applicable to the United States nationally or a part of the "laws of the United States." Republicans thus did not deny that common law words and phrases had a well-established meaning but essentially used Blackstone the same way they would a law dictionary. To say that the Constitution was written by men with a knowledge of the common law, against the backdrop of the common law, was decidedly different than saying that there was a single, federal set of common law principles that was equally in force over and above the common law as accepted and modified by each state. The first of these statements was undeniable and was thoroughly compatible with the Republican understanding of acceptance of the common law by each separate state. The latter of these statements potentially jeopardized the common law as it was practiced within each state. To Republicans, the assertion of a federal common law—even in Story's modified argument recognizing that federal jurisdiction was limited by the language of Article III—went far beyond the common-sense recognition of its applicability in interpreting familiar phrases; it promised to swallow up the common law distinctions between the states in favor of one national common law whose only limit was the creativity of federal judges in connecting their chosen common law object with some line or other in the Constitution.

Story, however, believed that the common law provided the only suitable foundation for interpreting federal law. And since the common law had demonstrably been accepted in America, there was no reason to deny federal justices the aid of these widely accepted principles in deciding cases. Thus, he began to seek out alternate methods of ensuring that the developing body of national case law would be based upon the firm foundation of the common law. In order to do so, however, he would have to account for the rather problematic issue that he had deftly skirted in *Coolidge*: the question of when and how this national common law, evidenced as it was throughout the language of the Constitution, had been adopted or accepted by the American people.

STORY'S THEORY OF ADOPTION

Story's assertion that the federal courts had a common law jurisdiction, albeit one limited by the parameters of the Constitution and the federal nature of the American government implied that the American people had at some point adopted the common law and accepted it as the basis of their federal Constitution and laws. If he could establish that the American people had, in fact, done so, then it was perfectly logical to assert, as Story had in *Coolidge*, that certain common law crimes against the government could be assumed to be within the federal courts' purview even in the absence of statutory authorization; other crimes, being affronts against the English crown or established church, obviously would not, as neither had ever enjoyed acceptance in America either before or after the Revolution.[65] On the other hand, if he could not prove that the common law had been adopted nationally the way it had obviously been adopted by each of the colonies, the common law would not have the same impact on the jurisdiction of the federal courts. Consequently, critics of the federal common law made much of the fact that there had been no formal common law adoption by Congress as there had been by the legislature of each separate colony when they had adopted the common law. In order to argue that the common law did, in fact, convey an additional jurisdiction to the federal courts, Story would first have to establish that such a federal common law had in fact been adopted by the American people in their national capacity.

Nor was it enough to merely point to the existence of the common law at the state level: to argue in favor of a national common law jurisdiction meant that the action of adoption would have had to be done *nationally* by the American people in their corporate capacity, taken as a whole and not just in their separate states. For although the common law was the foundation of every state legal system, it varied so greatly from one state to the next that any search for a substantial set of common law rules or principles that was universally acknowledged and identically practiced in every state would have been an impossible endeavor.

The difficulty of such an effort was described by Story's contemporary Nathan Dane in his *General Abridgment and Digest of American Law*, who, in his introduction to that work, recounted his early attempts "at the close of the American revolutionary war, when the United States became an independent nation . . . to inquire and to know what was law in them, collectively and individually."[66] Dane was interested in finding a single source that might aid in understanding the process by which English law had been adopted in America, "especially in selecting from the English laws in force in a monarchy once feudal, those parts of them adopted here, and remaining in force in our republic."[67] Unfortunately for Dane, such a search proved futile: "He early found that there was in the United States nothing like *one collected body of American law, or one collected system of American politics*; but all was found in scattered fragments"[68] (emphasis in the original). His own *General Digest* was an attempt to rectify this absence.

Although apparently a great frustration to him, Dane's failure to find a single compilation of American law that was nationally in force at the close of the revolution was, in a certain sense, predictable. After all, there was, in 1783, no singular body of "American law" to compile, nor was there a single agreed-upon standard of which British laws had been retained in the colonies and which had been abandoned. This is not to say that there was no American jurisprudence on this question up until this point, for common law composed an important component of the laws of every colony, or even to say that the statutory laws of each state had not been compiled and published. But it was apparent that none of the common law principles that existed in each colony was thought of as being in force nationally. In searching for a general digest of American law, Dane did find publications summarizing the laws of the newly formed states,[69] but no attempt to generalize these discordant state bodies of law into a national system of jurisprudence.

Nor was it of any help to Dane that every state had, since its inception, acknowledged the influence of the common law, for such a general similarity was not enough to override the differences between the common law tradition within each of the states. The common law of England had undoubtedly been Americanized over time, and the process of transformation had been carried out separately and differently by each state. St. George Tucker, in his essay *Of the Unwritten, or Common Law of England*, argued that the adoption of the common law within the colonies had failed to produce an overriding conformity between their legal systems, reliant as that adoption was on the "various modifications, limitations, and restrictions" of each colony and subject as the common law of each was to legislative alteration or override.[70] Absent a national legislature over all of the colonies, the choice by any one colony to adopt or reject any portion of the British common law could have had no effect outside its borders and whatever general symmetry might have been gained from the colonial legal systems all drawing on a common source was blemished by the countless alterations making the common law system of each state distinctive.

Consequently, assembling such a "collected body of American law" as Dane was searching for would doubtless have been very difficult, not only because of the difficulty in attaining sources—the publications of state statutory law had apparently all been published in England and very few of the state court decisions had been recorded in any regularly published court reporter—but also because of the divergences, some great and some small, from one state to the next. To truly summarize American law as it was actually practiced would have been an enormous undertaking, specifically because it would have had to summarize not one body of law, but thirteen separate ones. Tucker had twenty years earlier dismissed such attempts to uncover a general rule of what parts of the common law were in force within all the states as "hopeless."[71] Tucker's warnings are inadvertently validated by Dane's own experience: faced with such an impossible undertaking, Dane ultimately focused mostly on the law in Massachusetts. This concession by Dane, while eminently practical, demonstrates the unavoidability of focusing on state law in trying to examine the substantive law of the United States in this period. Indeed, there was little else Dane could have relied on.

Thus, to prove the existence of a general federal common law, or even to discuss the details of its adoption with any precision, was a formidable task, for although there was ubiquitous evidence for the adoption of the common law by each separate state, it was much harder to demonstrate that the common law had also been adopted nationally. At the moment of emigration, when the settlers of each separate colony had formally and publicly adopted the common law as it then existed in England, it would have been impossible for them to have done so corporately at that time, as they had no national body to effectuate or announce such an adoption, no national judiciary to develop and add to the body of law in the future, and no national legislature to amend it. Even after the Revolution, the evidence for a single body of national common law was, at best, implied rather than directly observed. This being the case, the formal declarations of a common law adoption by the governing bodies of the separate colonies-turned-states only made the absence of any such formal adoption by the federal government more noticeable, adding strength to Republican arguments that no such federal common law existed.

There were two additional barriers that Story had to overcome in demonstrating that the common law had been adopted nationally: both were anticipated by Tucker's comments on the adoption of the common law by the states. First of all, these original adoptions varied considerably due to the fact that each colonial settlement brought over the common law as it existed in England at that point in time. As the English common law continued to change and develop in the mother country, the common law as known and practiced within each already-established colony would generally be immune from many of these later developments, although other developments were willingly adopted by the colonists.[72] Consequently, the common law as adopted in colonies founded later was often substantively different from that of colonies founded earlier—as evidenced by the wide range of changes to the British constitution that were undergone between the founding of Jamestown in 1607 and the chartering of Georgia in 1732.

Moreover, being thus freed from any unifying or systematizing force, the common law systems of the several colonies had tended gradually to diverge from one another as they were developed by their respective judiciaries and amended by their respective legislatures. By the time of the Revolution, the common law practices of the several colonies had grown so disparate as to then essentially comprise thirteen distinct variations on the common law tradition and not, as was the case in England, one single legal system that was *common* to all in any substantive sense. James Madison makes this point in his *Report of 1800* where, in the context of explaining the Virginia Resolutions on behalf of the state House of Delegates, he argued at length against the federal common law doctrine: "The common law was not the same in any two of the colonies; in some, the modifications were materially and extensively different."[73] Nor was this divergence between the common law as it was practiced in different colonies at all surprising for Madison, who noted further the absence of any central authority to adopt, interpret, or apply the common law: "There was no common legislature, by which a common will could be expressed in the form of a law; nor any common magistracy, by which such a law could be carried into practice. The will of each colony, alone and separately, had its organs for these purposes."[74] Such a state of affairs fit naturally with the views of Madison's fellow Republicans, who saw an affirmation of the federal common law doctrine as wholly different from an affirmation of the role of the common law in each state's legal system. For Story, on the other hand, the divergence between different states' recognition and practice of the common law was deeply problematic, as Story's argument for a national common law foundation that could be used as a common reference point for all federal courts required that there be a single, *federal* common law foundation that the federal courts could have recourse to. In order for this theory to work, there must have been a moment, then, at which some corporate, national entity—either the American people as a whole or their agents in the federal government—had chosen to enact and adopt the common law.

Notwithstanding the central importance of common law adoption in establishing the federal common law foundation for the Constitution, Story had demurred to elaborate on the origins of the federal common law in his decision in *Coolidge*. Instead, he opted to simply demonstrate that a federal common law foundation did exist by pointing to textual evidence in the Constitution, as discussed before. As discussed earlier, Story held off on the thornier issue of describing a common law adoption, deeming the question of whether the common law had been "entirely adopted" by the United States to be unnecessary and warning that such a question "might lead to very elaborate inquiries."[75] For the present case, it had been enough to demonstrate that a common law foundation apparently did exist and to ignore the related questions of when, how, and to what extent that federal common law had been adopted. He thus limited himself to demonstrating merely that a common law foundation was assumed by the Constitution. Such evasion was not wholly unwarranted; his job as a jurist was—in a strict sense—to answer the case before him in as direct a manner as he could, without including extraneous historical or philosophical analysis that went far beyond the scope of the case immediately at hand. Admittedly, Story himself would not always strictly abide by this rule of avoiding broader analysis when not absolutely necessary. But he was not afraid to do so when it suited him or when such apparent self-restraint helped to evade the more problematic points of the broader claim that he was hinting at, yet not explicitly defending.

In order to understand Story's theory of a federal common law, however, the question of adoption cannot be dispelled quite so quickly. That requires an examination of the very question that Story avoids answering: the question of "whether," in Story's words, "the United States, as a sovereign power, have entirely adopted the common law."[76] Although Story deems it unnecessary to answer this question, its formulation here hints at two material questions:

the question of whether the common law foundation Story had uncovered included the *entire* British common law or only some portion of it, and second, the question of when and how that common law's adoption by the American people or their federal government had come to be. The first of these—the question of whether the *entire* British common law is in effect in American courts—was, in a sense, very easy to answer: all commentators on the issue, including Story, readily acknowledged that *some* aspects of the British common law were not in force anywhere in America, either federally or at the state level; two uncontestable examples would be those aspects of the common law dealing with royal prerogative or titles of nobility. This fact, however, only made the question of *which* parts of the common law had been accepted and which had not all the more problematic. Ascertaining this with any degree of precision or certainty would prove to be a very difficult task, but one that Story would willingly take on in the following years.

On the second question—asking when and how this national common law had been adopted—Story would never offer a thorough and comprehensive account, instead resorting to applying the asserted federal common law in various particular circumstances.[77] Nevertheless, an assumption of national adoption of the common law of Britain—whether "in its entirety" or not—is the unavoidable inference from Story's claim that the Constitution itself "presumes" a federal common law foundation. If the common law operates as a source of context or meaning, then there were only two possibilities: either there must have been a single identifiable moment at which the American people had chosen to embrace the British common law and set it up as the foundation of their legal system or else it had been chosen and established not in a single conscious act of endowment, but rather through its steady application through past generations and near-universal acceptance over a great span of time. Either option presented difficulties for Story's argument: if the former, where was the proof of its adoption? No national source—neither Congress, nor its predecessor under the Articles of Confederation, nor the constitutional architects at the 1787 Convention, nor the state ratification conventions, nor the wartime Continental Congress—had explicitly and unmistakably signaled such a national adoption of the British common law tradition in bulk. In fact, there were serious questions whether any of these bodies—with the possible exception of the Constitutional Convention—had the formal authority to do so. The latter option was likewise problematic because, though Story could easily demonstrate that common law precedents enjoyed widespread popular acceptance and were in everyday legal usage, this still did not necessarily prove the existence of a *federal* common law tradition, as the tangible evidence of common law acceptance might still only be proof of its acceptance by the legal systems of each separate state, and even there with significant differences in the common law traditions between them.

Consequently, Story's statement that the Constitution and the federal laws are "predicated upon the existence of the common law" is, at one and the same time, thoroughly unobjectionable and heavily laden with unspoken—and unprovable—ramifications. For while it is absolutely impossible to deny that the authors of the Constitution were trained in and fluent in the English common law tradition—and that they apparently assumed that the Constitution would also be read and interpreted by judges who were likewise steeped in the same common law tradition—the apparent presumption by Story that they were all drawing upon the *same* body of common law is deeply suspect, except perhaps in a very indirect sense. For although the authors of the Constitution had been trained in the common law of England through reading the same editions of Coke's *Institutes* and Blackstone's *Commentaries*, they all recognized that certain aspects of that tradition—for instance, Blackstone's emphasis on parliamentary sovereignty—were inapplicable to them.[78] Moreover, the practice of the common law that they were familiar with was in the common law as it had been modified and developed in each of their individual colonies-turned-states, between which traditions there were many material differences, as Story himself would point out in his *Commentaries on the Constitution*. Story himself was trained in the common law, it is true, but by the time it reached Story, the original English common law tradition had been filtered through the legal practices accepted in Massachusetts: his tutor in the law, Samuel Sewall, illustrated this point to him well: "While you shall acquire a knowledge of the law of England, you will read in discourse or as occasion may require, the Stat[utes] of the State of Mass[achusetts] & in them you will discover all the local & positive variations of the general system."[79] Sewall counseled that such "variations," due to "neglect or disuse of particular rules" from the law of England, would be made clearer by observing local court proceedings and listening to the arguments of local attorneys.[80] Sewallinstructions to Story underscore the general point well: that the common law of England may have been the foundation of legal practice in Massachusetts but had since been subject to endless variations from the original due to the "neglect or disuse" of particular portions of the English common law. Thus, while it is fair to assume a common law foundation in every state, it does not necessarily follow that the Constitution was predicated upon a body of *federal* common law.

Story's assertion that the Constitution "presumes" a foundation on a general federal common law thus balanced precariously on his assumption that the particular evidences of the common law that he readily cited were proof of the existence of a single, national body of common law and not thirteen distinct common law adoptions by the states—all drawn from the same tradition, to be sure, but nevertheless admitting of innumerable variations. It seems that Story, consistent with his general understanding of the Union—to be discussed in chapter 3—generally saw the American people as *acting as* a concerted whole, even if they were, at least physically, *acting through* the governing organs of their particular states. Consequently, he may have viewed the formal adoptions of the common law by the state constitutions as signifying—in the aggregate—a national common law adoption. And yet, even such a redefinition was difficult to maintain, as seen by looking at the adoptions of the common law by the preliminary state constitutions authored during the Revolutionary War. Such constitutions frequently contained pronouncements of common law adoption, but these pronouncements generally affirmed the preexisting legal practice in their own state, excepting only those parts that conflicted with the new state constitutions.

The early constitutions of Massachusetts and Delaware bear out this point. For instance, the 1780 Constitution of Massachusetts held generally that "All the laws which have heretofore been adopted, used, and approved in the province, colony, or State of Massachusetts Bay, and usually practiced on in the courts of law, shall still remain and be in full force, until altered or repealed by the legislature," making an exception only for any parts "repugnant to the rights and liberties contained in this constitution."[81] The 1776 Constitution of Delaware was even more direct in reaffirming the state's prior adoption of the British common law; there too, it was specified that the adoption applied only to such parts of the common law as had been previously practiced in the state: "The common law of England, as well as so much of the statute law as has been heretofore adopted in practice in this State, shall remain in force, unless they shall be altered by a future law of the legislature."[82] As in Delaware, the Constitution made an exception only for such portions of the common law "as are repugnant to the rights and privileges contained in this constitution, and the declaration of rights, &c. agreed to by this convention."[83] It is important to note that with both of these constitutions, the common law is declared to "remain in force," signifying that the common law tradition being affirmed was the same one that had then been developed and cultivated within each state from its colonial inception. Similarly, both constitutions clarified that the common law was subject to future alteration by the state legislature—as was considered a crucial element of the common law system—thus making it even less likely that the authors of the state constitutions were attempting to jointly affect a national common law adoption that would be in force equally over all Americans.

APPLYING THE NATIONAL COMMON LAW TO THE STATES

The pursuit of a precise moment of national common law adoption indeed appears to lead the examiner into the "very elaborate inquiries" that Story sought to avoid dealing with in *Coolidge*. Ultimately, Story avoids trying to answer the unanswerable question of *when* and *how* this federal common law was adopted. For him, it is enough to demonstrate that the American people have undeniably put the common law into practice, and that they have chosen to fill the United States Constitution with references to the common law, thus signaling to the federal judiciary which portions of the nationally accepted common law tradition were available for their use in answering cases. The precise origins of the federal common law might thus have been a mystery, but—for Story, at least—its existence was beyond any doubt.

Claiming a federal common law also opened up another round of problematic inquiries, however. As mentioned previously, both sides of the debate acknowledged that some parts of the British common law had apparently been deemed old-world vestiges inapplicable to the situation of the colonies and had thus not been adopted in America and consequently had no place in American jurisprudence at either the state or national level; the remaining question was who made the determination of what was "applicable" and what was not. Jeffersonians such as Tucker held that it had always been the prerogative of each state to decide what parts of the larger British common law adequately fit their particular situation and what parts were inapplicable. Because of the differences in the common law that occurred between the founding of the colonies, as well as because of different motives driving emigration to the various colonies, the parts of the common law that were accepted varied considerably from state to state.[84] There was thus no reason for the federal government to be concerned with the question of what parts of the common law had enjoyed acceptance in any particular colony and which had not. Such considerations were reserved solely to the governments of the several states.

On the other hand, for proponents of a federal common law, determining which portions of the British legal system had been adopted nationally was a question of utmost importance. If there was a federal common law, then it ostensibly would not include portions of the English system that had been uniformly rejected by the American people in every one of the states. But what about those innumerable portions of the common law that the states disagreed on? There, it would seem, the American people were in disagreement over what portions of the common law applied to the American situation and which did not. And, to the extent that the federal courts would be using the federal common law to decide cases, resolving these areas of disagreement became a concern of the federal government. In an 1802 interchange with John Randolph of Roanoke on the floor of the House of Representatives, Delaware Federalist James Bayard underscored this point by clarifying his position—and presumably the position of other adherents of the federal common law doctrine—and insisting that some parts of the common law of

England had no place in American law: "the law of the Ecclesiastical Establishment" and "any principle of monarchical tendency" had not been adopted, "but only such parts [of the common law of England] as were consonant to the nature and spirit of our Government."[85] Bayard argued further, however, that the determination of which parts of the old British system were part of the federally-in-force common law underlying the Constitution was a job best left for the federal judiciary: "What belongs to us, and what is unsuitable, is a question for the sound discretion of the judges."[86] It is important to note that Bayard is interested in ascertaining the suitability of the federal common law to the situation of the American nation, or to "the nature and spirit of *our* government" (emphasis added). Bayard thus appears to be asserting that it is the prerogative of the federal courts to determine which parts of the British common law are in force nationally and which are not. This is the federal judicial power that Republicans like Jefferson and Tucker feared lay behind the claim of a federal common law, and it is interesting to contrast the frankness with which Bayard asserts this power against the characteristic cautiousness with which Justice Story approached the issue in his judicial opinions.

For opponents of the federal common law, the determination of which parts of the common law were to be adopted as applicable to the colonists' situation and which were to be discarded was a determination to be made solely by each separate colony. Before the Revolution, each of the thirteen colonies made this determination for itself, and the results varied widely. Later, having declared independence, though ostensibly borrowing some from each other's declarations and state constitutions, the determination of which portions of the British common law applied to each state's separate condition was the driving determination in ascertaining which parts of the common law were adopted. Tucker describes the variations in original adoption by the different colonies as varying based on the different motives of the settlers of each: those who came to the New World seeking only to gain material wealth and then return might well be expected to endeavor to retain most, if not all, aspects of the British common law they were familiar with and presumably attached to and to "conform as near as possible both in doctrine and in practice to all the institutions of the mother country."[87] On the other hand, those who settled in the colonies fleeing persecution "must have carried with them prejudices against the laws and government of the parent state, which would induce a general rejection of all such as were inimical to those principles, which prompted them to migrate."[88] Tucker concludes that under such varying reasons for immigrating, it is natural for there to exist differences between the adopted laws of such colonies and "as two strait lines, which diverge from each other at the same point, can never after meet, or become parallel, so the institutions of two countries, founded upon such discordant principles, could never after be assimilated to each other."[89]

Thus, Tucker concluded, the determination of which portions of the common law are applicable was one that was historically made not by the aggregated American people in reference to their national situation, but by the people of each state in reference to their particular situation. Furthermore, just as it was ultimately the prerogative of each state to decide what parts of the common law were applicable to their situation, it was the sole prerogative of the colonial legislatures to amend and alter the adopted common law so as to make it "adapted to the views, principles, situation, and circumstances of their respective inhabitants and countries."[90] To search for a unified body of law in the varied common law practices of the several states was thus not only bound to be a fruitless and frustrating exercise but betrayed a basic misunderstanding of how the laws had come to be adopted and accepted in the first place.

Story, convinced as he was that there was a common law foundation underlying the Constitution, was not deterred by such complications. Although he never attempted to provide an exhaustive list of which portions of the common law of England had been adopted by the American people in their national capacity and which had not—and although he recognized also that there were considerable variations from state to state—Story apparently agreed with Bayard's claim that it was the province of the judiciary to determine, as needed in a decision, whether a particular component of the common law was applicable to the national American situation and thus available for use by federal judges. In his *Commentaries*, he recognized that ascertaining which parts of the common law had been adopted within a particular colony was difficult, noting that it was "a question of intrinsic difficulty to say what laws are or are not applicable" to the situation of the colonies.[91] "It is not perhaps easy to settle," continued Story, "what parts of the English laws are or are not in force in any such colony, until either by usage or judicial determination they have been recognized as of absolute force."[92] Story thus spoke of the original determination of applicability as one made independently by the people of each colony; practically speaking, it could not have been made on a larger scale in the absence of any national political body at the time. Still, in order for a federal common law foundation to underscore the Constitution, it would seemingly be necessary for this federal common law to be one that was *common* to the people in every state.

Such a national adoption was described by James Kent, a prominent jurist and chancellor of New York, who prefigured Story's nationalist reading of the American founding. In Lecture XVI of his *Commentaries on American Law*, Kent described the process of common law adoption as one carried out by the entire American people instead of by the separate people of each state: "It is the common jurisprudence of the people of the United States, and was brought with them as colonists from England and established here, *so far* as it was adapted to our institutions and circumstances."[93] Likewise, Story was prone to speaking of this test for applicability as if it were carried out nationally, noting in his *Commentaries* that the "uniform doctrine in America ever since the settlement of the colonies," in both principle and in practice, was "that the common law is our birthright and inheritance, and that our ancestors brought hither with them upon their emigration all of it which was applicable to their situation."[94] While this passage hints at a national common law adoption—describing the common law as "*our* birthright and inheritance" and saying such parts were adopted as were applicable to the *situation* rather than *situations* of the Americans—it still does not answer one of the underlying questions that would guide federal judges' application of a federal common law: in borderline cases where a common law rule's acceptance or applicability is unclear, would it be assessed according to its applicability to the situation of a particular state or to the United States as a whole? Story does not clearly answer this question in his *Commentaries*, but the casual way he transfers between talking about the two suggests that he sees the two standards of applicability as not greatly different from one another.

As a federal judge, Story took the lead in tackling the gray areas of uncertain adoption or usage. Little by little, case by case, Story began to develop a comprehensive federal common law that would answer—in particular cases—whether a disputed portion of the common law was a part of the American legal tradition or not. The Court's affirmation of the *Hudson and Goodwin* ruling in *Coolidge* seemed to preclude federal prosecution of crimes that had not yet been identified by a congressional statute, yet that affirmation arguably left open the possibility of a federal common law in civil cases. Chancellor Kent had already hinted at such a distinction when, after discussing the Court's opinions in *Worrall*, *Hudson and Goodwin*, and *Coolidge*, he summarized that these decisions "have not settled the general question as to the application and influence of the common law, upon clear and definite principles; and it may still be considered, in civil cases, as open for further consideration."[95] Kent went on to argue—in logic very similar to Story's in *Coolidge*—that, although the federal courts could not use the asserted federal common law as a source of jurisdiction in a case, they still were able to make recourse to the common law in deciding cases that the Constitution gave them authority to hear.[96] In other words, while the federal courts may not be able to prosecute crimes that had not been explicitly identified by federal statute, the common law still provided the most sure guide for the federal judiciary in answering federal civil cases, such as between citizens of different states. Applying the common law only to civil cases also helped avoid what Kent saw as one of the difficult and dangerous aspects of Story's argument in *Coolidge*: that it was ultimately up to the courts to determine what constituted an "offence against the United States" in the absence of a congressional statute defining it.

Shortly after his appointment to the Supreme Court, Story issued an opinion applying a common law rule to a civil case in the Vermont case *Town of Pawlet v. Clark*.[97] Article III, section 2 of the Constitution had given the federal courts jurisdiction over "controversies between citizens of the same State claiming lands under grants of different States" and *Town of Pawlet* dealt with a parcel of land that had been granted by the governor of New Hampshire to the Church of England before the Revolution, but which had later been granted to the town of Pawlet by the recently formed government of Vermont. In the meantime, an Episcopalian congregation took possession of the property and refused to surrender it to the town. Since the case involved conflicting land grants issued by different states, the Supreme Court had jurisdiction, and Story wrote the opinion of the Court. Story sided with the town, citing the relevant common law precedents regarding the establishment of Episcopal churches, which Story determined to be "applicable to the situation of the province," being regularly avowed and explicitly referred to in a long line of charters and acts of the provincial government.[98] Story was thus engaged in ascertaining what parts of the common law were relevant to the case at hand, but in choosing to decide the case according to the established principles and precedents of the states of New Hampshire and Vermont, he had not posed any great danger to the accepted common law within those states. Indeed, even Justice Johnson concurred in the decision, albeit noting that "The difficulties in this case appear to me to arise from refining too much upon the legal principles relative to ecclesiastical property under the laws of England."[99] The case could be decided, Justice Johnson seemed to be saying, without making reference to English legal precedents at all; all that mattered was the legal practices of New Hampshire and Vermont.

Indeed, Story could be less deferential toward state sources when they pointed against the common law tradition he sought to preserve. This can be seen in the 1829 case *Van Ness v. Pacard*,[100] in which Story found another opportunity to determine what parts of the British common law were applicable to the American condition. The case dealt with a tenant in the city of Washington D.C. who had built a house and stable on rented property and then removed the structures before his tenancy was through; the owner of the property brought a case against the tenant for the common law offense of waste, arguing that the structures had become part of the rented property and thus could not be removed by the tenant. Indeed, in England there was a well-established common-law rule forbidding the removal of structures from a property by a tenant, although there was no applicable local statute formally adopting that rule in the District of Columbia. In the absence of statutory direction on this issue, Story took it upon himself to determine the applicability of the relevant part of the common law to the American situation. "The common law of England is not to be taken in all respects to be that of America," he began.[101] "Our ancestors brought with them its general principles and claimed it as their birthright, but they brought with them and adopted only that portion which was applicable to their situation."[102] On this particular matter, Story questioned whether the common law's rules on the relation between landlord and tenant were so applicable to the situation in the American wilderness as to lead to a general presumption that such rules had been adopted, absent a definitive answer from the state legislature or courts.[103] Given the uniqueness of the American situation, then, Story held that this portion of the common law should not be read into the common law as practiced within a state, simply based on its existence in the common law of England.[104] Story thus ignored the relevant common law rule as not applicable to the American situation and therefore not binding in the case.

In a certain light, the outcome of the case was innocuous enough, even from the perspective of a critic of the federal common law: Story chose in this case not to bring into consideration a common law rule that had not yet been specifically adopted. And yet, there was something quite radical about Story's approach: Story had elected not to apply the general common law principle because he had adjudged that this particular aspect of the federal common law was not "applicable to our situation" or—at the very least—the situation of "our ancestors." Story presumed, in other words, that the federal courts were competent to decide—in the absence of a clear answer by the state legislature or courts—whether a particular element of the British common law was relevant to "our" situation or not. Justice Story had fulfilled Congressman Bayard's declaration that it was the province of the federal judiciary to answer what portion of the British common law was applicable to the American situation. In the present case, he held that it was not applicable, and thus would not be presumed by the federal courts to be a part of the law of the District of Columbia without a statute affirming it.

Two years later, in the case *Patterson v. Winn*,[105] Story followed a similar approach to answering the case and arrived at just the opposite conclusion. In a Georgia case dealing with whether a copy of a land grant was evidence of the original document, Story held that the old common law rule did apply. Georgia had not ever passed a state statute explicitly accepting the common law rule on the particular subject, but neither had its legislature or judges ever made an explicit variance from the common law. It was, in Story's mind, thus open for federal judges to decide whether the common law rule was applicable in the current case. Since, according to Story, the common law and its rules of evidence were fully in force in Georgia until modification by the state legislature or judiciary, the question was whether the state had explicitly departed from the common law on this matter.[106] Such a departure being absent, Story held that the relevant common law rule was binding here: "These statutes being passed before the emigration of our ancestors being applicable to our situation, and in amendment of the law constitute a part of our common law."[107] Story thus held that, in the absence of an explicit state rejection of a common law rule, that rule should be applied to the state.

What was the difference between the facts of the cases in *Patterson* and *Van Ness* that would lead to completely opposite results? Ostensibly, the different outcome in *Patterson* was due to the fact that, in this case, Story believed the common law rule on the use of copies of official state documents in court was "applicable to our situation" in a way that the common law rule against waste was not. At the very least, Story's position allowed federal judges a considerable degree of discretion in deciding which elements of the common law were applicable to the situation of "our ancestors" and which were not, instead of leaving that to the judges and legislators of each state to judge for themselves.[108]

It should be clarified that there is a curious ambiguity in these decisions. It is altogether unclear whether Story is judging common law rules based on their applicability to the situation of each particular state or to the situation of the whole American people. His references to "our ancestors" seem to point to the latter, and perhaps also give credence to the hypothesis that Story conceived of the original settlers in the colonies as collectively adopting a single body of law, albeit through their own particular colonial organs of government. However, his deference to state statutes, whenever available, seems curiously out of sync with this position: if "our ancestors" had been making a national determination of which portions of the common law were applicable to our national situation and which were not, then Story would ostensibly be justified in overturning or ignoring state statutes that went against his own interpretation, such questions being a matter of federal law. The deference that Story gives to state adoptions or rejections of the common law might therefore indicate that he saw such questions of applicability as relative to state situations and not a single national standard. Such a view, however, would seemingly undermine Story's own authority to answer such questions in lieu of an answer by state authorities.

The considerable discretion over common law principles that Story's theory of common law adoption gave to federal judges was not lost on Justice Johnson, who in *Patterson* wrote a dissenting opinion that took exception to Justice Story's process of answering cases. In addition to questioning Story's interpretation of the common law precedent, Johnson argued that the real underlying question in the case was "how far each state is to be permitted to fix its own rule of evidence as applicable to its own real estate."[109] In other words, Johnson held that Story's approach to solving such cases—deciding, as a federal judge, which portions of the common law were or were not applicable to the case at hand—violated the right of states to determine what their own laws would be. The fact that this case was heard in federal and not state court did not make a difference to Johnson: state law should determine the rules regarding evidence used in the case. Johnson's reasoning on this point followed that of Tucker almost exactly: the common law in Georgia was subject to modification based on "local views and settled judicial practice."[110] Thus, even if Story's analysis of the common law rule were perfectly right, "unless so recognized in Georgia, it is not the law of Georgia."[111] In other words, although the settlers of Georgia had indeed adopted the common law, that original adoption had been subject to subsequent changes that only Georgia legislators and judges were competent to make. Consequently, it was improper for Story to claim as simply as he did that "the common law is the law of Georgia."[112] The simple fact that Georgia judges had not yet issued a ruling on this question did not give Story the right to intrude upon their prerogative as a state. Until such a law as this be recognized by the government of Georgia, it was not applicable to the current case.

Justice Johnson's dissenting opinion notwithstanding, this string of opinions by Story did not seem to excite much opposition the way that earlier claims had. Without any such opposition, Story's opinions in these cases bolstered his argument for a federal common law and paved the way for a definitive declaration by the Supreme Court on the constitutionality of a federal common law in civil cases, the same as the Court had done for criminal cases in *Coolidge*. What was needed was a general rule that would distinguish what parts of the common law were applicable and which were not, or—alternately—which common law questions were left solely to the states to accept or reject and which were of a national enough character that the federal courts could answer them, even in spite of state decisions to the contrary. The latter type of case was hinted at by Story in the 1838 circuit case *Williams v. Suffolk Insurance Co.* in which Story held that a doctrine of the common law "being founded, not upon local law, but upon the general principles of commercial law," would provide the necessary rule for the case, even if the state courts were to rule in an opposite way.[113] Story went on to declare that this was because, in dealing with "commercial questions of a general nature," the federal courts operated upon equal authority to the state courts and were thus "not bound by the local decisions."[114] Thus, in *Williams v. Suffolk Insurance Co.*, Story hinted at a new type of federal common law jurisdiction: one in which the federal courts would not be bound by state court decisions on which parts of the civil common law were applicable and which were not, but instead would be freed to chart their own course, "guided," as it were, "by the greatest deference for the acknowledged learning and ability of the state tribunals,"[115] but ultimately endowed with the power to ignore state court decisions if they should disagree with the judgment. The stage was set, then, for perhaps the most influential—as well as controversial—opinion that Story would write in his long tenure on the highest court.

A FEDERAL COMMON LAW IN CIVIL CASES: *SWIFT V. TYSON*

Story's belief in a body of "general principles" that made up commercial law was founded, at least in part, on the belief that such general principles were currently in the process of shaping the increasingly uniform commercial codes of the several nations of Europe, and indeed all the countries of the commercialized world. In an 1835 legal essay entitled *A Discourse on the Past History, Present State, and Future Prospects of the Law*,[116] Story described a "natural tendency of maritime [i.e., commercial] usages to assimilation" and predicted that the maritime—or commercial—laws of the many nations would, over time, continue to move toward gradual assimilation through "mutual comity" as well as from "mutual convenience, if not necessity."[117] In other words, Story predicted that the imperatives of commercial growth would drive the legal codes of different nations together, at least with regard to commercial law. Story exulted in this coming legal homogenization:

> What a magnificent spectacle will it be to witness the establishment of such a beautiful system of juridical ethics,—to realize, not the oppressive schemes of holy alliances in a general conspiracy against the rights of mankind, but the universal empire of juridical reason, mingling with the concerns of commerce throughout the world, and imparting its beneficent light to the dark regions of the poles, and the soft and luxurious climates of the tropics.[118]

Embedded in the colorful and lively imagery employed by Story in this passage is a genuine optimism for the rising age of commerce. Alongside this general trend toward legal homogenization, Story believed that a string of federal cases, built upon the "general principles of commercial law" that he referenced in *Williams v. Suffolk Insurance Co.*, could serve as an example for the several systems of commercial law within the states, and the subsequent uniformity of legal codes could lead to remarkable economic growth on the American continent.[119] State adherence to this common standard would not be legally coerced,[120] but Story expected—given the growing general confluence around these principles across national borders—that they would gradually move toward the rules propounded by the federal courts.

In order for the federal courts to show the way in deciding cases on these universal principles, however, they must have some constitutional basis for doing so, either in an act of Congress or the text of the Constitution itself. For Story, who had maintained since his early days on the Court that the United States Constitution is predicated upon the common law, the constitutional and historical grounding for this "universal empire of juridical reason" was obvious. Thus, the first step in this process of legal evolution was an accomplishment that had heretofore eluded Story: a recognition by the Supreme Court of a federal common law foundation underlying the Constitution.

The case came in *Swift v. Tyson*,[121] a complex diversity-of-citizenship case dealing most immediately with the question of whether a pre-existing debt constituted a valuable consideration respecting negotiable instruments. More importantly for Story's purposes, however, the outcome of the case hinged on whether the case would be decided according to the common law of New York, where the case had been brought in a federal district court, or according to the general common law principle in place elsewhere. If the latter were to govern, Story emphatically held that a pre-existing debt did constitute valuable consideration, calling this position "a doctrine so long and so well established, and so essential to the security of negotiable paper, that it is laid up among the fundamentals of law."[122] On the other hand, Story conceded that the issue had not been settled by New York statute and that more recent cases in New York appeared to lean against considering a pre-existing debt to constitute sufficient consideration. Story, however, considered the question to still be open, especially since the New York Court of Errors had not ruled either way on the matter.[123]

Richard Dana, the lawyer for the defendant in the case, argued that New York law should rule in the case,[124] an argument based on settled judicial practice as well as congressional statute: chapter 20, section 34 of the Judiciary Act of 1789 dictated "that the laws of the several states, except where the Constitution, treaties, or statutes of the United States shall otherwise require or provide, shall be regarded as rules of decision in trials at common law in the Courts of the United States, in cases where they apply."[125] Ostensibly, then, if the "laws of the several states" included the common law as practiced by the courts within the states, then the Judiciary Act would have bound Story to apply the decisions of the New York courts, regardless of his own feelings on the essentialness of the traditional common law rule. In other words, the question before Story was whether the federal courts were bound to apply the common law as practiced by the several states, or whether—alternately—they were free to have their own, based on general principles of law.

What Story held in *Swift* was that the "laws of the several states" referenced in section 34 of the Judiciary Act did not apply to the decisions of local state courts: that including such decisions under the umbrella of "laws" went beyond the ordinary use of language, that such decisions are prone to be frequently "reexamined, reversed and qualified by the courts themselves," and that the Supreme Court had previously considered state law to constitute only the statutes passed by the state legislature, as well as their subsequent interpretation by the state courts.[126] In other words, Story held that the Supreme

Court was not bound to abide by the common law rules of each state, at least in cases such as this one where the subject matter dealt with "questions of a general nature" and which had to be decided based on the "general principles and doctrines of commercial jurisprudence" and not on the will of the state legislature.[127] Likewise, Story noted, the state courts in New York based their commercial law rulings not on statutes or local custom, but upon general commercial principles; in such cases, state courts "are called upon to perform the like functions as ourselves that is, to ascertain, upon general reasoning and legal analogies, what is the true exposition of the contract or instrument, or what is the just rule furnished by the principles of commercial law to govern the case."[128] Thus, in *Swift v. Tyson,* Story drew a distinction between two types of cases: those dealing with "state laws, strictly local"—defined by Story as those dealing with the statutes of the state and their construction by the local state courts—and those dealing with "questions of a more general nature, not at all dependent upon local statutes or local usages"—such as cases dealing with the construction of contracts and written instruments or other general questions of commercial law that did not substantially vary state-to-state.[129] On this latter category of cases, Story declared the federal courts competent to base their decisions upon the general principles of commercial law, regardless of what the state courts said on the matter. On its face, Story's achievement in *Swift v. Tyson* seemed rather moderate, and indeed the case did not cause the uproar that one might have expected given the ferocity of the federal common law debate 30 years prior. Even in the legal class in New York—the group that should ostensibly have been the most outraged that the federal courts had ignored their own common law rule—there was a remarkable lack of interest in the outcome of the case.[130] The precedent that the case created, however, ultimately led to considerable legal debate, with opposition to the "*Swift* doctrine" mounting throughout the era of progressive state enactments from the 1890s until *Swift* was finally overturned[131] in the 1938 case *Erie Railroad Co. v. Tompkins.*[132] Along the way, future judges would expand Story's doctrine from a relatively limited application of generally accepted commercial law in contracts cases to deal with a wide range of cases that Story never envisioned, such as tort claims.[133] Indeed, by the time of the eventual demise of the "*Swift* doctrine," it had been expanded to include "all matters of contracts and torts not positively governed by state enactments," as Justice Pierce Butler noted in his dissent in *Erie.*[134] Judging by the sheer number of cases that drew on its reasoning, it stands as Justice Story's most wide-reaching contribution to Supreme Court doctrine, perhaps rivaled only by *Martin v. Hunter's Lessee* in this regard.

It also marked the culmination of Story's career-long drive to recognize a uniquely federal body of common law underlying the Constitution. Interestingly, the only reference to the common law in *Swift* is when Story quotes section 34 of the Judiciary Act. In a certain sense, Story was indeed reaching even beyond the laws of England in his attempt to connect American commercial jurisprudence to the "universal empire of juridical reason" that he had read of in Cicero and Lord Mansfield,[135] but the common law had always been thought of as having been drawn, at least in part, from reason and natural law. At the same time, the "general principles" of commercial law that federal judges had recourse to after *Swift v. Tyson* were essentially getting at the same object that Story had sought after in *United States v. Coolidge*: the ability of the Court to propound and develop a uniquely federal set of common law principles that could be used to decide cases on which Congress had not passed a statute. In diversity-of-citizenship cases, of course, this included the ability of the federal courts to have a unique body of common law in matters on which Congress had no constitutional authority to legislate. Story's desire to establish a federal common law foundation for the federal courts thus went through several phases, and the end result—a federal common law on contracts and other matters of general commercial law—was quite different in substance from the federal jurisdiction for common law crimes that he had pursued in his first days on the Court. This transition likely had as much to do with changing political necessities and the hard realities of what accomplishments were judicially feasible, but also seemed to reflect a shift in Story's own thoughts on the common law: By 1835, Story seemed to be questioning whether greater uniformity in applying the common law in different states would be a good thing.[136]

Story's theory of a federal common law might have shifted considerably over the years, but there are still discernible certain common threads that tie together the various stages of his quest to recognize a federal common law. One, certainly, is the consistent desire to link American jurisprudence to some larger and older body of venerable legal tradition than the infant American jurisprudence had been able to produce; to tap into what Story's revered statesman Edmund Burke had termed the "general bank and capital of nations and of ages."[137] A second would be a long-term commitment to discovering and promulgating a uniquely national body of American law. Like his fellow pioneer in legal education Nathan Dane, who had endeavored first to locate, then to create, a "collected body of American law," Story's efforts from *United States v. Coolidge* through *Swift v. Tyson* were designed to grant federal judges a single common law tradition that would be purely national, instead of having to rely on the various common law practices of the states. Story's decisions in *Town of Pawlet v. Clark, Van Ness v. Pacard*, and *Patterson v. Winn* all presupposed that a national body of common law had been adopted by "our ancestors" and that it was federal judges who were competent to discover what the parameters of that common law adoption were. In short, it was Story's theory of the union that drove his career-long pursuit of a federal common law and that connected together its various stages into a quest to recognize a truly national system of accepted American common law.

NOTES

1. In *Life and Letters of Joseph Story*, ed. William W. Story (London: John Chapman, 1851), I:299. Quoted in McClellan, 170.
2. Story, *Commentaries*, Sec. 158, 1:107n2.
3. Ibid.
4. *United States v. Wonson*, 28 Fed. Cas. 745 (C.C. Mass. 1812) (No. 16,750); 1 Gall. 5.
5. Ibid.
6. Ibid.
7. Ibid.
8. *Van Reimsdyk v. Kane*, 28 Fed. Cas. 1062, No. 16,871 (1812).
9. Notably, Section 34 provides an exception that the laws of the several states might not apply "where the constitution, treaties, or statutes of the United States shall otherwise require or provide." There is, of course, no mention of a federal common law in diversity cases in either the federal constitution nor in federal statutes or treaties. To argue, as Story later would in *United States v. Hoar* (26 Fed. Cas. 329), that the Constitution required an exception to the general rule thus rested, again, on some implicit or understood limitation on the states.
10. Newmyer, 100.
11. *Van Reimsdyk*, quoted in Herbert Hovenkamp, *Enterprise and American Law, 1836–1937* (Cambridge: Harvard University Press, 1991), 87.
12. Ibid.
13. Newmyer, 100.
14. Ibid., 100n86.
15. Ibid.
16. Ibid., 100.
17. Story, *Life and Letters*, I:299.
18. Ibid.
19. *United States v. Clark*, 25 Fed. Cas. 441, No. 14,804.
20. Palmer Robert, "The Federal Common Law of Crime." William & Mary University, *Faculty Publication*, Paper 900 (1986): 322.
21. Mark Tushnet, "*Swift v. Tyson* Exhumed." *The Yale Law Journal* 79, no. 2 (1969): 284–310, 287n15.
22. *United States v. Coolidge*, 24 Fed. Cas. 619, No. 14,857; 1 Gall. 488 (1813).
23. *United States v. Coolidge*, 14 U.S. 415 (1816). The 1816 Supreme Court ruling in the case included a brief summary of the facts of the case. The previous citation, along with most of the succeeding citations referring to the case, will refer instead to Justice Story's Circuit Court decision in the case in 1813. Citations referring to Justice Johnson's opinion for the Supreme Court will be designated *Coolidge* (1816).

24. *Coolidge*, 415.
25. Newmyer, 103–104.
26. Ibid., 104.
27. Peter Stephen Du Ponceau, "A Dissertation on the Nature and Extent of the Jurisdiction of the Courts of the United States." Valedictory address at the Law Academy of Philadelphia, April 22, 1824. Available online through The Constitution Society at http://www.constitution.org/cmt/psdp/juris.htm.
28. Ibid.
29. *Coolidge*, 621.
30. Ibid.
31. Ibid.
32. Joseph Story. Manuscript on "a bill further to extend the judicial system of the United States," ostensibly sent to Charles Pinckney. 1816. Reprinted in *Life and Letters*, I:293–303.
33. *Coolidge*, 619.
34. Ibid., 621.
35. "Instructions to Virginia Senators," passed by the General Assembly of Virginia on January 11, 1800, and reprinted in Tucker, 369.
36. *Coolidge*, 619.
37. Ibid.
38. *Swift v. Tyson*, 12. Quoted in McClellan, 171.
39. *Coolidge*, 61,9
40. United States Constitution, Article I, Section 8.
41. Ibid.
42. Tucker, 369.
43. Judiciary Act of 1789, chapter 20, section 34. 1 Stat. 73.
44. *Coolidge*, 619–620.
45. Ibid., 619.
46. Ibid.
47. Ibid.
48. Ibid.
49. Ibid., 620.
50. Ibid., 621.
51. Ibid., 620.
52. Ibid.
53. Ibid..
54. McClellan, 172.
55. Ibid., 415–416.
56. Ibid., 416.
57. Ibid.
58. Ibid.
59. Ibid., 416–417.
60. *Coolidge*, 620.
61. Ibid.
62. Story, *Commentaries*, I, sec. 158, 141–142, n. 2.

63. Randolph, "Floor Speech on February 20, 1802." Recorded in *The Annals of Congress, House of Representatives, 7th Congress, First Session* (Washington: Gales and Seaton, 1801), 652.

64. Ibid.

65. That some parts of the common law were never a part of American legal practice, either by the states or the federal courts, seems to have been universally agreed upon. See, for instance, the opinions of James Bayard and St. George Tucker, both discussed later in this section.

66. Nathan Dane, Introduction to *General Abridgment and Digest of American Law*, quoted by Story in his essay "Digests of the Common Law." Reprinted in *The Miscellaneous Writings of Joseph Story*, ed. William W. Story (Boston: Charles C. Little & James Brown, 1852), 379–407, 394.

67. Ibid.

68. Ibid.

69. Dane, 395.

70. Tucker, 341.

71. Ibid., 345.

72. See, for example a letter to Story from his law tutor Samuel Sewall on February 12, 1799. Sewall writes that, to the original adoption of the common law "in use & force at the departure of our fathers from their native country" could be added "the changes wrought by the Stat[utes] of the Engl[ish] Parl't in which the colonies were expressly named & which were formerly holden to be binding therein; & some States which on account of their reasonableness and utility were admitted by the Courts of Law here, as modifications of the common law in certain instances, altho[ugh] enacted at much later periods than the emigration of our ancestors." Quoted in McClellan, 163.

73. Madison, "Report of 1800."

74. Ibid.

75. *Coolidge*, 619.

76. Ibid.

77. McClellan, 163.

78. Stoner, *Common Law and the Constitution*, 13.

79. Sewall to Story, quoted in McClellan, 163.

80. Ibid.

81. 1780 Constitution of Massachusetts, Chapter IV, Article VI. Available at http://www.nhinet.org/ccs/docs/ma-1780.htm.

82. 1776 Constitution of Delaware, Article 25. Available at http://www.nhinet.org/ccs/docs/del-1776.htm.

83. Ibid.

84. Tucker, 326.

85. James Bayard, "Floor Speech, February 20, 1802." Recorded in *Annals of Congress, House of Representatives, 7th Congress, First Session* (Washington: Gales and Seaton, 1801), 614.

86. Ibid.

87. Tucker, 325–326.

88. Ibid., 326.
89. Ibid.
90. Ibid., 327.
91. Story, *Commentaries*, Sec. 149, 1:100–101.
92. Ibid.
93. Kent, Part II, Lecture XVI, p. 322.
94. Story, *Commentaries*, Sec. 156, 1:105.
95. Kent, 318. Kent later seems to favor allowing a federal common law jurisdiction in criminal cases as well. Kent, 320–321.
96. Ibid., 318–319. Also similar to Story, Kent held that without recourse to this common law foundation, federal judges would be "left to a dangerous discretion, and to roam at large in the trackless field of their own imaginations." Kent, 321.
97. *Town of Pawlet v. Clark*, 13 U.S. 292; 9 Cranch (1815).
98. Ibid., 334.
99. Ibid., 337.
100. *Van Ness v. Pacard*, 27 U.S. 137; 2 Peters 137 (1829).
101. Ibid., 144–145.
102. Ibid.
103. Ibid.
104. Ibid.
105. *Patterson v. Winn*, 30 U.S. 233; 5 Peters 233 (1831).
106. Ibid., 241.
107. Ibid.
108. Even McClellan, who otherwise seems largely sympathetic toward Story's position, notes about the discrepancy between *Van Ness* and *Patterson* that "Clearly, Judge Story's theory of adoption as applied in these decisions granted wide discretionary authority to the Court in deciding whether a particular state had or had not adopted certain common law rules, or whether such rules were, in the eyes of the Court, 'applicable,' to the state's situation." McClellan, 170.
109. *Patterson*, 245.
110. Ibid., 246.
111. Ibid.
112. Ibid., 241.
113. *Williams v. Suffolk Insurance Co.* 3 Sumner 270; Fed. Cas. 1406, No. 17,739 (1838).
114. Ibid.
115. Ibid.
116. Story, *A Discourse on the Past History, Present State, and Future Prospects of the Law* (Edinburgh: Thomas Clark, 1835). Digitized by the University of Michigan and available online at https://babel.hathitrust.org/cgi/pt?id=mdp.35112203495983;view=1up;seq=9. Hereafter referenced as Past History.
117. Ibid., 23.
118. Ibid., 24.
119. McClellan, 179.
120. Ibid.

121. *Swift v. Tyson*, 16 Peters 1 (1842).
122. Ibid., 15.
123. Ibid., 17–18.
124. McClellan, 180.
125. Judiciary Act of 1789.
126. *Swift*, 18.
127. Ibid., 18–19.
128. Ibid., 19.
129. Ibid., 18–19. Story's position here would be reasserted and expanded in a case later that term, *Carpenter v. Providence Insurance Co.*, 16 Peters 495 (1842), which extended the ruling from dealing exclusively with negotiable paper to applying to all cases dealing with contracts. McClellan, 182n77.
130. Newmyer, 336.
131. Ibid., 334–335.
132. *Erie Railroad Co. v. Tompkins*, 304 U.S. 64(1938).
133. Newmyer, 342.
134. *Erie Railraod*, 87.
135. McClellan, 182–183.
136. Story, *Past History*, 21.
137. Edmund Burke, *Reflections on the Revolution in France* (London: Penguin Books, 2004), 183.

Chapter 3

Story and American Nationhood

The connection between Story's arguments for a federal common law and his understanding of the union should not be surprising. One of Story's signature career achievements was the creation of a systematic narrative of American nationhood and the development of a comprehensive constitutional theory drawn from that narrative. As a result of this achievement, Story has become so heavily identified with the argument of the Nationalist Theory that it is easy to forget that the basic premise of the theory—that the union was the creation of the national "American people"—dated all the way back to the very origins of American independence. To be sure, this premise was contested at various points by those who adhered to the essential premise of the Compact Theory—that the union had been created as a compact or confederation between the separate peoples of the several states. Story was not the first commentator to theorize the existence of a national American people and his contemporary John C. Calhoun—who played a systematizing role for the Compact Theory similar to the one Story played for the Nationalist Theory—was not the first to deny the existence of any such people. Just as Story's theory of a federal common law, which was built upon prior Federalist claims of a body of non-statutory federal law underlying the Constitution, the foundations of Story's Nationalist Theory were already laid by previous constitutional theorizing and the basic outline of Story's historical narrative had already been expressed by an unbroken line of commentators and political actors stretching back to the Continental Congress.

Story played two essential roles in the development of the Nationalist Theory: he provided its most complete articulation and defense, most notably in his *Commentaries on the Constitution*, and he also systematized the Nationalist Theory of the union by purging from the ranks of Federalist commentaries certain accepted premises that Story felt subtly denied the federal government the full scope of its powers. The former effect is attested to by the number of Compact Theory works singling out Story's analysis for refutation.[1] Among his fellow nationalists, one of the most lasting impacts of Story's *Commentaries on the Constitution* would be his success in working out a historical narrative that, to his supporters, laid out an incontrovertible refutation of the claim that the United States Constitution was a "Compact" between the states.

The latter effect is attested to by the fact that early Federalist constitutional commentaries, while urging a broad reading of the federal government's powers, could still depart from the basic premise of the Nationalist Theory and instead suggest that the union was the creation of the several states. Indeed, among early Federalist thinkers, there seems to have been, on the whole, a considerable diversity of opinion, coupled with a good deal of ambiguity, on fundamental questions, such as whether the union was the creation of a single national people and whether the states were in any sense sovereign. This ambiguity reflects well the general lack of clarity on the questions of American nationhood before the issue could really be crystallized through the writings of Federalists like Story and his fellow nationalist Nathan Dane.

Of these early nationalists with at least an ambiguous record on the question of state sovereignty, one prime example would be Chancellor Kent. In his *Commentaries on American Law*, Kent argued that the organization of the U.S. Senate disproved those who argued against the sovereignty of the states: "On the principle of consolidation of the states, this organization would have been inadmissible, for in that case, each state would have been merged in one single and entire government."[2] The election of senators by the state legislators was further recognition of the "separate and independent existence" of the states.[3] Similarly, the Pennsylvania Federalist William Rawle also had a relatively complicated view of the union, culminating in his allowance of state secession from the union. Rawle saw the Declaration of Independence as acting as a sort of Social Compact binding on individuals,[4] but one that the people of an individual state could unilaterally break,[5] suggesting that the decision to join the compact was ultimately made by the separate communities of individuals, and not by an undifferentiated collection of "American" citizens, as later nationalist writers would insist.

This shift can be seen by contrasting two speeches made by Story's friend and political collaborator in the Senate Daniel Webster. In 1812, Webster's views on pre-constitutional state sovereignty were substantially different from the Nationalist Theory as later expressed by Story. In a speech denouncing Northern secessionist agitation during the War of 1812,[6] Webster noted that, in the immediate aftermath of American independence, the former colonies were completely sovereign and independent of one another: "that 'The war [i.e. the American Revolution] left the States individually sovereign and independent. . . . They had all Constitutions, and Governments, and Laws. They were in truth thirteen separate and independent NATIONS."[7] Story would argue against this very point at length in his *Commentaries*, claiming that the states had never enjoyed such "individually sovereign" status as Webster here indicated. Story was apparently successful in changing the opinion of his friend, who, after the publication of Story's *Commentaries*, was arguing the exact opposite position. In an 1833 speech on the floor of the Senate, Webster asserted that "Before the Confederation of 1781 [i.e., the Articles of Confederation], they had declared independence jointly, and had carried on the war jointly, both by sea and land; and this not as separate States, but as one people."[8] Webster went on in the speech to argue that any description of the separate states *acceding* to the union was inappropriate, as the states were already bound together: "Such language would have been ill-suited to the occasion. It would have implied an existing separation or disunion among the States, such as never has existed since 1774."[9] The fact that this later speech was given only a month after the publication of Story's *Commentaries* lends credence to the suggestion by some later scholars that the content of the speech was heavily influenced by Story.[10] It was thus Story, in conjunction with Dane, who helped systematize nationalist constitutional theory, resting their new system on an absolute insistence that the states had never been the separate, sovereign political entities that adherents of the Compact Theory made them out to be. It was Dane and Story who, in a pair of works published against the backdrop of the Nullification Crisis in 1832 and Calhoun's subsequent re-articulation of the Compact Theory, would help organize the nationalist reading of the American founding into something resembling a systematic constitutional and historical ideology.

In her *Commentaries on the Constitution, 1790–1860*—an overview of the constitutional commentary genre—Elizabeth Kelley Bauer fittingly described Dane, Story, and subsequent nationalist writers under the heading "The Orthodox Nationalists."[11] Such a denomination is very apt: Dane and Story both worked to systematize their constitutional and historical reading into something resembling a comprehensive religious creed, taking the place of Rawle's vague, general sense that the a strong federal union ought to be preserved on practical grounds. Although Bauer did not extend the analogy this far, her use of the term perhaps subtly invites the reader to witness the "orthodox nationalists" taking care to expunge heretical interpretations such as Rawle's that disagreed on singular points and thus deviated from fundamental tenets of the nationalist faith.[12]

Thus, although Story was not the first to assert that the union was the creation of the national American people, his contributions to the theory distinguish him as one of the most influential theorists of American nationalist thought. Story's argument for American nationhood has undeniably had a formative impact on the constitutional imaginations of subsequent generations, but before launching a study of Story's theory of the union, it will also be necessary to briefly consider the other early claims of American nationhood that Story was consciously and explicitly building upon. This series of assertions of American nationhood culminates in the Nationalist Theory of Nathan Dane, whose narrative of a pre-constitutional American nationhood in his 1829 *General Abridgment and Digest of American Law* in many ways paved the way for Story's much more memorable and influential argument for American nationhood in his *Commentaries on the Constitution*. Once some of the early assertions of the emerging Nationalist Theory have been considered, Story's own understanding of the union will be examined, starting with the speech that marked Story's entry into the political arena and that gives a unique perspective on his nationalism. For although the young Story's political theory—like his theory of a federal common law—would change greatly as he aged, it was his unwavering attachment to the union that provided a steady and consistent basis that cuts a straight line throughout both his early and mature constitutional thought.

EARLY CLAIMS OF AMERICAN NATIONHOOD

On the whole, it is very difficult to ascertain *exactly* how widespread acceptance of the Nationalist Theory was among the American Framers. At the outset of this investigation, it is important to note that this nationalist conception of the American Union coexisted side-by-side with the opposing view that the states had won their separate independences from England, with each state subsequently making the decision *as a state* to join the union. These two theories thus coexisted in obvious tension with one another—both could not simultaneously be true—but their respective advocates, with more urgent matters to attend to, apparently opted to put aside such disagreements in order to keep the fragile union in place in spite of the fundamental disagreement over what it, collectively, was. Despite these efforts at unity, the controversy obviously could not be staved off forever, and would occasionally bubble up to the surface in the midst of some dispute over representation in the shared central government, or over how far federal power should extend, or over the existence of a unique federal common law. The widespread nature and early origins of the claims on both sides of this debate point to both positions being widespread throughout the union, even under the Articles of Confederation.

Despite this original coexistence of the two mutually exclusive viewpoints, as the question of American nationalism increasingly became associated with early partisan divisions—and, later, with the antebellum regional division between North and South over slavery—both viewpoints would insist that theirs was the one "true" account of the American founding and that the rival theory, once unheard of, had arisen only recently out of the wily machinations of their partisan foes. Emblematic of this attitude would be Luther Martin's response to Elbridge Gerry's denial of state sovereignty at the Constitutional Convention. Madison's *Notes of Debates in the Federal Convention of 1787* recorded Martin's assertion that "the language of the States being *sovereign & independent*, was once familiar & understood; though it seemed now so strange & obscure. He read those passages in the articles of Confederation, which described them in that language."[13] Similarly, in 1829, Dane observed that the use of terms such as *sovereign states*, *state sovereignties*, and *state rights* had only "grown into very popular use in party times,"[14] the obvious implication being that such and similar terms, while obviously present in various state constitutions and the Articles of Confederation, had later undergone a shift in meaning or importance, transforming such phrases from their original meaning—understood by all—into something they never were intended to be. Somewhat ironically, although both sides claimed that their position was supported by recorded historical events that could be objectively verified, the fact that both understandings of the union date back to the beginning of American independence hinted that the exact nature of the American Union would continue to elude agreement. And despite the fact that early adherents of the Nationalist Theory obviously recognized the fundamental divergence of opinion underlying the union itself, none appeared to have undertaken a comprehensive refutation of the contemporary claims of pre-constitutional state sovereignty and independence; the first attempt to do so in any systematic manner would be Dane's *General Abridgment and Digest*.

A perfect example of this early ambiguity over the nature of the union can be seen in an episode touched on briefly in the Introduction: the debates of the Second Continental Congress not even a full month after the signing of the Declaration of Independence. As the delegates debated the scheme of representation for what would become the Articles of Confederation, two distinct understandings of the American Union rose to the surface. On one side of the debate were the delegates from larger states—Massachusetts and Pennsylvania—who advocated proportional state representation based on population and on the other were the delegates from smaller states—Connecticut, New Jersey, and Rhode Island—who advocated equal representation for all states. The struggle between the two sets of delegates, which would carry over into the Constitutional Convention, is often cast as a purely self-interested power struggle between the large states and the small states with both sides trying to maximize their own political influence in the new federal government; indeed, those delegates from larger states stood the most to gain from a system of proportional representation, while those delegates from smaller states stood to lose the most political influence from a system of proportional representation. Such an interpretation of the debate, however, obscures the added importance that the debate took on when the delegates based their respective arguments on the nature of their association together: whatever the motivation of individual delegates, the arguments made by each side began to reflect a fundamental disagreement over whether America was a single political community or several political communities.

James Wilson of Pennsylvania illustrated this connection well in his argument for proportional representation, asserting that "as to the matters which are referred to Congress, we are not so many states; we are one large state. We lay our aside our individuality whenever we come here."[15] More bluntly, Benjamin Rush declared in the same exchange that "I would not have it understood that I am pleading the cause of Pennsylvania; when I entered that door, I considered myself a citizen of America."[16] John Adams would put it slightly differently, hinting that the separate states were *currently* independent but that in joining the union they would *become* a single nation, noting that "the confederacy is to make us one individual only; it is to form us, like separate parcels of metal, into one common mass. We shall no longer retain our separate individuality, but become a single individual as to all questions submitted to the confederacy."[17] Such language goes far beyond any pragmatic argument in favor of one form of representation over another: the delegates from Massachusetts and Pennsylvania were arguing that America was a single nation and not a collection of political communities. Rush would even make this connection explicit, declaring "We are now a new nation."[18] In his mind, the Declaration of Independence had marked the starting point for a new political community. The argument against equal state representation flowed easily out of this assertion.

From the perspective of those who, like Rush and Wilson, saw the American colonists as comprising one great political community, to give the smaller states equal representation to the larger ones was to, in effect, provide for an *unequal* representation of individual citizens. It is thus that Benjamin Franklin argued against equal state representation that "If we had been born and bred under an unequal representation, we might bear it; but to set out with an unequal representation, is unreasonable."[19] If indeed the Continental Congress—or for that matter the new Confederation government that would take its place—was supposed to be truly representative of the American people as a whole, then any scheme of equal representation was patently imbalanced, as citizens of smaller states would be given a much larger per-capita voice in the federal government than the citizens of smaller states.

On the other hand, if the proposed union was to be nothing more than a confederation of sovereign states, then the role of the central government would be to represent the interests of the separate state governments and not individuals. To this effect, Connecticut delegate Roger Sherman asserted that

"We are representatives of States, not individuals" and Dr. John Witherspoon of New Jersey argued that "nothing relating to individuals could ever come before Congress; nothing but what would respect colonies."[20] Under such a system, the confederating states would be treated as coequal political communities, and the principle of equal representation would mandate that each *state* receive an equal voice, regardless of its comparative size. Witherspoon illustrated this confederal conception of the union in his response to Rush, asking, "Must I have three votes in a county, because I have three times as much money as my neighbor?"[21] To Witherspoon, the separate colonies were at that moment gathered together "as individuals making a bargain with each other, and of course had a right to vote as individuals."[22] It is apparent then that Witherspoon and Sherman considered the somewhat vague general principle of "equal representation" to dictate the exact opposite result than it did to Rush, Adams, and Wilson: it mandated that all the constituent parties to the national agreement—that is, each individual state as a separate political community—receive an equal voice in creating it.

The debate over representation in the Continental Congress was thus much more than a mere power struggle between the representatives of the large and small states: it demonstrated that, from the very beginning of American independence, there was a fundamental disagreement over the nature of the American Union. Rush, Adams, Wilson, and Franklin all apparently conceived of America as comprising something more than a collection of sovereign, independent states; they already perceived themselves to be, in Rush's words, "a new nation," and this conception of American nationhood and the sovereignty of the entire American people would form the historical starting point of the nationalist understanding of America that Story would take for granted in writing his *Commentaries*. At least some, then, of the signers of the Declaration of Independence saw that document as effecting one *national* independence instead of thirteen different *state* independences.

To those who believed otherwise, the evidence against this claim lay even in the use of previously recognized terms like calling the former colonies *States* or calling the collection of state delegates a *Congress* or the government over such states a *Confederation*: such words had always been used to denote that the separate political communities being discussed were, in their own right, sovereign and independent political units. The fact that the Declaration of Independence had declared the former colonies to be "free and independent states" and made no reference at all to the "new nation" that the delegates of Pennsylvania and Massachusetts were advocating provided some early textual evidence for the advocates of state sovereignty. Further evidence was provided by the final language of the Articles of Confederation, which, in addition to securing equal votes for all states, clearly announced that "Each state retains its sovereignty, freedom, and independence."[23] Moreover, the

Articles explicitly purported to be exactly what the proponents of American nationhood said they were not: a mutual agreement between separate states and not a social compact binding the American people together as a whole. This can be seen in the preamble of the Articles, which described the agreement as "The Articles of Confederation and perpetual Union *between the states*"[24] (emphasis added) and then reaffirmed this concept in Article III by declaring, "The said States hereby severally enter into a firm league of friendship with each other."[25] Thus, throughout the Articles, the language seemed to support the contentions of Witherspoon and Sherman that the Declaration had effected independence for each of the thirteen states separately and not for the American people as a whole. With the collapse of American confidence in the Articles, however, came a renewed push for the realization of the American nation that had been articulated by the members of the Massachusetts and Pennsylvania delegations.

As delegates of the states met in Philadelphia for the Constitutional Convention of 1787, the proponents of American nationhood would make their case again. Madison's *Notes of Debates* record that on June 19, Rufus King rose to argue on behalf of the Nationalist understanding of the American Union: "He [King] conceived that the import of the terms 'States,' 'Sovereignty,' '*national*,' 'federal,' had been often used & applied in the discussions inaccurately and delusively," wrote Madison. King elaborated that "the States were not 'Sovereigns' in the sense contended for by some" since "they did not possess the peculiar features of sovereignty, they could not make war, nor peace, nor alliance nor treaties."[26] King further argued that, even if they were "a confederacy in some respects" have a separate existence, they were still decidedly national in another: "If the states retained some portion of their sovereignty, they had certainly divested themselves of essential portions of it."[27] Thus, according to King, the Articles of Confederation had done precisely what the proponents of American nationhood had argued they had in the Continental Congress. Disregarding all language to the contrary in the Articles, King argued that the federal government not only held some of the political attributes of nationhood—making war, signing alliances, etc.—but that it had a distinctly "national character" arising as it did out of a "a Union of the men" within the states. *Confederation* and *consolidation* were not two distinct possibilities, King argued, but any confederation of the states would have necessarily meant consolidation.

This argument was then taken a step further by Wilson, who had argued on behalf of American nationhood in the Continental Congress and who rose after King finished speaking to argue for it again. Wilson, according to Madison, "read the declaration of Independence, observing thereon that the *United Colonies* were declared to be free and independent, not *individually* but *Unitedly* and that they were confederated as they were independent, States."[28] If indeed Wilson was right and the Declaration had declared the colonies to be "free and independent states" not separately but as a whole, then the later claims of state sovereignty that were being sounded by other delegates in the Convention—delegates such as Maryland's Luther Martin who argued on the contrary that the Declaration of Independence had effected a separate independence for each distinct state and had thus "placed the 13 States in a state of Nature towards each other"[29]—were thus completely baseless.

Wilson was thus arguing that America had always been a single nation, dating back at least to the Declaration of Independence. Story would eventually place the starting point for American nationhood even before this, but even Wilson's interpretation of the Declaration thus leads the reader to the federal government being the creator of the state governments instead of the other way around. By implication, this theory would lead to the principle that the states had never been *sovereign* political societies in any real sense of the word. Elbridge Gerry of Massachusetts made this implication explicit when he argued later in the Convention that "we never were independent States, were not such now, & never could be even on the principles of the Confederation."[30] Such provocative claims would not go by unopposed by Martin, who contrasted Gerry's assertions with what he saw as the plain meaning of the Articles of Confederation.[31] These exchanges in the Constitutional Convention demonstrate that, just as in the Continental Congress, there was no consensus between the delegates on questions of American nationhood or of state sovereignty.

Following the conclusion of the Convention and the submission of the proposed Constitution to the state ratifying conventions, the devotees of American nationhood would become, on the whole, much cagier in their advocacy of a full-throated sovereignty for the national American people—at least while the debates over ratification waged on. Even Wilson toned back his nationalism, reminding his listeners in his famous "State House Yard Speech" of October 6 that the Constitutional Convention had been "not limited to the views and establishments of a single state, but co-extensive with the continent, and comprehending the views and establishments of thirteen independent sovereignties."[32] One notable exception to this general rule was Charles Cotesworth Pinckney, who, at the South Carolina ratifying convention in 1788, declared that nothing could have been further from the intentions of the signers and authors of the Declaration of Independence than "The separate independence and individual sovereignty of the several States."[33] The absence even of the names of the separate states from the Declaration seemed to Pinckney also to drive home the point that American independence was only possible as a byproduct of the union.[34] This was far from an idle academic question, according to Pinckney, but instead was bound to have significant consequences for the viability of the union: "Let us then consider all attempts to weaken this union, by maintaining that each State is separately and individually independent, as a species of political heresy, which can never benefit us, but may bring on us the most serious distresses."[35] If accepted, Pinckney's argument would certainly have undercut Anti-Federalist claims that the Constitution went too far in infringing upon state sovereignty: the states had never been sovereign to begin with, according to Pinckney's interpretation of the Declaration. But such forthright denials of state sovereignty also provided ammunition for those who held the opposite interpretation. Outside of the closed-door, secrecy-sworn environment of the Pennsylvania State House, even the most avowed nationalists strove to avoid unnecessary damage to the cause of ratification.

For their part, many of the Anti-Federalists feared that the proposed Constitution would amount to a "consolidation" of the separate states into a national system, particularly drawing attention to the fact that the Constitution's preamble claimed an authority drawn from "We the people of the United States," suggesting the new Constitution to be more akin to a national social compact between the individuals of a society than a union of preexisting sovereign political communities. To this effect, the Anti-Federalist faction of the ratifying convention in Pennsylvania issued a statement warning that the Constitution effected a "consolidation" of the states into a single political society, arguing that the Preamble's declaration to be speaking for "We the people of the United States" was more emblematic of a social contract between individual citizens entering into a society together, rather than a confederation of preexisting states.[36] The Pennsylvania minority argued that this consolidation was the unavoidable intention of the Constitution's framers: "In short, consolidation pervades the whole constitution. It begins with an annunciation that such was the intention. The main pillars of the fabric correspond with it, and the concluding paragraph is a confirmation of it."[37] This was obviously not the same sentiment as that expressed by Wilson and Gerry at the Constitutional Convention: the concern of the Pennsylvania Minority was premised upon the idea that the states were currently sovereign and were in danger of losing that sovereignty through an act of national consolidation; the starting point of the early Nationalist theorists was that the states had never been sovereign and that America had always been a single nation. Still, it is noteworthy that many of the Anti-Federalists saw the Constitution as another example of the creeping menace of national consolidation, and it is entirely plausible that such fears were at least partially due to the earlier Nationalist claims by those like Wilson and Gerry, who believed such a consolidation had already been accomplished in the Declaration.

Another piece of historical evidence from the ratification debates stands out in this regard. George Washington's letter introducing the Constitution to the Confederation Congress—sometimes referred to as the Constitution's "cover letter"—spoke frankly of "our country," "our Union," and "our national existence," prompting historian Daniel Farber to surmise that the letter "implies that a union already exists and that Americans are in some sense already one people" and that "in some sense, there is already a national existence capable of being at risk, which is to say that the United States under the Articles of Confederation was already a nation of sorts rather than a league."[38] On its face, this seems to be a plausible argument, but upon further examination of the letter, complications with this interpretation arise. While the letter obviously indicated that Washington—and, most likely, many Americans—thought or spoke of themselves as a "country" or a "nation" in some sense, that does not necessarily mean, absent from affirmative language to the contrary, that they didn't also think of the constituent states as political societies—even as "countries" of their own—the apparent contradiction between the two thoughts arising out of the imprecise nature of such terms. In fact, a close examination of Washington's letter suggests that he saw the states as currently holding some degree of independent sovereignty under the Articles. In the second paragraph, Washington wrote that it was "obviously impracticable in the federal government of these states, to secure all rights of independent sovereignty to each, and yet provide for the interest and safety of all; Individuals entering into society, must give up a share of liberty to preserve the rest."[39] From this sentence, Farber declared that "the drafters did not portray the Constitution as merely an agreement between states that retained their separate existence. The letter compares the Constitution with the social compact, which is an irrevocable creation of a unified society."[40] Yet, it is apparent in the sentence above that Washington is analogizing between states joining a union *as states* and the decision of individuals to join a social compact *as individuals*. This analogy does the exact opposite of what Farber claimed it does: rather than give textual evidence of the Constitution's creation of a single society under a unitary government, it affirmed the claim that the states represented distinct legal personalities, each of which could choose to join the union and thus sacrifice some of their own independent sovereignty—the recognition of which also cuts against the Nationalist Theory understanding of pre-constitutional America—in exchange for the interest and safety of the whole union. Farber is right in drawing attention to the letter's mention of "that country so dear to us all,"[41] but he overstates his case in suggesting that this letter substantiates the claim that the Constitution was the creation of the American people as a whole instead of the people of each individual state.

In the years following the ratification of the Constitution, scattered references to a pre-constitutional American nationhood continued, with both sides continuing to assert their previous position. David Ramsay, a South Carolina Federalist, published the two-volume *History of the American Revolution* in

1789 in which he restated the nationalist interpretation of the Declaration of Independence: "The rejection of British sovereignty not only involved a necessity of erecting independent constitutions, but of cementing the whole United States by some common bond of union."[42] The creation of this union thus being the primary purpose of the Declaration, the document itself was said to announce the independence not of thirteen distinct political communities, but rather "a common sovereignty of the whole in their united capacity."[43] Ramsay recounted the debate over state representation, noting the assertion of the smaller states "that the states confederated as individuals, in a state of nature, and should therefore have equal votes."[44] Ramsay thus was familiar with the opposing view that the Declaration created thirteen independent sovereignties, although he explicitly discarded this theory. He also added a nationalist interpretation of the creation of state governments, noting that "The Americans agreed in appointing a supreme executive head to each state, with the title either of governor or president. They also agreed in deriving the whole powers of government, either mediately or immediately from the people."[45] Embedded in this statement is Ramsay's assertion that the creation of the state governments was made by "the Americans" and not by the people of each state.

Ramsay's book also provided an insight into how early Nationalists may have been able to reconcile the tension between their interpretation of the Declaration and the language of the Articles of Confederation. Many points of evidence within the Articles of Confederation seemed to directly contradict the Nationalist Theory: the equality of state representation in the Confederation Congress, the language pointing to an agreement or contract between the peoples of the several states, and the explicit recognitions of state "sovereignty, freedom, and independence," to name a few. Ramsay—although interested more in the larger historical narrative than in the finer points of legislative or constitutional theory—seemed to be at least aware of this tension. He wrote that the delegates of the larger states were willing to concede the debate over state representation "from fear of weakening their exertions against the common enemy,"[46] ostensibly referencing the fact that the delegates from some of the smaller states had threatened to withdraw from the confederation if they were not treated as equal parties to the compact. Madison had recorded Gerry making a similar argument during the Constitutional Convention, conceding that he voted for equal representation "but it was against his Judgment, and under the pressure of public danger, and the obstinacy of the lesser States."[47] Thus, while making a passing statement that the Constitution of 1787 did nothing to abridge the "Rights of the States,"[48] Ramsay largely treated pre-constitutional America as already endowed with the sovereignty of nationhood and chalked up any recognition of state sovereignty in the Articles to the necessities of wartime and the obstinacy of the smaller states.

Between the publication of Ramsay's *The History of the American Revolution* in 1789 and Joseph Story's *Commentaries on the Constitution of the United States* in 1842, there were other voices repeating the Nationalist narrative that Wilson and Gerry had espoused at the Constitutional Convention. A few of those came in key Supreme Court decisions aimed at affirming the extent of federal power. In his seriatim opinion in the 1793 case *Chisolm v. Georgia*,[49] Chief Justice John Jay argued that, prior to the Revolution, the American colonists were "in a variety of respects one people" and that they shared a political bond stronger than that which was shared by the ancient peoples of the various Roman Provinces: whereas the people of Gaul, Britain, and Spain merely shared a common sovereign over them, the American colonists considered themselves to be a united people, as evidenced by the creation of the Continental Congress.[50] Story would approvingly cite Jay's decision in his *Commentaries*, but Jay's analysis—without any actual historical evidence to explicitly affirm his suspicion that the American colonists thought of themselves as a single people—necessarily stayed vague.

In a later decision, John Marshall made the case perhaps most persuasively by reframing the debate as hinging on the role of "the people" in creating the Constitution. Writing for a unanimous court in *McCulloch v. Maryland*,[51] he combatted the contention made by the counsel for Maryland that the Constitution was the creation of the "sovereign and independent States."[52] Marshall rejoined that the Constitution had been created, not by the state governments, but by the people.[53] The delegates to the Philadelphia convention had indeed been appointed by the state legislatures, but, argued Marshall, the Constitution was then simply a proposal; it was entirely up to the people to decide whether to put it into practice.[54] It was referred by the convention to the Congress, and from there to the legislatures of the states, and from there was ultimately referred to the people "for their assent and ratification."[55] The people thus received the proposed Constitution and directly made the decision over its ratification: "They acted upon it in the only manner in which they can act safely, effectively, and wisely, on such a subject—by assembling in convention."[56] Marshall thus very persuasively set up the two contrasting positions: on the one hand, Maryland's contention that the Constitution had been created by the states—subtly reframed by Marshall as the easily refutable assertion that the Constitution had been created by the state *governments*—and on the other hand, the indisputable position that the Constitution was the creation of "the people," as evidenced both by the Preamble's invocation of "we the people" and by the uniform use of popular ratifying conventions instead of by a vote in the state legislative organs. As far as Marshall could see, the only outcome of emphasizing the creative role of the several states would be to call into question the direct agency of "the people" in ratifying the Constitution.

Of course, Marshall's framing of the two alternative ratification narratives ignored one other possibility. The early proponents of the Compact Theory did not argue that the Constitution was created by the state legislatures, they argued instead that it was the direct creation of the people of each state, with the decision of the people in one state being in no way binding on the decision of the people in another. The Constitution was thus, according to the "Compact Theory," the creation of thirteen different peoples and not as one national people. Marshall foresaw this argument and promptly turned to refute it: "It is true, they assembled in their several States—and where else should they have assembled? No political dreamer was ever wild enough to think of breaking down the lines which separate the States, and of compounding the American people into one common mass."[57] Marshall preceded to explain that although "when they act, they act in their States," still the people themselves maintain a fundamental distinction from their representatives in the state governments: acting *within* their particular states does not, in other words, mean that they act *as* the people of separate states. Nor was the Constitution ratified by the state governments; they had given their assent in calling for ratification conventions and submitting the Constitution before the people, "but the people were at perfect liberty to accept or reject it, and their act was final. It required not the affirmance, and could not be negative, by the State Governments."[58] The Constitution—and by extension, the union—was thus, as Marshall emphatically maintained, the direct creation of the people and did not in any way owe its existence to a decision of the separate states.

Here Marshall's claims begin to seem rather curious in relation to his broader argument: on the one hand, he maintained that "compounding the American people into one common mass" was an act too radical to be even dreamt of, but on the other, he seemed incapable of conceiving of the American people as representing anything other than a common, compounded mass. For Marshall, to discuss the separate and sovereign *states* meant necessarily to discuss the state *governments* which had been, like the federal government, erected by the people. For all of his protestations, any conception of the people of each state as representing a distinct sovereign populace seemed as much removed from Marshall's mind as the possibility of removing the state governments altogether. Marshall's reasoning in this case shows him to be fully convinced that the Constitution was the creation of a sovereign national people and not the sovereign people of each state. For whatever reason, Marshall was never as explicit as Story in denying the separate political existence of the people of each state, but the implication of Marshall's argument in *McCulloch* is clear: the American people may have "acted in their States," but that fact did nothing to change their corporate status as a single people.

Prior to Marshall, another Nationalist had made a similar argument, drawing a contrast between the state *governments* and the national *people*. The publication of the *Virginia Resolutions* and *Kentucky Resolutions*—authored, respectively, by Madison and Jefferson—provoked several caustic Federalist responses, many of which denounced the *Resolutions* as dangerous or even treasonous, but one of which echoed the early claims of American nationhood. Virginia Federalist Henry Lee III published a response that took exception to Jefferson and Madison's implicit belief that the states were sovereign under the Constitution. Against the Compact Theory, Lee argued that the state governments "are not parties to the . . . [Constitution], they did not form or adopt it, nor did they create or regulate its powers. . . . The people, and the people only, were competent to those important objects."[59] In elaborating on the role of "the people" in ratifying the Constitution, Lee further distinguished his view from Madison and Jefferson's assertion that it was the people of the several states who had ratified the Constitution, noting that the Constitution "was sanctioned by the people themselves, assembled in their different states in convention."[60] Lee thus hinted that he viewed the Constitution as the product of the American people acting corporately as a single people, even if they were *assembled* in their separate states in doing so.

NATHAN DANE'S THEORY OF AMERICAN NATIONHOOD

By the late 1820's, both the Nationalist and Compact Theories' interpretation of the Founding had thus been asserted many times; often times, as at the Constitutional Convention, the contrast between the two interpretations came vividly into focus. But it was not until the "Nullification Crisis" of 1828 that advocates of the Nationalist Theory set about providing a comprehensive defense of their understanding, which of course would have doubled as a comprehensive refutation of the Compact Theory. In 1829, ten years after Marshall's ruling in *McCulloch*, Dane provided the most extensive—if also, perhaps, the most convoluted—defense of the Nationalist interpretation that had yet been published. Dane's argument was published as an appendix to the ninth volume of his *General Abridgment and Digest of American Law* and would soon serve as an important aide to Story in writing his *Commentaries*.

In a lengthy passage, Dane set out to demonstrate that the contemporary use of such terms as *sovereign states* or *state rights* was not founded upon the language of the Constitution or the Declaration, but that it rather had been discovered later and was thus a faulty understanding of the American constitutional order.[61] While acknowledging that such language had been used in the Articles of Confederation and in some state constitutions, Dane argued that the word was then used in a "subordinate sense" and did not signify that the American states were endowed with the full range of attributes sovereign states enjoyed;[62] in other words, the states were not fully sovereign in a technical sense, even though a recognition of the "sovereignty" of the states—as the word was used colloquially and in a much more loose sense—had worked its way into popular discourse. In order to prove this, Dane directed his readers back before the Declaration to the calling together of the First Continental Congress in January 1774: A moment at which, according to Dane, "the Thirteen States existed *constitutionally*, in the condition of 13 *British Colonies*, yet *de fact, the people* of them exercised original sovereign power in their institutions in 1774, of the Continental Congress."[63] Particularly important to Dane's argument was the decision of the people in June 1775 to vest the Second Continental Congress with "the great national powers that will be described; scarcely any of which were resumed"[64] by the people thereafter. With the American people thus composing a *de facto* nation in 1774, the Declaration of Independence's announcement that the former colonies were "free and independent states" becomes the action of the whole American people, thus precluding any claim of original state independence or residual state sovereignty and making the states the creatures of the federal government and not the other way around. Dane emphasized this in his description of the Declaration: "the State Governments, and States, as *free and independent States*, were, July 4th, 1776, created by the General Government, empowered to do it by the people, acting on revolutionary principles, and in their *original, sovereign capacity*."[65] Consequently, the states were not only the creation of the American people but also, in fact, owed their very existence to that people's representatives in the Second Continental Congress. Dane emphasized this point by insisting that "the State Governments, *as such*, have been instituted during the existence of the General Government, and in subordination to it,"[66] and thus enjoyed a subservient role not only to the national American people but also to the general government of the union. Thus, Dane became the first constitutional theorist to assert that the states were the direct creation of the national government, as it was authorized by the sovereign American people. Put thus, the states have no more claim to a sovereign status than the counties do that make up a state. If the American people as an undifferentiated aggregate were the true creators not only of the federal government but of each state government as well, the people of each state would be reduced from a sovereign people in their own right to a constituent part of the national sovereign.

Dane supported this claim that the states are the creatures of the federal government by arguing that with the passage of the Declaration of Independence, the states were transformed from subordinate, dependent colonies into subordinate parts of the American Union.[67] According to Dane, the people of each separate colony—by virtue of "assuming their original sovereign power"[68] and of exercising that power upon "revolutionary principles"[69]—had appointed agents to represent them, as a nation, in the Continental Congress. At this point, Dane's rendition of the political history of the Declaration puts him in direct opposition to the Compact heorists' interpretation of the same actions.

According to Dane, the actions of the American people then shifted from the people of each separate colony acting separately—in appointing delegates—to the people of all the colonies acting jointly—through the actions of the Congress, including the Declaration of Independence.[70] Consequently, from the moment of the Continental Congress' creation, the people of each state were no longer free to act in their "original sovereignty" but rather were a part of the whole American people. Thus, from even before the Revolution, the people of each colony conducted themselves, even in their internal affairs, "in *subordination* to those national powers," to which they had previously lent their support.[71] When the time had come to declare American independence, it was the Continental Congress that acted as a national governing body and, empowered by the sovereign American people, transformed the former colonies into new state governments.[72] These governments had thus, since their creation, always been subordinate to the national government.[73]

In assessing Dane's theory of national sovereignty, it must first be acknowledged that the theory is noteworthy inasmuch as it represents the first systematic articulation of the "Nationalist Theory." Following the publication of Dane's lengthy appendix, Nationalist thought on the Constitution was much more uniform on the foundations of the federal government and the source of its supremacy in the sovereign American people. Nevertheless, the theory is plagued by a number of difficulties, not least of which is the comparative complexity and convolutedness of Dane's theory compared to the other competing narratives that came before and after it.

On this note, Dane's conception of the people of each state's simultaneous removal from British rule and entrance into the American Union is particularly vexing. Dane curiously describes this phenomenon as an instantaneous divorce and remarriage. By the Declaration of Independence, the people of the states "at the very same instant, were divorced, and freed from their British subjection and connexion, married into the American family, and, by their full consent, brought under federal subjection and power," then seated in the Continental Congress.[74] Consequently, said Dane, "there has never been a moment since they were so made a State, when they had power of right, to make war, or peace, or treaties, or to exercise any one of many other powers, which were properly vested in Congress and the Union."[75] Confusing the matter further is that this absorption of the people of each state into the American "family" apparently occurred subsequent to the people of each state jointly deciding to form the Continental Congress. The fact that this decision was made by the people of each state instead of the people of a national whole makes Dane's iteration of the Nationalist Theory unique, but it also raises problems when the thrust of his argument is that the states never held the status of independent sovereign political communities in their own right. The whole matter is complicated further by Dane's central reliance on vaguely defined concepts of "original sovereignty" and "revolutionary principles." Whatever value it provided to the advocates of the Nationalist Theory by focusing attention on the Continental Congress, the unnecessarily convoluted nature of Dane's theory raised as many questions as it answered.

1804: THE THREAT OF DISUNION

Story's theory of the American founding presented in his *Commentaries on the Constitution* closely adhered to the historical narrative and subsequent argument for state subordination and national primacy set forth by Dane. When Story set forth this Nationalist narrative, he was thus asserting a position that had been expressed many times since the Revolutionary period. Indeed, Story considered the point to be well established and cited many of the previously referenced sources to demonstrate that his interpretation had once been commonly accepted. The implication was clear: nobody at the time of the Founding thought of the states as sovereign political units, and any attempt by the Jeffersonian Republicans—or, later, the Calhounian Democrats—to portray them as such after the fact was an act of historical revisionism. Given the enormous importance that these disagreements on the historical origins of the Constitution had for contemporary controversies in constitutional interpretation, Story devoted a considerable amount of space in the early part of his *Commentaries* to disproving the Compact Theory narrative.

The defense of American nationhood was not completely new to Story. Although no Nationalist Theory explication of this magnitude had ever been attempted—by Story or by anyone else—Story was no stranger to questions of American sovereignty or to defending what he considered to be the essential prerogatives of the federal government; such endeavors had been a mainstay of Story's public career since its earliest days. Many aspects of Story's constitutional and political thought would change over the years, but his commitment to the union appears to lend an essential continuity throughout his life.

The young Story's Nationalist strain can be seen in a commemorative speech delivered by Story in Salem, Massachusetts, on Independence Day 1804.[76] Styled simply "An Oration," the speech stands as Story's contribution to what was once a prominent tradition of "July 4th Orations," where the chosen speaker would exhort his audience to cultivate republican virtues and remind his fellow citizens of their revolutionary inheritance. Story was then not yet twenty-five years old and was still one year away from his eventual election to the Massachusetts House of Representatives, four years away from his election to Congress, and eight years away from his astonishingly young appointment to the Supreme Court. For the young Story, this oration also has the distinction as his earliest public statement of his beliefs, if one discounts an 1800 eulogy for George Washington that Story would later disavow as "poor and in bad taste."[77] Similarly, Story would also later distance himself from his "July 4th Oration" as well, given its significant democratic overtones and other considerable differences with his later positions.

Story had already publicly identified himself as a Republican,[78] which made him a social outlier in Boston[79] and although Story's mature thought was marked by a distinct cultural elitism and opposition to Jacksonian democratic leveling, the language of Story's "Oration" was markedly more in line with the general sentiment of democratic egalitarianism that pervaded his chosen party. The young Republican partisan took the opportunity to harangue "the crafty SINONS who would exchange republican simplicity for royal trappings"[80] and asked, "Why are the splendor and tranquillity of monarchies blazoned in all the pomp of eloquence; and the miseries and oppressions and frauds of hereditary prerogative forgotten or concealed?"[81] Story also betrayed an openness to innovation in stark contrast to his later Burkean conservatism: "Why is the alarum bell forever ringing charges against innovation, reform, and philosophy?"[82] Such language, while noteworthy for its distance from Story's later thought, was not entirely out of place for the young Story. Story's biographer James McClellan—who generally emphasized Story's conservative streak—observed a tinge of radicalism in Story's youth, which he attributes to Story's "romantic temperament," as well as independence of mind: as Story's classmates at Harvard encouraged him to check his idealism through a "careful perusal of the Bible," it drove him even further into an idealistic celebration of *Reason*: the title of a poem he wrote for his graduation. Story later burned the poem in what McClellan described as "one of his many fits of protest against the age in which he lived, embarrassed that he, the archfoe of metaphysics, should have ever been drawn to its captivations."[83]

Nevertheless, Story's youthful Jeffersonianism did not extend to then-president Jefferson's conception of the union as a compact between sovereign states; Story also demonstrated a firm nationalism. Even his celebration of "republican simplicity" and his contempt for the crypto-monarchical enemies of republicanism do nothing to blunt his unwavering commitment to national union. Story himself, in his *Autobiography*, saw no tension between his identification as a Republican and his firm commitment to the union: "A Virginia republican of that day was very different from a Massachusetts republican and the anti-federal doctrines of the former state then had and still have very little support or influence in the latter state, notwithstanding a concurrence of political action upon general subjects."[84] His partisan affiliation might have also been partially due to the fact that, somewhat ironically, there was more of an emphasis on national unity among Republicans than Federalists in New England, some of whom even maintained secessionist sympathies[85]—a sentiment that Story specifically targeted in his "Oration." As corollaries to his lifelong commitment to the union, Story was always wary of excessive devotion to the interests or prerogatives of individual states over the national interest and powers of the federal government, and adamantly opposed to any action of a state government that would threaten *disunion*.

This call for national unity was closely linked to another major theme of the speech: the dangers of the party factionalism. These two themes—opposition to partisanship and a call for national unity—are intertwined in Story's thought, as Story considered party factionalism to be a danger chiefly because it weakened the bonds between the states, endangered the national character, and—in short—threatened to "sap the foundations of national union."[86] This link explains Story's utilization of frightening, even violent language to convey the dangers of party factionalism: "Civil dissension has everywhere opened the way to slaughter; and unprincipled faction made a charnel house of the earth."[87] Similarly, Story saw the "petty prejudices of states"[88] as inextricably linked to the same factionalism and dissension that he saw poisoning the young republic. Both were equally dangerous, and Story apparently saw both as posing an existential threat to the national union.

Story's fear that state prejudices and party factionalism pose an existential threat to the union may seem unusual when considered in the abstract, but it is worth remembering the broader political context in which Story delivered this speech. Story had a very concrete and very real danger in mind when he spoke of the twin dangers of disunion and party faction: the literal dissolution of the American Union through state secession. Midway through the *Oration*, Story turned his attention to efforts by unnamed enemies of the public good to threaten such dissolution: "Why are projects darkly hinted which tend to dissolve the Union and restore us again to anarchy and confusion? These are evils which all good men should unite to repress; for all are interested in the preservation of their country."[89] The answer, according to Story, was that "party spirit" had "blurred the public vision" and darkened the eyes of his contemporaries.[90]

Here it becomes apparent that Story's general wariness of factionalism and division were tied to a very tangible threat. When he said that such discord threatened to "sap the foundations of national union," he was not thinking merely of a national unity of purpose in some vague, metaphysical sense, but rather of a very tangible political peril that he apparently saw as imminently threatening. This helps make some sense of Story's dire, calamitous language that would seem out of place if describing merely a lack of national consensus: "France has not alone wept over the massacres of ROBESPIERRE; Britain has not alone been clothed in sackcloth by the wars of her HENRIES."[91] To take this language seriously, Story saw partisan bickering and the "petty prejudices of States" as threatening to bring civil war and anarchy to American shores.

What then were these "projects darkly hinted" that threatened dissolution? Again, Story seems to be focusing his attacks on the actions of New England Federalists. During Jefferson's presidency, many leading Federalists in the region considered the prospect of a New England secession much preferable to continued participation in a union under a Republican president. Such northern secessionist sympathies would eventually culminate in the Hartford Convention of 1814–1815 over the War of 1812, but in 1804, the issue prompting most calls for New England secession centered on what were perceived as the heavy-handed and unconstitutional policies of the Jefferson Administration. Among the northern Federalists seriously advancing the prospect of secession was former Secretary of State and current United States Senator Timothy Pickering of Salem, Massachusetts—the site of Story's Independence Day speech. Pickering's advocacy for New England secession is recorded in a letter to George Cabot in January of 1804, where he laid out the moral danger posed by Jefferson's presidency: "Men are tempted to become apostates," under the current administration, "not to Federalism merely, but to virtue and to religion and to good government."[92] The real danger to Federalists, though, lay in the fact that the Jefferson administration was steadily, gradually eroding the constitutional protections for Federalists and for "the protection of the best, and therefore to him the most obnoxious, part of the community."[93] Faced with the threat of extinction, the best option for Federalists was thus to effect a permanent separation from the union before Jefferson's plans for their ruin could come to their full fruition: "The principles of our Revolution point to a remedy—a separation. . . .The people of the East cannot reconcile their habits, views, and interests with those of the South and the West. The latter are beginning to rule with a rod of iron."[94] These irreconcilable tensions made any continuation of the union impracticable; the only viable possibility would be for each part of the union to go their separate ways: "A Northern confederacy would unite congenial characters and present a fairer prospect of public happiness; while the Southern States, having a similarity of habits, might be left 'to manage their own affairs in their own way.'"[95] Pickering would go on in the letter to argue that such a separation should be made immediately, "lest [New England] should be overwhelmed, and become unable to attempt its own relief."[96] It certainly seems from this context, then, that the push for New England secession and the establishment of a "Northern confederacy" were the targets of Story's virulent denunciations of disunion and faction.

Pickering's push for a New England separation generated considerable discussion in its day, and the various responses to it give a fascinating insight into the constitutional theory of the young republic, not least of all because of the irony of Federalists proposing a dissolution of the union. One of the main reasons proposals for secession could be taken seriously at this time in a way that they could not in the modern era is that there was, at this stage of national development, no fixed understanding of the nature of the union, but rather a few varied working assumptions that had not been fully fleshed out yet by their supporters on either side. Republican jurist St. George Tucker did not address the subject of secession in his 1803 *View of the Constitution of the United States*—widely held to be the first extended, systematic examination of the United States Constitution. The first fully articulated theory of the right of a single state to withdraw from the union was William Rawle's assertion in his 1825 book *View of the Constitution* that while states undeniably had the right to leave the union, they should nevertheless resist the temptation to do so "with the same feelings that we should avert the dagger of the parricide."[97] The theory of secession would, of course, later achieve its fullest exposition by South Carolinian John C. Calhoun in his posthumously published *Discourse on the Constitution and Government of the United States*, which began with a restatement of the Compact Theory and then declared that the principle of state secession "results, necessarily, from the nature of a compact between sovereign parties."[98] Preceding Calhoun's defense of the doctrine, however, were a series of systematic Nationalist refutations of it: first in volume 9 of Nathan Dane's *General Abridgment and Digest of American Law* in 1829, and then in two works published four years later in 1833: William Alexander Duer's *Outlines of Constitutional Jurisprudence* and Joseph Story's *Commentaries on the Constitution*. Even before the first of these works attempted to provide a systematic constitutional theory, constitutional and legal commentators issued varying responses to the question of secession. These responses, no less than those of the constitutional theorists listed above, drove to different conclusions based on differing conceptions of the American Union.

When faced with the prospect of northern secession, Story found the proposal utterly repulsive. Other northeasterners with a similar commitment to the union also rejected such arguments. One of Story's most prominent intellectual and political allies, Daniel Webster, gave a July 4th Oration of his own eight years later, in 1812.[99] There, although he opposed the war that had just begun against England, Webster insisted that New Englanders should support the war and not threaten disunion: "Resistance and Insurrection form no parts of our creed. The disciples of WASHINGTON are neither tyrants *in* power, nor rebels *out*."[100] By rejecting "insurrection" and "rebellion," Webster apparently anticipated the reemergence of Federalist calls for secession that would eventually be voiced in the Hartford Convention.

It is worth noting that at this time, there were those on the Republican side who, although obviously not as troubled by recent election results, were surprisingly sympathetic to the actions of New England secessionists. Jefferson's views were surely representative of many others in his party when he addressed the movement in an 1816 letter to William H. Crawford.[101] There, Jefferson identified a love of "licentious commerce" and "eternal war" as the root sources of New England secessionism but declared that he had "no hesitation in saying 'let us separate.'" Jefferson continued that he would rather see the union break into two confederacies: one based on "unlimited commerce & war" and the other seeking "peace and agriculture."

Jefferson's reaction could not have been more different than that of Story and Webster, but it echoed the attitude of the Virginia jurist St. George Tucker at the time of Aaron Burr's trial for treason in 1807. Burr had been arrested on the grounds that he had plotted to cause the secession of the western states from the union.[102] Tucker and Chief Justice John Marshall were at a party in Richmond, where a spectator recorded their dispute over whether such states had the right to leave the union should they so wish: Tucker held that states had that right and that "any State in the Union is at any time competent to recede from the same," an argument which Marshall "strongly opposed."[103] Tucker seems not to have explicitly addressed the question of secession in any of his writings, but the acceptance of the doctrine by some political actors and jurists from both the north and south, and within both political parties, points to the fact that the acceptance of the doctrine was apparently widespread, although far from undisputed. By the time Rawle published his work in 1825, state secession had been a part of the political discourse for the past two decades.

What was it that led these thinkers to such different views on the question of state withdrawal from the union? How could Tucker consider it to be an obvious right of any state to unilaterally withdraw from the union and Webster consider the same actions to be "insurrection" and "rebellion"? These varied responses to the prospect of state secession can best be understood as growing out of diverging understandings of what America was. Indeed, it is over this issue and the related question of state nullification that we see the formation of two substantive constitutional theories: the Compact Theory and the "Nationalist Theory." To Republicans like Jefferson and Tucker, the United States Constitution was essentially a compact, or agreement, between the separate people of each state. Under such a "Compact Theory," allowing one of the member states to secede was no large matter since the union had been voluntarily assented to by each. Moreover, the logic of the Compact

Theory seemed to lead unavoidably toward a right of state secession. In his *Discourse on the Constitution and Government of the United States*, Calhoun argued that such a right was the unavoidable consequence of treating the Constitution as a compact between sovereign states: "That a State, as a party to the constitutional compact, has the right to secede—acting in the same capacity in which it ratified the constitution—cannot, with any show of reason, be denied by any one who regards the constitution as a compact . . ."[104] The entire argument for a constitutional right to secession hinged upon the interpretation of the Constitution as a legal contract between the sovereign people of each state.

The Nationalist rejoinder against the doctrine of secession similarly fought the battle over first principles, asserting that Calhoun's starting premise in his *Discourse* was wrong: the union was not merely a compact between separate sovereign parties, but was instead the direct creation of the whole American people, who, considered in the aggregate, had exercised ultimate sovereignty since the passage of the Declaration of Independence. This Nationalist Theory of the American Union thus rested on demonstrating a series of historical propositions: that the Declaration of Independence, the Articles of Confederation, and the Constitution were the creations of the American people as a whole, and not the people of each separate state. Under such a formulation, an attempt by any state to leave the union would be an improper attempt by one portion of the sovereign national community to come between the American people and their national government.

What is interesting about the discussion of secession in this period is that, prior to the nullification controversies surrounding the Tariffs of 1828 and 1832, support for the right of a state to secede did not neatly follow the partisan or geographic divides that it would eventually be identified with. Similarly, although the basic features of the Compact Theory would remain largely the same from Jefferson and Madison's *Kentucky Resolutions* and *Virginia Resolutions* in 1798 to Calhoun's *Discourse* in 1851, support for the most basic underlying tenet of the Nationalist Theory—that the United States, as a nation, predated the separate states—would only gain uniform acceptance over time, even among those with a broad view of the federal government's constitutional powers. Of course, as has already been shown, certain Nationalist thinkers accepted this premise from the inception of the union, but such acceptance was not universal. After its publication, it was Story's microscopically detailed analysis of revolutionary history and constitutional language that would provide evidence for the central claim of the Nationalist Theory: that the American people had always been the ultimate sovereign authority above the people of any particular state. Persuasively defending this central assertion would be the subject of some of Story's most vigorous scholarly and judicial endeavors.

STORY'S *COMMENTARIES ON THE CONSTITUTION*: THE ORIGINS OF THE UNION

Unlike some of the forerunners of the "Nationalist Theory," Story was early on convinced that the American Union must be understood as the creation of the American people as a whole and not the creation of the distinct people of each state. Long before setting out to provide evidence for this claim, he would describe the Declaration of Independence in his 1804 *Oration* as "the sublime declaration that America was free and sovereign"[105] and declare that "this day our country has reached the twenty-ninth year of her sovereignty and independence."[106] In a song composed by Story for the occasion and included at the end of the published *Oration*, he wrote, "all hail to the day, when assembled as one / Our gallant forefathers proclaim'd us a nation."[107] These passages suggest that Story interpreted the Declaration of Independence as announcing that the American people as a whole were an independent nation, free of British rule. Elsewhere, however, Story suggests that the actual starting point for American national identity goes back much further than this.

Story noted in the *Oration* that it was the first settlers from England who "established a nation, not by the aspiring vassals on feudal seignories . . . but they established the whole on the legitimate basis of popular consent."[108] Thus, the American colonial experience was not so much the experience of thirteen distinct political communities, all united under the British Crown, but rather the experience of a singular people, comprising an embryonic nation. British rule over the colonies was thus part of a systematic "infringement of natural right,"[109] although the colonies were unable in their undeveloped and infant state to stand up to British encroachments.[110] The American people were the true source of sovereignty even before the ratification of the Constitution; plots of state secession were thus indeed existential threats to the union of the American people and calls for the dissolution of the American national civil society itself.

From such passages as these, one can gather a general—though not complete—compatibility between the assertions of American nationhood in Story's "Oration" and similar assertions in Dane's later *General Abridgment*. Indeed, in his *Commentaries on the Constitution*, Story largely reaffirmed Dane's treatment of the founding in his *General Abridgment*, and a footnote in Section 214 of the *Commentaries* carried an enthusiastic recommendation of Dane's history for understanding the nature of the Second Continental Congress."[111] Not surprisingly, Story was in agreement with Dane that the Continental Congress represented a "general government . . . created and acting by the general consent of the people of all the colonies."[112] Thus, like his predecessors in the emerging "Nationalist Theory," Story's history of the

Revolution considered the American people, since before the Declaration of Independence, as acting as a single sovereign nation and creating a national government over themselves through the Continental Congress.

On the whole, Story's narrative as laid out in the *Commentaries* is naturally much more detailed than the one presented in *An Oration*. Still, as Story proceeded with a detailed review of colonial America, the sovereign status of the separate colonies before the establishment of this national government remained ambiguous. On the one hand, Story generally treated the colonies as separate and, for the most part, self-contained political communities. Although undeniable from a historical perspective, with regard to his Nationalist reading of colonial history, this was a major concession. Story acknowledged that each colony held more legal authority to pass its own legislation than if they were "mere civil corporations of the realm," and that the government of each colony—while dependent upon England and subject to the laws of the realm—had been endowed with "the general powers of government and rights of sovereignty."[113] He concluded from this that each of them was endowed with some of the basic traits of an independent sovereign community, going as far as to note that "each, in a limited sense, was sovereign within its territory,"[114] excepting of course their dependency on Great Britain.[115] Furthermore, he noted that while each of the colonies separately held a considerable degree of authority to govern themselves, there was no governing body above them nor any political ties to each other apart from all being "dependencies" in the same relation to the British Crown.[116] Though all the colonists were British subjects, in other words, "they had no direct political connection with each other" and "the assembly of one province could not make laws for another; nor confer privileges which were to be enjoyed or exercised in another, further than they could in any independent foreign state."[117] There were various scattered attempts to forge treaties or confederacies between them, but these alliances were of questionable legal standing and proved always to be informal and short-lived.[118]

Nevertheless, Story insisted that the American people were in some sense united, noting that in spite of each colony's limited sovereign status and unchallenged prerogative over all taxation and legislation within its territorial borders, the people of the many colonies still "were not wholly alien to each other."[119] In a certain sense, this should not be surprising, given that the American colonists shared many elements of a common political culture: Story emphasized that they "had a common origin, and owed a common allegiance, and the inhabitants of each were British subjects."[120] Nevertheless, Story saw the colonists as bound together by something more than a shared history or a shared status as dependencies of the realm: "for many purposes," Story wrote, the American colonists represented "one people."[121] To support this claim, he cited Chief Justice Jay's opinion in *Chisolm v. Georgia*, where, in describing the situation of the colonists before the Revolution, Jay had described them as a singular people: "All the people of this country were then subjects of the king of Great Britain, and owed allegiance to him; and all the civil authority then existing, or exercised here, flowed from the head of the British Empire."[122] The American people were thus, according to Jay, "in a strict sense, *fellow*-subjects, and in a variety of respects *one people*."[123] Jay, and by extension Story, thus linked a shared colonial allegiance to the King and a shared British citizenship to a shared identity by all Americans as part of "one people."

This is, at first blush, in stark contrast with the political reality in the colonies as already described by Story: what evidence is there that the people of the several colonies represented *one people* at a point when they had no common government over them and were ruled, exclusively, by their separate colonial governments? For Story, however, there was no contradiction: the American people continued to entrust the traditional powers of self-government to the colonial governments that they were most familiar with; for them to create a general shared government over all of them would require a break with their status under the King. The crises of the 1770s was apparently impetus enough for this act, as it led them to create such a general government in the Continental Congress; this creation was itself a revolutionary act. Thus, Story followed Dane in describing the Continental Congress as the "revolutionary government," in consideration of how "in its origin and progress it was wholly conducted upon revolutionary principles."[124] For Story, as for Dane, the Continental Congress was more than a meeting place for the delegates of the several semi-sovereign colonies: it was the national representative body of the whole American people and thus a crucial piece of evidence pointing to a pre-revolutionary common *American people*. Thus, it is not at all surprising that the First Continental Congress played a key role in both Story's and Dane's interpretation of the founding, just as it did for Jay in his opinion in *Chisolm*. If the American colonists were indeed "one people," as Jay and Story were suggesting, then one should expect the revolutionary government to be national rather than confederal in its powers.

Due to the central role that the Congress of 1774 played in his historical narrative, Story spent a considerable amount of time describing the formation of the Congress and also the various political roles that it played. His intention in doing this was to demonstrate beyond any doubt that the body was the direct creation of the sovereign American people and that from the moment of its creation it had "exercised *de facto* and *de jure* a sovereign authority; not as the delegated agents of the governments *de facto* of the colonies, but in virtue of original powers derived from the people."[125] Thus, it became crucial for Story to demonstrate that the Congress was, in fact, the direct creation of the American people writ large, and not authorized or directed by the colonial governments. If Story's contention were true, then it would indicate that, in sending delegates to the Continental Congress, the American people were casting aside their old colonial governments and creating a new national government to replace them. If the Congress had been called by the state governments, on the other hand, it would indicate that the colonists were coming together not as a new people but rather as the representatives of their several colonies. Put differently, to assert as Story did that the Continental Congress constituted a national government required it to be the spontaneous creation of the American people as a whole, disregarding the old colonial boundary lines. By arguing that the Continental Congress was founded upon "revolutionary principles," he thus was presenting its formation as something vaguely resembling a social contract among pre-political individuals.

Story's claim that the Continental Congress represented a *de facto* and *de jure* national government also required him to demonstrate that it considered itself to be a national government and not a voluntary confederation of sovereign states, as the very title *congress* might denote. Story, like Dane, argued that the actions of the Continental Congress pointed to it operating as a national government with a direct connection to individual American citizens, instead of as a confederal government dealing solely with the sovereign states composing it and with little regulatory power of its own. On this point, Story ran into difficulty squaring the historical record with his theory: in 1774, the delegates of each state were given appointment commissions detailing the parameters of their authority as delegates to the First Continental Congress. By Story's admission, the duties that these commissions recognized for the delegates—and by extension for the Continental Congress that they made up—were "principally of an advisory nature,"[126] and thus more closely resembled a loose confederal association making recommendations to the governments of each state than a sovereign government in its own right. Story maintained, however, that the delegates still opted to follow "the wishes and objects of their constituents"[127] rather than quibble over the limits of their formal power, indicating that the delegates themselves knew that their expected role was something much broader and more authoritative than the one laid out in their formal instructions from their colonial governments.

When the Second Continental Congress convened in 1775, the delegate instructions appeared to grant more powers to the Congress, but Story's argument for a national sovereign authority still relied more upon the broad language of the delegate instructions than any direct acknowledgment of a sovereign authority. Story considered this absence of a formal recognition of the Congress' legislative or regulatory authority to be more indicative of the peculiar cautionary constraints of the revolutionary situation than a true indication of the intentions of the people authorizing the delegates; their language may have thus appeared "more guarded than the objects really in view would justify," but they nevertheless understood the true scope of their power and anticipated too "that the spirit of the people would eagerly second every measure adopted to further a general union and resistance against the British claims."[128] Thus, while Story conceded that there is little in the formal authorizations of the Congress to indicate that it was designed to be either a *de jure* or *de facto* national government, the people's ready acceptance of the Continental Congress' assumption of these roles indicated that they had intended all along for Congress to take on these roles, even in the absence of a formal recognition of their full powers.[129]

For Story, the proclaimed devotee of Edmund Burke, the study of government should always rely more on actual historical practice than on its theoretical underpinnings: in this case, the formal legal authority of the Continental Congress was less significant for understanding the scope of its authority and powers than was the popular acceptance or rejection of the Congress' actions by the people. He had written in the Preface to the *Commentaries* that his purpose was to provide the reader with a description of the powers of the federal government "illustrated by its actual practices."[130] He then contrasted the "common-sense of the people" that he meant to appeal to with the work to the "metaphysical refinements" that Burke had so eloquently denounced in his *Reflections on the Revolution in France*. Thus, the fact that the American people had "eagerly second[ed]" the Congress' actions was more important in ascertaining the scope of Congress' authority than a strict adherence to the formal instructions that the delegates had received.

Having dealt with the problem of the Continental Congress' limited formal authorization, Story proceeded to argue that the actual practice of the Congress during the Revolution pointed to its status as a *de facto* and *de jure* national government. The fact that the Congress had been called directly by the united American people and that the people apparently readily accepted expansive actions by the Congress only served to confirm the sovereign role that the Congress was playing as the official national government over the united American nation. When the Second Continental Congress convened and wrote Story, they immediately assumed "some of the highest functions of sovereignty" to themselves: passing measures dealing with national defense, trade restrictions with Britain, raising money and taking out debts on behalf of the nation, emitting bills of credit, creating a national post-office, and establishing for their own body an appellate jurisdiction over prize cases.[131] Similarly, as the war progressed and the nation moved closer to declaring independence from Britain, the Congress continued to conduct itself increasingly like the national government that Story claimed it to be, exerting a sovereign authority which could only be explained by "the supposition that a national union for national purposes already existed, and that Congress was invested with sovereign power over all the colonies for the purpose of preserving the common rights and liberties of all."[132] Thus, the Congress continued to exert control over wartime and military measures, began to engage in commerce with foreign nations—claiming for themselves the power to regulate imports and exports—directing the colonies that had not already done so to form new functioning governments to replace those disbanded by the British, and then finally issuing the act that would securely establish the American people as a nation beyond any doubt: the Declaration of Independence.[133] All of these actions were positively received by the American people,[134] leaving no doubt in Story's mind that, in spite of the limited nature of the congressional delegates' formal authority, the American people had intended the Continental Congress to be endowed with sovereign authority and to act as a national government over them.

Story argued further that the exercise of these powers by the national government, on behalf of the sovereign American people, answered the vexing question of precisely when the American people came together to form a nation and when they had vested a sovereign legislative authority in the Congress: "as soon as Congress assumed powers and passed measures which were in their nature national, to that extent the people, from whose acquiescence and consent they took effect, must be considered as agreeing to form a nation."[135] Thus, the formation of the American nation was not, as one might expect, the result of a sudden formal pronouncement to that effect. Rather, it was based upon the gradual claiming of powers by the Congress that were—in a strict sense, at least—ungranted, and upon the acceptance of these power claims by the people that the Congress was designed to represent. The fact that this national formation process took place during a time of war and political revolution made such extra-legal actions of the Congress even more legitimate. Measuring nationhood in this way—as the product of the practical actions of Congress and their popular acceptance—solved the pressing problem of why there was no formal declaration of American nationhood and why the American people—if creating a national government—had not ever voted on these delegates by national elections.

Still, Story's theory of how the American nation came about was not devoid of defining moments. Story, like all future adherents of his "Nationalist Theory," placed heavy emphasis on the issuing of the Declaration of Independence as a central moment in the formation of the new American people. Story had already approvingly quoted Chief Justice Jay's characterization of the American colonists before the Revolution as composing "in a variety of respects *one people*" and had described the First Continental Congress as "organized under the auspices and with the consent of the people, acting in their primary, sovereign capacity,"[136] hinting that the birth of the American people as a cognizable political entity must have occurred at an unidentified earlier moment in time. Still, in Story's interpretation, the passage of the

Declaration of Independence marked the first formal assertion of American nationhood, sovereignty, and independence and the moment at which the Continental Congress—speaking, again, on behalf of the whole American people—made the people of all the colonies free from British rule.

Story emphasized that it was the Continental Congress that encouraged each state to write their own constitutions and conduct themselves as state governments free of British control.[137] In Story's words, then, it was the Continental Congress that officially "authorized the formation of new governments in the colonies"[138] and that later, through its own act, "absolved them from all allegiance to the British Crown."[139] The chronological ordering here is important for understanding Story's Nationalist Theory: the people of each colony did not create their own revolutionary governments until doing so "in pursuance of the recommendation of Congress," and thus the creation of the revolutionary governments within the colonies flowed from the sovereign authority of the national American people and not from their own status as colonies—which, by the terms of their royal charters, lacked the sovereign authority to conduct themselves independently[140]—or from the authority of the people of each colony. The creation of these governments was, instead, "the achievement of the whole for the benefit of the whole,"[141] and therefore not truly the work of the distinct people of each colony, even if they were the ones tasked with crafting the new governments. Story supported this by arguing that the Declaration itself purported to be "a declaration made by the representatives of the United States of America in Congress assembled."[142] Likewise, the Declaration of Independence had been declared on behalf of the whole people and not on the behalf of the people of any particular colony. "The colonies did not," insisted Story, "severally act for themselves, and proclaim their independence."[143] Rather, since their independence from Britain had been declared to them by the representatives of the new American nation, the colonies-turned-states owed their very existence and independence to the actions of the Congress and thus, indirectly, to the American people as a whole.

Thus, for Story, the issuance of the Declaration of Independence became the moment at which the people of the whole nation broke off whatever remained of their subjugation to British rule and declared the former colonies, taken together, to be "free and independent states"—a step that any one of the colonial governments was incapable of taking on their own and that had to have been taken by the people of all the colonies acting together: "It was," stressed Story, "emphatically the act of the whole *people* of the united colonies, by the instrumentality of their representatives, chosen for that among other purposes."[144] Consequently, with the American people thus asserting their total independence from Britain, through the organ of the national government, and thereby establishing the governments within the several states, the Declaration of Independence marked the moment at which the existence of an American nation came palpably into existence, whereas previously it could only be demonstrated by speculation over whether the colonies considered themselves to be "one people" in some vague, ill-defined, and ultimately unprovable sense. Now, the Declaration of Independence—as carried out by the representatives of the whole American people—was unequivocal proof of that people's existence. "From the moment of the declaration of independence, if not for most purposes at an antecedent period, the united colonies must be considered as being a nation *de facto*, having a general government over it, created and acting by the general consent of the people of all the colonies."[145] Story's depiction of the event thus signified both the vague sense in which the American people constituted—at least "for most purposes"—a nation and also the significance of the Declaration as a singular watershed moment securing and proclaiming that nation's existence. Story readily conceded that the nature of this national government was, in some sense, still murky, for instance in identifying the particular powers of the Congress: "The powers of that government were not, and indeed could not, be well defined. But still, its exclusive sovereignty, in many cases, was firmly established; and its controlling power over the States was in most, if not all, national measures universally admitted."[146] The Declaration's pronouncement of a total separation from Britain thus marked the creation not only of the several state governments but of the national government as well. Although the people of the colonies had acted as if they were a nation prior to this point—with the Congress likewise acting as if it were their national legislature—this was the moment that formally and unequivocally announced American nationhood to the world. As the effective creation of both national and state governments, the Declaration was thus "an act of paramount and sovereign authority" by the American people.[147]

It is worth pointing out that under this narrative, the states—considered both as the state governments and as the political communities of the people of each state—are the creatures of the national government and not the other way around. Thus, the relationship of the federal government to the states becomes analogous to that of a state government to a county or municipal government, or of the British Crown to a royal corporation. Under such an arrangement, the states essentially exist at the pleasure of the national government, which called them into being for its purposes. If one accepts Story's claim that the Declaration of Independence was an act by the representatives of the whole American people that created the states as political communities, then it is entirely appropriate to argue, as Lincoln did in his *Message to Congress in Special Session*, that the federal government was not only historically prior to the state governments but that it directly created them.[148] According to Story's Nationalist Theory, the states, as separate political societies, have no legal status and no historical existence outside of the entire union, and owe their entire existence to the continued pleasure of the whole American people.

Story also turned his attention in this section to one of the principal challenges to his theory. In claiming that the Declaration of Independence was an action taken by the whole American people, he had to contend with that document's climactic pronouncement that the several former colonies now existed as "free and independent states." The fact that the Declaration made no explicit reference to the formation of a unified American nation or to the status of its signatories as the representatives of a nation complicated the problem, as did the Articles of Confederation's stipulation that "each state retains its sovereignty, freedom, and independence."[149] Story was thus faced with explicit language in both the Declaration and the Articles that seemed to directly contradict the narrative of pre-constitutional American nationhood that he had been theorizing. How could the Declaration of Independence at one and the same time be primarily intended to declare the American people, as a nation, to be "free and independent" and then declare only its several constituent communities to be so?

In response to this objection, Story argued that such words as *sovereign* and *state* admit multiple interpretations. In particular, he argued that the word *sovereign* could mean either "supreme, absolute, uncontrollable power, the *jus summi imperii*, the absolute right to govern"[150] or else "such powers as in the actual organization of the particular state or nation are to be exclusively exercised by certain public functionaries, without the control of any superior authority."[151] Similarly, the word state could denote either "the people composing a particular nation or community"[152] or else "merely the positive or actual organization of the legislative, executive, or judicial powers."[153] It is apparent that in both of these instances, the first interpretation is the broader of the two and connotes that the person or body being described is ultimately and fully vested with all of the various attributes of sovereignty or statehood that Story had been describing as existing purely in the American people as a whole and in their national government; on the other hand, in both instances, the second interpretation is much narrower and signifies only that the person or body being described exercises some particular power or else enjoys some particular attribute of sovereignty or statehood without necessarily being endowed with every such attribute.

If the Declaration had meant to declare the former colonies to be "free and independent *states*" in the fullest sense of the word, then Story's narrative fell apart, for the Congress could not have been declaring independence on behalf of the entire American people if it were setting up the colonies as entirely sovereign and autonomous communities in their own right. But, Story argued, this was not the sense in which the Declaration used the term:

"it is apparent that none of the colonies before the Revolution were, in the most large and general sense, independent or sovereign communities," all of them being subject to the British Crown.[154] "If in any sense they might claim the attributes of sovereignty, it was only in that subordinate sense to which we have alluded as exercising within a limited extent certain usual powers of sovereignty."[155] Thus, Story argued that the language of "free and independent states" in the Declaration did not detract from or endanger his narrative of the Founding.

For one thing, Story insisted that in republican governments, it was always "the people of the nation" and not their "public functionaries" who would be endowed with "the absolute sovereignty of the nation"[156] and thus, any interpretation of the Founding that emphasized the roles played by the colonial governments in setting up the Congress or declaring independence ignored the ultimate sovereignty of the American people. Again, relying on the actual practice of the Continental Congress as the highest proof of its status as a *de jure* and *de facto* national government, Story held that the independence declared by the Continental Congress in 1776 could not have possibly been that of thirteen autonomous *states*, in the full sense of the word: "Whatever, then, may be the theories of ingenious men on the subject, it is historically true that before the declaration of independence these colonies were not, in any absolute sense, sovereign states; that the event did not find them or make them such."[157] On the contrary, each of the states was, "at the moment of their separation," subjected to the power of the general government and thus "under a dominion of a superior controlling national government whose powers were vested in and exercised by the general Congress with the consent of the people of all the States."[158] Thus, Story argued, the historical practice of the Congress and of the people it represented demonstrated that the states were not, either before or after the Declaration of Independence, sovereign states in the full sense.

The states owed their very existence as states—in any sense of the word—to the people of the whole nation, since it was this national popular body that had authorized the creation of the Continental Congress that had in turn authorized the creation of the several state governments and declared the states independent of Britain—all with the ready approval of the national American people. It stood to reason, then, that it was the American people as a whole that remained sovereign throughout the existence of the Articles of Confederation. Furthermore, there was also no other power than this sovereign national people that was capable of ratifying the proposed Constitution that came out of the convention in Philadelphia. Story's next task in spelling out the implications of his Nationalist reading of American history was proving that the Constitution was created as an act of the sovereign national American people.

STORY'S *COMMENTARIES ON THE CONSTITUTION*: "NATURE OF THE CONSTITUTION,— WHETHER A COMPACT"

Story's detailed history of the colonies and of the Revolution culminated in Chapter III of the *Commentaries*, which Story titles "Nature of the Constitution,—Whether a Compact": a lengthy section in which he examined the assertion of Jefferson and his allies that the Constitution was compact or agreement between the several states, as separate political communities, and not—as Story's understanding of the Founding required—as the national creation of the American people as a whole. The prominence of this section in Story's overall work should not be surprising: indeed, whether or not the national union—or the federal Constitution that provided the foundation for its central government—could rightly be considered a "compact" was far from a semantical concern. Given the importance of this question for assessing the scope of federal powers and the very function of the Constitution, as well as the extent to which Story relies on his prior historical narrative in answering this question, it is a fairly safe conjecture to suggest that the previous detailed examination of American history—from its roots in the colonial experience through its experience in the Articles of Confederation—was placed in the *Commentaries* in order to lend credence to Story's emphatic insistence that the Constitution was not a compact between the people of each state.

This is the interpretation of the Jeffersonian jurist Abel Upshur in analyzing the role of Story's pre-constitutional narrative in the overall framework of the *Commentaries*. In the most thorough published Republican response to Story's *Commentaries*, Upshur emphasized the central role that Story's historical narrative plays in his overall constitutional theory; Story's historical analysis, according to Upshur, "contains much to enable us to understand fully the relation which they bore to one another and to the mother country."[159] Upshur, like Story, understood that the answers given to this underlying question about the relationship of the colonies to one another would be of key significance to understanding the scope of the federal government's powers, as well as of its relationship to the state governments: "Many of the powers which have been claimed for the federal government" by Story and other partisans of a stronger federal government "depend upon a denial of that separate existence, and separate sovereignty and independence, which the opposing party has uniformly claimed for the States."[160] Given the importance of these historical questions for understanding the scope and power of the contemporary federal government, Upshur found it to be absolutely essential to correctly understand the original situation of the colonies, "and by tracing the colonies from their first establishment as such, through the various stages of their progress up to the adoption of the Federal

Constitution, we shall be greatly aided in forming a correct opinion as to the true character of that instrument."[161] Thus, Upshur argued, the reason that Story spent so great a portion of the *Commentaries* on the historical background before the Constitution's ratification was that it asserted his basic premise that the Constitution was the creation of the American people as a whole and not—as proponents of the Compact Theory would claim—an agreement between the people of each state. Story's insistence that it was the people of the whole nation who authorized the creation of the state governments and declared their independence is central to his later claims of how the federal government is to interact with the state governments and how the constitutional grants of power to the federal government should be interpreted.

More broadly, Story's claim that the Constitution was created by the national American people would also have consequences for how the Constitution would be interpreted. If indeed the union was never a mere compact or agreement between separate peoples, but rather the direct creation of the sovereign American people acting together, the function of the Constitution changed, and so did the lens through which it would be read and interpreted. The very nature and function of the Constitution hinge largely upon the question Story turned to address in Chapter III: Is the Constitution nothing more than a compact between the peoples of the several states, or is it the direct creation of a larger national people?

Story began this examination into the true nature of the Constitution by addressing the opinion of "a learned commentator"—St. George Tucker—on the matter.[162] In his *View of the Constitution of the United States*, Tucker had described the Constitution as "an original, written, federal, and social compact, freely, voluntarily, and solemnly entered into by the several states of North-America, and ratified by the people thereof, respectively."[163] Story quoted Tucker's definition almost word-for-word and then proceeded in like manner to provide descriptions for what Tucker means by each component of this definition. Story contrasted Tucker's interpretation of the Revolution as securing the independence of thirteen independent states and contrasted this to Dane's theory of the founding.[164] Tucker's opinion on the matter was not, as Story observed, his alone, but was rather shared by "a large body of statesmen and jurists in different parts of the Union, avowed and acted upon in former times, and recently revived under circumstances which have given them increased importance if not a perilous influence."[165] Ultimately, Story rejected the Compact Theory on two grounds. The first was more prudential: the "perilous influence" that Story feared the theory would have was largely due to what Story saw as the negative consequences of endorsing the theory, but he also resisted the Compact Theory in principal, based on his historical narrative already laid out as well as the text of the Constitution.

Practically, Story held that the Compact Theory would lead to disastrous results that would undermine the Constitution and threaten to destroy the union. The recent circumstances he cited included, most notably, the nullification controversy surrounding the tariff of 1828, and Story conceded that the right of each state to judge the constitutionality of federal actions for themselves would "flow naturally" from the basic premises of Compact Theory.[166] He further reasoned that the Compact Theory would allow an individual state to effectively dissolve the union if they felt that the terms of the federal compact creating the union had been broken.[167] This construction, Story argued, would thus defeat the entire purpose of the Constitution by threatening to bring back the powerlessness of the central government under the Articles of Confederation. Even if the Constitution was to be considered a contract, Story reasoned, then it should be read as a contract, meaning that it should be interpreted in a way that accurately reflects the purposes and objectives of the parties contracting together.[168]

Story was quick to acknowledge multiple meanings of the word "compact" or "contract,"[169] and pointed out that the nature of the agreement—as well as the rights and duties of the compacting parties—depended entirely upon the status of who was doing the contracting: whether such parties were individuals entering into a "social compact" to create a society and a government, or whether the parties were sovereign states in their own right entering into a treaty or alliance. Story examined the Compact Theory in the light of the first possibility—of a "social compact" creating a new society out of members previously in a pre-political state of nature—and argued that if this were the case, any claims of a continued existence for the states as separate political entities after having compacted together were self-defeating. According to Story, if there were a "social compact" between the states creating the Union—the same way that individuals compacted together to create civil society as an original political act—then the states would have then lost their status as distinct contracting parties in signing onto the Constitution.

To this effect, he quoted the constitution of Massachusetts, which identified a government as "a social compact, by which the whole people covenants with each citizen, and each citizen with the whole government."[170] Story then likened any constitutional role for the states as distinct parties *after* ratifying the Constitution to the ability of an individual under the social compact, having once joined civil society, to renounce that society and restore his full autonomy the moment he as an individual supposed the compact to have been violated or infringed.[171] Such an interpretation would defeat the entire purpose of the Constitution by dissolving any hope of permanence or security in government and ushering in the very same sense of anarchy and chaos that the creation of government had been hoping to avoid.[172] Thus, according to Story, when private individual citizens have contracted together to form a government over themselves, they subsequently lose their ability to interpret the contract themselves, or to determine for themselves that the original agreement had been breached, and must instead submit their case to the public functionaries—usually the judiciary—established by the government itself.[173]

On the other hand, in the case of compacts or agreements between separate nations, very different rules of construction apply. Such nations, Story wrote, "in their sovereign character, are all upon an equality," and thus do not acknowledge any superior power over them, although they may invest some entity with the authority to serve as a common arbiter over them.[174] This sense of the word appears to be closer to the way that it was used when Calhoun and other Compact Theorists described the Constitution as a compact.

Story held that a constitution, inasmuch as it established a fundamental law for a government, may, in a limited sense, perhaps be considered to be the product of an original compact among the citizens establishing it, but that from the moment of its ratification, it ceased to be a compact—in the second sense of the word, dealing with sovereign nations—and instead became "a fundamental law of absolute paramount obligation."[175] To this effect, Story noted that all of the state constitutions seemed to be worded more as the first type of compact—an agreement among private citizens to establish a sovereign government over them—and not the second, thus preventing individual citizens from being treated as coequal sovereign states would.[176] This was the meaning of language in the state constitutions declaring that these governments were "ordained and established" by the people of the state.[177] Similarly, Story argued that constitutions—both state and federal—inasmuch as they purport to create a *government*, inherently bring with them some degree of supremacy over individuals,[178] and when that government created involves the merging of several political societies into a larger society, that larger society is entrusted with all the same supremacy and sovereignty over individual citizens, as well as the composite parts.[179]

Story then turned his attention to the central question prompting this lengthy examination: Should the Constitution of the United States be considered to be "a mere compact, treaty, or confederation" between each of the states, or between the people of each state, or as establishing a government with supreme, sovereign power over them?[180] Throughout the remainder of the chapter, Story went on to argue at considerable length that both the language of the Constitution itself and the historical record of the founding era weighed heavily against the notion that the Constitution is a compact between separate parties that continued to exist in their full sovereign capacity after the ratification of the document. In examining the language of the Constitution, Story noted that it—like the state constitutions already discussed—purports itself to be "ordained and established" by the people; more precisely, it purported to be the creation of "the people of the United States" and not the people of any particular state.[181] Moreover, unlike the Articles of Confederation—curiously described here by Story as "mainly of a pure federative character, and . . . treated as stipulations between States for many purposes independent and sovereign"—or the abortive New England Confederacy of 1643, the Framers of the Constitution nowhere in the document described the union as a *confederation* or *compact*, instead calling their national founding document a *constitution*: a word which, according to Story, carried with it strong inferences against it being a treaty between sovereign nations;[182] such inferences are then made explicit in the Supremacy Clause.[183] After examining the ratification debates and finding there no reference to the Constitution as a voluntary confederation between sovereign states, he turned to address statements by Tucker and Madison that the states are parties to the federal compact in the Constitution. Such a view of the states, wrote Story, "having no foundation in the words of the Constitution, is altogether a gratuitous assumption, and therefore inadmissible."[184] If the Constitution then was not the product of a voluntary compact between the people of the several states, Story was free to offer an alternative explanation of the origins of the union.

In addition to Story's careful examination of the text of the Constitution, his denial of the Compact Theory was linked also to his claim that the Constitution was the creation of the people of the whole United States. Much as Marshall had done in *McCulloch v. Maryland*, Story distinguished this claim first from the notion that the Constitution was the creation of the many *state governments*. If indeed the Constitution were the creation of the already-established state governments, it would thus not be a creation of "the people" at all. Under such a theory, the state governments essentially acted as intermediaries between the people of the nation and the new federal government: the state governments had been delegated certain powers by their people, and they in turn delegated some of their powers to the federal government. Such a delegation, Story argued, would go beyond the state governments' authority.[185]

Furthermore, nothing was clearer from the history of the ratification than that the Constitution was submitted to a vote of the people of each state and not to the state legislatures. Thus, in criticizing a quote by Jefferson holding the Constitution to be a compact between the states, Story pointed out what he saw as the historical complications attending such a proposition: "It would, I imagine, be very difficult to point out when and in what manner any such compact was made."[186] The Constitution, according to Story, "was neither made nor ratified by the States as sovereignties or political communities," but rather was "framed by a convention, proposed to the people of the States for their adoption by Congress; and was adopted by State conventions,—the immediate representatives of the people."[187] Consequently, it was "the people of the United States"—as evidenced also by the Preamble—that created the Constitution, and did so on their own, save for being called into convention by the governments of their state.[188] It was the people who had created the Constitution as an exercise of their underlying sovereignty, and so any effort on the part of any state government to stand in the way of the operation of the federal government denied the sovereign and supreme power that had created the state governments as well.

This argument, however—that the Constitution and the union were assented to by the state governments—was never advanced by any proponent of the Compact Theory. On the contrary, it should be noted that advocates of the Compact Theory uniformly held that the Constitution was the direct creation of *the people* of each state, operating directly through popular ratification conventions instead of going through their regular process of governing through their elected representatives in the state governments. The consequence of this distinction was that Compact Theorists held that ultimate sovereignty under the Constitution rested in the people of each state and not in the state governments, which were likewise creatures of the sovereign people of each separate state. Thus, for instance, James Madison in his *Report of 1800* acknowledged, like Story, several definitions of the word *state*, but placed emphasis on only one of those meanings: "the people composing . . . political societies, in their highest sovereign capacity. . . ."[189] It was in this sense—the *people* of the state—that the Constitution had been submitted to, and ratified by, the states, according to Madison. Neither Madison nor Jefferson argued that the Constitution was assented to by the people's functionaries in the state governments; they argued instead that the Constitution was a compact between the separate peoples of each state instead of by some national aggregate people. For Marshall and Story, on the other hand, any discussion of "the people" could refer only to the people of the entire union; to the extent that the states were recognizable as distinct political units at all, it was only inasmuch as that national people had created state governments: "the people" themselves existed solely in their national capacity.

Story did briefly address this argument of the Compact Theorists that the Constitution was compacted not by the several state governments, but by the people of each state. Under such a formulation, adherents of the Compact Theory agreed with Story that the Constitution was created by the people directly instead of going through their normal representatives in the state governments, while still maintaining that ultimate sovereignty rested in the separate people of each state, and not in a united body of people that transcended state lines. Such an understanding of the union, Story noted, was made immediately suspect by the wording of the Preamble: by claiming to be the direct action of "the people of the United States" instead of "the people of the several States," the Constitution in effect "pronounces that it is established by the people of the United States in the aggregate."[190] Ultimately, it is this phrasing in the Preamble that led Story to reject the claim that the Constitution was assented to by the people of each state: a theory by which its adherents are thus "obliged to depart from the words of the instrument" and which "can serve no better purpose than to confuse the mind in relation to a subject otherwise clear."[191] For Story, the language of the Preamble was evidence enough—at least when coupled with the purpose of creating the Constitution and the lack of any textual evidence that it was originally conceived to be a Compact between the states—to demonstrate that the Constitution was the creation of the American people acting as one single national sovereign body and not several state political bodies.

It may be noted here that proponents of the Compact Theory had at least one incontrovertible piece of historical evidence on their side: the Constitution was assented to *not* by the people of the United States in a national convention, but was instead voted on separately by the people of each state.[192] Furthermore, when the states of North Carolina and Rhode Island had failed at first to ratify the Constitution, they were treated—in a variety of respects—as foreign countries;[193] if indeed the Constitution were the creation of the "American people" writ large, then ostensibly the approval of the Constitution within a few small states should not have had any effect on the people of those states, inasmuch as they too were part of the pre-constitutional American nation that Story had previously described. Story, however, explained away this contradiction by arguing that, in retrospect, the people had acted corporately, albeit within their separate states: "Doubtless the people of the several States, taken collectively, constitute the people of the United States. But it is in this their collective capacity, it is as all the people of the United States, that they establish the Constitution."[194] Here Story seemed to be relying on his earlier demonstration that the Constitution does not, on its face, purport to create a compact or treaty between the states. Therefore, he inferred that the seemingly separate actions of the people within each state were, in actuality, part of a larger collective action. This inference is, of course, enhanced by Story's previous demonstration that certain previous political acts—most notability, the creation of state governments and the issuance of the Declaration of Independence—were actions taken by the people of the entire nation as a whole. Once this statement was accepted, it became much easier to see the actions of the people within each state as mere parts of a larger corporate whole, at least on matters of national significance.

Thus, Story reasoned, the Constitution owed its existence not to the separate political communities of the several states, but rather to the whole body of the national American people acting in their collective, sovereign capacity. It is this understanding of the union that had already formed the basis of one of Story's most influential decisions he would write in his long tenure on the

Court. In the 1816 case *Martin v. Hunter's Lessee*, the Supreme Court of the United States established its own supremacy over state supreme courts in interpreting questions of federal law. Here, the usually prolific Chief Justice Marshall recused himself from the case, citing a financial conflict of interest, and it fell upon Justice Story to write the opinion for a unanimous court. Story used the opportunity to elaborate on his understanding of the ratification of the Constitution: "The Constitution of the United States was ordained and established not by the States in their sovereign capacities, but emphatically, as the preamble of the Constitution declares, by 'the people of the United States.'"[195] Again, Story—like Marshall in *McCulloch*—tended to speak of the "states" merely as the state governments and not as so many people representing distinct political communities, which, according to Story, they were not.

Throughout his career, Story was insistent that the union had been created by the national American people, and it was this basic premise that drove virtually every aspect of his constitutional theory. The rejection of the Compact Theory in Story's *Commentaries* represents the final culmination of this constitutional theory and the strongest argument that has yet been made in favor of the proposition that the union and the Constitution were the creations of the national American people. Story understood well that the question of whether the Constitution was a Compact between the states had significant implications for the scope of its powers as well as for the standard by which it would be interpreted. Story declared in *Martin* that it was "competent to the people" of the United States to give the general government any and all powers that they might see fit; following this, it was thus also "competent to the people" of each separate state to give to their state governments whatever portion of the remaining powers they chose. The chief ramification of all of this was that there was no substantial difference in kind between the federal government and the states, both drawing their authority directly from the people—except, of course, inasmuch as the federal government drew its powers first and thus had the right to preempt certain state powers.

It is clear from this examination of Story's Nationalist Theory that his historical theory was thus not only an integral part of his overarching philosophy of constitutional interpretation, but that it had profound ramifications for his understanding of federal powers. Not only did it allow him greater latitude in interpreting the Constitution, but it also created different expectations of what federal powers might be necessary or might be reasonably expected in order for the federal government to fulfill its obligations. For while the enumerated powers of the federal government might all be either explicitly or implicitly enumerated in the Constitution, the body of powers that were necessary for operation as a functioning member of the community of nations was not only much more broad but also much less clearly defined. In a variety of ways, then, Story's Nationalist Theory allowed for—and required—the existence of a broad field of federal rights, powers, and duties that did not exist under the Compact Theory.

That the existence of a federal common law—and the consequent right of the federal courts to interpret and develop it—was included among these powers will be established in the following chapters. First, however, it remains to be demonstrated that opponents of the federal common law doctrine were operating out of an opposing constitutional theory. Indeed, when Jefferson and his allies opposed the doctrine of a federal common law, they did so not only by pointing out the absence of any positive evidence of a federal common law adoption, but also by arguing that the existence of a federal common law violated the very nature of the union as a compact between otherwise-sovereign states granting specified limited powers over to the central government. Opposition to the federal common law doctrine was thus inextricably bound up in support of the basic premise of the Compact Theory.

NOTES

1. The most famous of these is the first: Abel Parker Upshur's *A Brief Enquiry into the Nature and Character of Our Federal Government* (Petersburg, 1840). Later rebuttals, largely similar in their criticism of Story's adherence to the Nationalist Theory, include: Henry St. George Tucker, *Lectures on Government* (Charlottesville, 1844), Nathaniel Beverly Tucker, *Lectures on the Science of Government* (Philadelphia, 1845), Alexander Stephens, A Constitutional View of the Late War between the States (Philadelphia, 1868).
2. Kent, I:225. Quoted in Elizabeth Kelley Bauer, *Commentaries on the Constitution 1790–1860* (New York: Columbia University Press, 1952), 220.
3. Ibid.
4. Bauer, 272–273.
5. Ibid., 274–276.
6. Daniel Webster, "An Address Delivered Before the Washington Benevolent Society," at Portsmouth, July 4, 1812. Digitized by the University of Missouri-Columbia and available online at https://babel.hathitrust.org/cgi/pt?id=mou.010507016961;view=1up;seq=2.
7. Ibid., 11.
8. Daniel Webster, "The Constitution Not a Compact Between Sovereign States." Floor Speech in the United States Senate, February 16, 1833. *Register of Debates in Congress, Senate, 22nd Congress, 2nd Session* (Washington: Gales and Seaton, 1833), 553–587, 556.
9. Ibid.
10. Bauer, 152n146. Bauer also cites Vernon Louis Parrington, *Main Currents in American Thought*, Vol II (New York: Harcourt Brace And Co., 1927), 311–312.

11. Bauer, 276.
12. See, for instance, Story's denunciation of Rawle at Bauer, 284–285.
13. Madison, *Notes of Debates in the Federal Convention of 1787* (New York: W.W. Norton & Co., 1987), 217.
14. Nathan Dane, *A General Abridgment and Digest of American Law*, Vol. IX, Appendix (Boston: Hilliard, Gray, Little, and Wilkins, 1829), 10.
15. Ford, *Journals of the Continental Congress*, VI:1105.
16. Ibid., 1081.
17. Ibid., 1104.
18. Ibid., 1081.
19. Ibid., 1082.
20. Ibid., 1103.
21. Ibid., 1082.
22. Ibid., 1103.
23. Articles of Confederation, Article II.
24. Ibid., Preamble.
25. Ibid.,, Article III.
26. Madison, *Notes of Debates*, 152–153.
27. Ibid.
28. Ibid, 153.
29. Ibid.
30. Ibid., 217.
31. Ibid.
32. James Wilson, "State House Yard Speech." Reprinted in *Collected Works of James Wilson*, ed. Kermit L. Hall and Mark David Hall (Indianapolis: Liberty Fund, 2007), 1:171–177, 173.
33. Quoted in Story, *Commentaries*, Sec. 212, 1:150.
34. Ibid.
35. Ibid.
36. "The Address and Reasons of Dissent of the Minority of the Convention of Pennsylvania to their Constituents," December 12, 1787. Available online through the Constitution Society, http://www.constitution.org/afp/pennmi00.htm.
37. Ibid.
38. Daniel Farber, "The Constitution's Forgotten Cover Letter: An Essay on the New Federalism and the Original Understanding." *Michigan Law Review* 94, issue 3 (1995), 615–650, 638–639.
39. George Washington, "Letter of the President of the Federal Convention, Dated September 17, 1787, to the President of Congress, Transmitting the Constitution." Available through The Avalon Project: Documents in Law, History, and Diplomacy of Yale Law School, available online at http://avalon.law.yale.edu/18th_century/translet.asp.
40. Farber, 638.
41. Washington, "Letter."
42. David Ramsay, *The History of the American Revolution*, ed. Lester H. Cohen (Indianapolis: Liberty Fund, 1990), I:332.
43. Ibid.

44. Ibid.
45. Ibid., 328.
46. Ibid., 332.
47. Madison, 217.
48. Ramsay, 656.
49. *Chisolm v. Georgia*, 2. U.S. 419 (1793).
50. Ibid., 470.
51. *McCulloch v. Maryland*, 17 U.S. (4 Wheat.) 316 (1819).
52. Ibid., 402.
53. Ibid., 403.
54. Ibid.
55. Ibid.
56. Ibid.
57. Ibid.
58. Ibid.
59. Henry Lee, *Plain Truth: Addressed to the People of Virginia* (Petersburg: William Prentiss, 1799), 22. Quoted in Kenneth Stampp, "The Concept of a Perpetual Union." *The Journal of American History* 65, no. 1 (June, 1978), 5–33.
60. Ibid., 20.
61. Dane, Vol. IX, Appendix, 10.
62. Ibid.
63. Ibid., 11.
64. Ibid., 11.
65. Ibid.
66. Ibid.
67. Ibid., 18–19.
68. Ibid., 21.
69. Ibid.
70. Ibid., 19.
71. Ibid., 21.
72. Ibid., 8.
73. Ibid., 19.
74. Ibid., 18–19.
75. Ibid.
76. Story, "An Oration," Speech delivered in Salem, MA on July 4th, 1804. Original printing. Available online at https://archive.org/stream/orationpronounce00stor#page/n3/mode/2up.
77. *Life and Letters*, I:84. Quoted in McClellan, 19.
78. McClellan, 19.
79. Ibid., 18.
80. "An Oration," 23.
81. Ibid., 21.
82. Ibid.
83. McClellan, 8–9.
84. Story, *Miscellaneous Writings*, ed. William W. Story (Boston: Charles C. Little & James Brown, 1852), 27. Quoted in McClellan, 19.

85. Ibid.
86. Ibid., 27.
87. Ibid., 28.
88. Ibid., 34.
89. Ibid., 21–22.
90. Ibid.
91. Ibid., 28.
92. Timothy Pickering. Timothy Pickering to George Cabot, January 29, 1804. Reprinted in *The Founder's Constitution*, ed. Philip B. Kurland and Ralph Lerner (Chicago: University of Chicago Press, 1987), 1:235–236.
93. Ibid., 236.
94. Ibid.
95. Ibid.
96. Ibid.
97. Rawle, *A View of the Constitution of the United States of America*, 2nd ed. (Philadelphia: Philip H. Nicklin, 1829), 307.
98. Calhoun, *A Discourse on the Constitution and Government of the United States*, reprinted in *Union and Liberty: The Political Philosophy of John C. Calhoun*, ed. Ross M. Lence (Indianapolis: Liberty Fund, 1992), 79–284.
99. Webster, "Benevolent Society."
100. Ibid., 21.
101. Thomas Jefferson. Thomas Jefferson to William H. Crawford, June 20, 1816. From *Founders Online*, National Archives, https://founders.archives.gov/documents/Jefferson/03-10-02-0101.
102. Bauer, 179.
103. Anecdote cited in Bauer, 179, citing William Harrison Safford, ed., *Blennerhassett Papers, Embodying the Private Journal of Harman Blennerhassett* (Cincinnati: Moore, Wilstach, Keys, & Co., 1864).
104. Calhoun, *Discourse*, 212.
105. "An Oration," 6–7.
106. Ibid., 6.
107. Ibid., 35.
108. Ibid., 9.
109. Ibid., 11.
110. Ibid., 10.
111. Story, *Commentaries*, Sec. 214n1, 1:152.
112. Ibid., Sec. 215, 152–153.
113. Ibid., Sec. 161, 111.
114. Ibid., Sec. 177, 124.
115. Ibid., Sec. 171, 120.
116. Ibid., Sec. 177, 124.
117. Ibid.
118. Ibid.
119. Ibid.
120. Ibid.

121. Ibid., Sec. 178, 124.
122. *Chisolm v. Georgia*, 470. Quoted in Story, *Commentaries*, Sec. 178, 1:125.
123. Ibid.
124. Story, *Commentaries*, Sec. 201, 1:140.
125. Ibid.
126. Ibid., Sec. 213, 151.
127. Ibid.
128. Ibid.
129. Ibid.
130. Ibid., viii.
131. Ibid., Sec. 213, 151–152.
132. Ibid., Sec. 214, 152.
133. Ibid.
134. Ibid.
135. Ibid., Sec. 213, 151.
136. Ibid., Sec. 201, 140.
137. Ibid., Sec. 211, 149.
138. Ibid., Sec. 214, 152.
139. Ibid., Sec. 211, 149.
140. Ibid.
141. Ibid.
142. Ibid.
143. Ibid.
144. Ibid.
145. Ibid.
146. Ibid., Sec. 215, 152–153.
147. Ibid., Sec. 211, 149.
148. Lincoln, "Special Session."
149. Articles of Confederation, Article II.
150. Story, *Commentaries*, Sec. 207, 1:144.
151. Ibid., Sec. 207, 145.
152. Ibid., Sec. 208, 145.
153. Ibid., Sec. 208, 146.
154. Ibid., Sec. 210, 147–148.
155. Ibid.
156. Ibid., Sec. 208, 147.
157. Ibid., Sec. 214, 152.
158. Ibid.
159. Abel Parker Upshur, *A Brief Enquiry into the Nature and Character of our Federal Government: Being a Review of Judge Story's Commentaries on the Constitution*. Reprinting (Philadelphia: John Campbell, Publisher, 1863). Full text available online from The Constitution Society at http://www.constitution.org/ups/upshur.htm.
160. Ibid.
161. Ibid.
162. Story, *Commentaries*, Sec. 310, 1:215.

163. Tucker, 91.
164. Story, *Commentaries*, Sec. 314, 218n1.
165. Ibid., Sec. 319, 1:221.
166. Ibid., Sec. 321, 223.
167. Ibid., Sec. 322, 224.
168. Ibid., Sec. 331, 231.
169. Ibid., Sec. 323, 224.
170. Ibid., Sec. 333, 232.
171. Ibid., Sec. 333, 232.
172. Ibid.
173. Ibid., Sec. 334, 233.
174. Ibid., Sec. 335, 233–234.
175. Ibid., Sec. 348, 242.
176. Ibid., Sec. 338, 235.
177. Ibid.
178. Ibid., Sec. 340, 237.
179. Ibid.
180. Ibid., Sec. 350, 243.
181. Ibid., Sec. 352, 244.
182. Ibid., Sec. 353, 245.
183. Ibid., Sec. 354, 246.
184. Ibid., Sec. 361, 252.
185. Story, *Commentaries*, Sec. 362, 1:253.
186. Ibid., Sec. 311, 1:215n3.
187. Ibid.
188. Ibid., Sec. 362, 1:252.
189. Madison, "Report of 1800."
190. Ibid., Sec. 363, 255.
191. Ibid., Sec. 365, 257.
192. Even the language of the Preamble, heavily relied on by Story, can largely be explained by the fact that, at the moment of the Constitution's writing, it was unclear which states were eventually to ratify the document, and thus would have been impossible to list the people of each ratifying state specifically. Indeed, a first draft of the Constitution, before being sent to the Committee of Style, instead began "We the people of the states of New-Hampshire, Massachusetts, Rhode-Island . . ." Max Farrand, ed., *Records of the Federal Convention of 1787* (New Haven: Yale University Press, 1911), 2:565.
193. As one example of this, see Washington's conspicuous avoidance of visiting Rhode Island while on a tour of the states following his election as president. Pauline Maier, *Ratification: The People Debate the Constitution, 1787–1788* (New York: Simon & Schuster, 2010), 458.
194. Story, *Commentaries*, Sec. 363, 1:255.
195. *Martin v. Hunter's Lessee*, 14 U.S. 1 Wheat. 304, 324–325 (1816).

Chapter 4

Understanding the Opposition to the Federal Common Law

In a 1799 letter to Charles Pinckney, Jefferson singled out the federal common law doctrine as uniquely dangerous among what he saw as federal encroachments on the powers of the state governments: "I consider all the encroachments made on that heretofore, as nothing, as mere retail stuff, compared with the wholesale doctrine, that there is a common law in force in the U.S. of which & of all the cases within it's provisions their courts have cognizance."[1] Jefferson's reaction would seem to suggest a deeper fear than that the federal courts would be able to prosecute non-statutory offenses, but what was that deeper fear, and what about the federal common law doctrine stoked such fears? If all the debate centered on was the theoretical existence of some body of legal precedents that were already, by and large, recognized in every state and thus were already *common* throughout the United States, then such vehement objections would seem rather incongruous; certainly, such the suggestion of a federal common law jurisdiction for the federal courts would not seem at first glance to be a greater threat to Republican principles than any of the other controversial Federalist policies that drew criticism from the Jeffersonians. And yet, claims of a federal common law seemed to draw out a more forceful response than any other perceived threat. The intensity of Republican opposition to the assertion of the federal common law indicates that the Jeffersonians saw some larger danger lurking underneath the surface of the debate.

What was this larger danger? By studying the Republican responses to Federalist claims of a single, national common law, it becomes clear that Jefferson and his fellow Republicans saw such claims as threatening to alter the fundamental framework of the American federal republic. Their views on the nature of the union and the Constitution were wholly incompatible with even the possibility that a single, federal common law adoption—open as it would be to interpretation and development by the federal courts and to repeal or modification by the federal legislature—might bind all Americans together.

In short, it was their acceptance of the Compact Theory that led Jefferson and his followers to vigorously reject the federal common law doctrine. That understanding of the union led them to maintain at one and the same time two principles that seemed so contradictory for proponents of a federal common law jurisdiction: that the common law had unquestionably been adopted as the foundation for the legal system in every state, but that the United States as a whole was completely incapable of ever having a national common law of its own. For Story, who conceived of the federal government and the state governments as essentially similar in their origins—both being empowered by the American people—such a distinction was impossible: if the American people were competent to give power to the judiciaries of the states, surely they were competent to give such power to the federal judiciary. Given his Nationalist framework for understanding the union, Story could conceive of no rationalization for the opponents of the federal common law other than that they must be driven by an animus against the common law itself. Consequently, this is how he treated opponents of the federal common law in his *Commentaries.*

THE COMMON LAW VS. THE "RIGHTS OF MAN"

In a footnote in his *Commentaries on the Constitution,* Story offered a suggestion as to what lay behind Jefferson's opposition to the federal common law doctrine. Following a passage where he made the unobjectionable observation that the "whole structure of our present jurisprudence stands upon the original foundations of the common law," Story noted that Jefferson was opposed to this principle that he found to be so clear in the historical record.[2] Jefferson, according to Story, rejected the notion that American jurisprudence was built upon the common law, treating that doctrine "with an extraordinary degree of derision if not of contempt."[3] As evidence of Jefferson's critical views of the common law, Story quoted a letter from Jefferson to John Tyler: "I deride with you the ordinary doctrine, that we brought with us from England the common law rights."[4] Jefferson suggested that this reliance on the inherited common law was merely an initial instinct, but that time had shown American rights to be grounded in something more universal: "This narrow notion was a favourite in the first moment of rallying to our rights against Great Britain. But it was that of men, who felt their rights, before they had thought of their explanation. The truth is, that we brought with us the rights of men, of expatriated men."[5] Thus, according to Story, Jefferson was opposed to the very notion that the American colonists brought with them the common law, and consequently, he opposed the notion that American jurisprudence was built upon the foundation of the common law. Such an argument also had significant ramifications for interpreting the motivating factors behind the American Revolution; Jefferson appeared to be downplaying the extent to which the claims of rights made by the colonists against the British Crown were based on violations of the colonists' traditional common law rights and instead emphasizing the extent to which the Revolution was fought to preserve the universal "rights of men." Story, indeed, countered Jefferson's claim by quoting the First Continental Congress' *Declaration of Rights of the Colonies*, which asserted that the colonists were entitled to the rights "of free and natural born subjects within the realm of England."[6] They based their claim, as Story emphasized, not on the universal "rights of men" but upon their traditional British liberties, which is to say, on the common law.[7]

Establishing the widespread reliance on the common law for the jurisprudence in all of the states was a crucial first step in Story's own argument for a federal common law; Story surely could see the connection between Jefferson's apparent denial of a common law adoption and his opposition to the federal common law doctrine. Jefferson's argument, though, had deeper significance than this one debate, however. If Jefferson were denying that American legal rights were derived from the common law, then he would view any claim of a common law adoption in the United States—at either the federal or state level—as not only wrong but also as undermining the true purpose of the American Revolution: The establishment of the American system not on the "rights of Englishmen" as Story argued but on abstract Enlightenment principles. The claim of a federal common law thus betrayed the philosophical foundations of American independence, and instead of those universal principles that the revolutionary generation had once asserted, now embraced instead the traditional body of rights that they had fought to rid themselves of. In short, Story used the quote by Jefferson to recast the debate over a federal common law as a philosophical dispute between the advocates of traditional common law "rights of Englishmen" and the advocates of abstract Enlightenment "rights of men." Such a dispute, if true, would surely go a long way in explaining Republican opposition to the federal common law doctrine: Republicans would have fought against any trace of the common law at either the state or federal level. Following Story's example, it is easy to understand the appeal of interpreting opposition to the federal common law as Story did. One way to explain the philosophical divide between the Federalists and Republicans is to view them as taking opposite sides in how they treated the British tradition.

The question of how much of the inherited British tradition the American revolutionaries had chosen to retain in the years following the Revolution is an important one, and one that is undeniably key to understanding the legal and constitutional ideas that were popular in the early years of the American republic. Those who view the partisan debates in this period through this lens portray Federalists as wholeheartedly embracing the federal common law as part of their general attempt to stay as close as possible to their British heritage. Meanwhile, Jeffersonian Republicans are presented as disregarding that inherited British tradition in favor of a more abstract, universal foundation. Thus, if the partisan divide between Federalists and Republicans is viewed through this lens, the debate over the federal common law can be seen as essentially centering on the much broader question of what rights the Revolution was fought to protect and what rights should govern the young republic.

In his book *Joseph Story and the American Constitution*, James McClellan portrayed the federal common law debate in this way, writing that in the aftermath of the Revolution "there were Jeffersonians who opposed the adoption of the common law and aspired to create an entirely new code of rules patterned along the lines of abstract rights, which the common law denied to men."[8] By contrast, McClellan described Story as a jurist "who wished to build the American constitutional and legal edifice upon common law foundations."[9] Elaborating on this point, McClellan laid out Story's theory of where the federal common law originated from, beginning with Story's observations of the several common law traditions within the states. From there, he proceeded to lay out what he sees as the origins of the debate over the federal common law, tracing it back to these differing notions of rights: Story's jurisprudence was grounded on belief that "a general body of law, consisting of common law and general legal principles . . . constituted the foundation of the American legal system in the several states," while "to Jeffersonian Republicans, of course, such an interpretation was wholly unacceptable."[10] Jefferson's followers rejected Story's belief in an underlying common law tradition not only because it was sympathetic to the English legal tradition, which they were trying to get away from, but also because it went against their understanding of the Revolution as a struggle over natural, universal rights, identified by McClellan as "a basic premise of the Jeffersonian creed."[11] McClellan later repeats this claim that Republican campaign against a federal common law ultimately stemmed from a competing interpretation of the American Revolution, summarizing Jefferson's argument as claiming "that the several states had adopted natural rights rather than common law rights."[12] This being the case, the Republican objection to a federal common law jurisdiction must be based upon a rejection of the British common law *as such*.

If this interpretation of the federal common law debate is correct, then the Republican critics of the federal common law were ostensibly opposed to the use of common law precedents by *any* court system, and their rejection of a *federal* common law jurisdiction was merely part of this larger rejection of the inherited British tradition. Thus, McClellan—like Story—presents the federal common law question as intimately linked to the question of whether the American Revolution was fought to protect traditional British common law rights or the universal, natural "rights of man." This, of course, is a very interesting and important question, and one that scholars of the American founding continue to debate to this day. It is not, however, an adequate explanation of the dispute over the federal common law. Primarily, this interpretation of the common law dispute fails because it gives an inaccurate depiction of the opponents of the federal common law. If it were true, one would expect Jefferson, Madison, Tucker, and others who spoke out against the doctrine to also ardently deny the acceptance of the common law within the several states. On the contrary, these Republican critics of the federal common law not only acknowledged the distinct common law tradition in each state, but they opposed the idea of a federal common law specifically because they thought it might endanger these common law traditions within the states.

This fear was the direct result of the differences in the common law in each state: a facet of the common law foundation that commentators on both sides of the issue acknowledged. These differences in the common law as practiced within the various states were due to a number of factors, all of which were highlighted by Tucker in his essay *On the Unwritten, or Common Law of England*, included as an appendix to his edition of William Blackstone's *Commentaries on the Laws of England*. For one thing, each state, in adopting the bulk of the British common law tradition, had brought over the common law as it existed at the moment of migration, thus giving each state a wide range of starting points to the common law as adopted there.[13] Second, notwithstanding the fact that each of the colonies was formally obligated to accept all of the laws of England, such a literal adherence to every portion of the common law would have been impracticable,[14] and the actual practice within each of the colonies had been to decline at the outset to adopt some portions of the British common law—those parts that they found to be unsuited to their new conditions[15]—and to legislatively amend other portions at their discretion since that point.[16] Consequently, many Republicans feared that a separate *federal* common law jurisdiction might subject the citizens of the states to features of the British common law that they had already explicitly rejected through their state legislature. Tucker described the danger that he thought a federal common law jurisdiction would pose to the separate common law traditions of each state, describing such a common law jurisdiction as a grant of power to the federal government to "revive, and enforce such parts of the common law, or statutes of England" as had already been explicitly rejected or repealed by the state constitutions "as dangerous, absurd, or incompatible with that system of government which they had, respectively, established."[17] Given that the portions of the British common law that had been explicitly rejected as incompatible with republicanism varied from state to state, Tucker recognized that any federal common law would necessarily revive some portions of the common law that the people of each state—through their constitutions and their chosen agents in their courts and legislatures—had chosen to reject. For Tucker, then, opposition to the federal common law was motivated more by a desire to *defend* the accepted common law practice of each state, rather than by a desire to undermine the British common law tradition as it existed everywhere in the states.

Second, viewing the federal common law debate as an expression of a debate between the defenders of the British tradition on the one hand and the proponents of universal rights on the other hand is overly simplistic. It would be a gross oversimplification to pronounce all Republicans—and by extension, all opponents of the federal common law—to be staunch proponents of natural rights, just as it would be a gross oversimplification to pronounce all Federalists and all advocates of the federal common law as staunch opponents of natural rights. It is true that many, though not all, of the opponents of the federal common law were in some ways amenable to the idea of universal, abstract "rights of man," as were many of the Federalists of the day. One notable exception to this widespread acceptance of the doctrine of natural rights would be Republican congressman John Randolph of Roanoke, who, although a critic of natural rights and steadfast defender of the British tradition,[18] nonetheless called the doctrine of a federal common law "a doctrine more abhorrent, if possible, to the feelings of the Republican Party in the United States, than the law [i.e., the Sedition Act] itself."[19] Similarly, Thomas Cooper of South Carolina—one of the most high-profile Sedition Act prosecutions of Republican editorialists during the Adams administration—also wrote critically of natural rights doctrine, albeit considerably later in 1826.[20] On the other hand, while it is true that Joseph Story was at times opposed to the idea of natural rights, this aspect of his thought was far from consistent; moreover, other proponents of the federal common law were prone to thinking of rights not just as arising from the British tradition but as arising from nature. One prominent example would be John Adams, who, although undeniably an admirer and defender of the British tradition, also relied heavily on the doctrine of natural rights in his 1765 publication, *A Dissertation on the Canon and Feudal Law*.[21] Finally, as noted above, even among the Republicans who supported "natural rights" doctrine, none were opponents of the use of the common law at the state level, indicating that their opposition to the federal common law was not an opposition to the common law *as such*. Additionally, it will be remembered that as President, Jefferson ordered the cessation of all prosecutions at federal common law, but not prosecutions based upon the common law as accepted by a particular state,[22] as evidenced by his position in *Hardin's Case* as discussed in chapter 1.

It is clear from the foregoing that any presentation of this debate as arising from a Republican rejection of the common law *as such* misses a crucial element of what motivated Republican opposition to an asserted federal common law jurisdiction. Critics of the doctrine apparently distinguished between common law jurisdiction at the federal and state level. Moreover, their rejection of a federal common law jurisdiction was motivated by a desire to protect the common law traditions of the separate states rather than by a desire to tear down any remnant of the British common law tradition in America. Story's assessment of Jefferson's views on the common law thus appears incomplete; Jefferson—like Madison, Tucker, and Randolph—was apparently comfortable with affirming the adoption of, and continued reliance upon, the common law at the state level, but this position seems difficult to square away with the letter to Tyler quoted in Story's *Commentaries*. Understanding Jefferson's views on the adoption of the common law generally becomes crucial to understanding what motivated objections to the federal common law doctrine.

JEFFERSON AND THE COMMON LAW

In a certain sense, Jefferson was not the primary political or intellectual force behind Republican opposition to a common law jurisdiction for the federal courts: he never used his political influence to oppose the doctrine directly through formal political institutions the way that James Madison had or through the federal judiciary as William Johnson did, nor did he ever write a systematic exposition of the Republican theory of common law adoption as Tucker had done. While Jefferson's opposition to the doctrine remained consistent, the historical record of it comes from a few scattered references in his correspondences, as well as the absence of his use of the doctrine as president. Still, perhaps due to the central political and intellectual role that he played in the Republican Party that he helped to build, Jefferson's views on the federal common law are the only ones directly countered by Joseph Story in his *Commentaries*. Story's targeting of Jefferson may also have been partly due to the fact that the unguarded Enlightenment liberalism that Jefferson periodically displayed in his correspondences made him an easy target for straw man arguments.

If Story's views on Jefferson were right and Jefferson were a staunch opponent of the common law generally, then his opposition to a federal common law jurisdiction could easily be seen as a natural outgrowth of this general position. The general narrative flowing out of this characterization provides an easy, if somewhat overly simplistic, philosophical contrast: Story and other nationalist proponents of the federal common law are presented as defenders of the inherited British legal and political traditions, with their support of a common law jurisdiction for the federal courts seen as part of their broader attempt to preserve the British heritage in the young republic and ground American jurisprudence in a concrete tradition, while Jefferson and his collaborators opposed the federal common law because they hated the British legal tradition due to its inevitable failure to live up to the ahistorical, abstract principles that formed the basis of their own legal thought. Thus, according to such a reading of the debate, Jefferson's opposition to the federal common law doctrine would be based on an opposition to the despotic monarchical traditions that the Revolution had been fought to throw off. If this interpretation of Jefferson's thought on the common law were right, we should expect him to oppose any recognition of a common law tradition at the state level as well as the federal level.

As an accurate depiction of Jefferson's views on the common law, however, this assessment does not hold up well. Throughout his career, Jefferson decidedly treated the common law in Virginia as different from the doctrine of a federal common law; the former he treated as historical fact, the latter he considered a constitutional impossibility. Obviously, there was something more at stake than a preference for abstractly derived, rather than historically inherited, rights. Unfortunately, Jefferson does not seem to have written extensively on the subject of the common law—apart from an essay and subsequent series of correspondences asserting the controversial position that the common law of England was not a product of Christianity—but his views on the doctrine of the federal common law are largely born out of three letters he wrote on the subject: one to Edmund Randolph, dated August 18, 1799;[23] one to Charles Pinckney on October 29, 1799;[24] and one to John Tyler, dated June 17, 1812.[25] The last of these included the reference to the "rights of expatriated men," as quoted by Story and McClellan.

Although Jefferson allowed that he personally preferred a written code of *civil law* to the unwritten body of *common law*, he nonetheless never denied the dual incontrovertible historical facts that Virginia had chosen to govern itself by the rules of the inherited common law and that, furthermore, it continued to largely be governed by the common law subsequent to the Revolution. In the 1799 letter to Randolph, Jefferson noted that before the revolution the "nation of Virginia" had chosen to embrace the common law and that "when by the declaration of Independence they chose to abolish their former organs for declaring their will, the acts of will already formally & constitutionally declared, remained untouched."[26] This included the common law, which "continued to be our law, because the nation continued in being, & because tho' it changed the organs for the future declarations of it's will, yet it did not change it's former declarations that the common law was it's law."[27] Jefferson thus agreed with Story that the law of Virginia—and presumably, although Jefferson doesn't explicitly make the extension, the rest of the states—were currently and had always been based upon the common law. He steadfastly held that it was the prerogative of the people of Virginia to choose to be governed by that law, as they had done at their inception and as they continued to do. Jefferson's opposition to the doctrine of federal common law must therefore arise from some distinction between the federal and state governments and not from a general opposition to the common law in principle.

Nor is this letter from 1799 an outlier from Jefferson's statements on the common law in Virginia throughout his career. Jefferson's recognition of the use of the common law in Virginia, as in all the states, is also born out in other passing references to the common law, such as a letter to James Monroe about the government of Virginia's prohibition against granting river and creek beds to individuals and which overturned the relevant portion of the common law "which," Jefferson noted, "was the law here till this act."[28] Jefferson thus obviously treated the acceptance of the common law in Virginia as substantially different from the idea of it being adopted federally.

Still, Jefferson's recognition of Virginia's adoption of the common law seems to be irreconcilable with the statement made in the letter to Tyler, which Story relied on in his presentation of Jefferson's views on the subject. Indeed, taken alone and without context, Jefferson's statement about the English emigrants bringing with them the "rights of ex-patriated men" seems squarely opposed to the common law in principle, and yet elsewhere, Jefferson seems to not be overly troubled by the use of the common law in Virginia courts. Reconciling the two letters, however, is not difficult, if one reads the letter to Tyler in its entirety. In the same passage quoted by Story, Jefferson indicates that he does in fact recognize the use of the common law by these same "ex-patriated men": "On our arrival here the question would at once arise, By what law will we govern ourselves? The resolution seems to have been, By that system with which we are familiar, to be altered by ourselves occasionally, and adapted to our new situation."[29] Story quoted these sentences in the same footnote as the foregoing ones, but ignored their obvious implication, instead choosing to paint Jefferson as an unequivocal opponent of American common law adoption and leaving the reader with the incorrect impression that Jefferson maintained that the American colonists did not bring the common law with them when they settled the colonies. Nevertheless, it is plain from this letter that Jefferson acknowledged that the Virginia emigrants did indeed adopt the common law.

Jefferson then went on in the letter to cite several pieces of historical evidence to illustrate this adoption, including a 1631 oath to uphold "the lawes and customes of this colony, and as neere as may be after the lawes of the realme of England and statutes thereof made"[30] and the preamble to the laws of 1661 that formally adopted the common law but noted that any subsequent laws made within the colony "be reputed the laws of this country."[31] Thus, while obviously objecting on some level to the "ordinary doctrine" of common law adoption, Jefferson was here reiterating a point that seems to have been virtually unanimously agreed upon: that the common law currently in force in each colony was the common law as it stood at the moment of adoption, "adapted to [each colony's] new situation," and subject to occasional alteration by the colonial courts and legislature. If they indeed brought over nothing more than the "rights of men," they apparently did not wait long in that position, as they very quickly moved to adopt the common law rights of Englishmen.

Far from denying any colonial adoption of the common law, it seems that what Jefferson was asserting in this letter was that the introduction of the common law to the new colonies was not *automatic* or legally compelled, but rather the conscious and free choice of the settlers in Virginia. This can be seen in the emphasis he placed on the freedom the settlers had in choosing to be under the laws they were most familiar with. Similarly, in the earlier letter to Randolph, Jefferson had noted that "the common law therefore . . . was not in force when we landed here, nor till we had formed ourselves into a nation, and had manifested by the organs we constituted, that the common law was to be our law."[32] Thus, Jefferson's position on the adoption of the common law in Virginia is, at most, only slightly different from the position shared by Story and Tucker: Jefferson asserted that the colonists came to American shores and then promptly *chose* to adopt the common law, while Story and Tucker held that the adoption of the common law had happened automatically. In essence, then, Jefferson's position on the common law as it had existed, and continued to exist, in Virginia was not substantively different in what it meant for the legal practice of the colonies, even if Jefferson held that the people of Virginia could have made another choice had they been so inclined.

Similarly, Tyler, in the letter that prompted Jefferson's already-quoted response, demonstrated that he also believed that the common law then in Virginia was the product of an affirmative assent to it by the people of Virginia, although he differed from Jefferson in considering the common law to have been forced upon them while yet a colony, claiming the doctrine of a shared legal code with England to have been "just enough while we remain'd Subjects of the British Gov't."[33] Having declared, independence, however, the installment of the common law as English citizens "was done away until we thought fit to establish as much of it as did not contravene our Republican System."[34] Thus, although Tyler and Jefferson disagreed on some smaller points, both parties in this correspondence fully agreed that the British common law was a part of the laws of Virginia, even if both men would have preferred that the Virginia settlers had chosen differently, with Tyler lamenting that the settlers had not "form'd a Code of our own" distinct from every "foreign Authority" and Jefferson admitting his preference for a civil code over the system of common law.

In fact, the main thrust of Jefferson's objection in the letter appears to be focused on the introduction of later common law developments in England that were alien to the common law tradition as it had developed in Virginia. In the same letter to Tyler, Jefferson went on shortly to write "the state of the English law at the date of our emigration, constituted the system adopted here. We may doubt therefore the propriety of quoting in our courts English authorities subsequent to that adoption, still more the admission of authorities posterior to the declaration of Independence."[35] This comment was directed at a decision by John Marshall that prompted Tyler to ask Jefferson his views on the adoption of the common law by Virginia. In the case of *Livingston v. Jefferson*, Marshall relied on recent British court decisions that had overturned contemporary interpretations of the common law rule of trespass and instead reintroduced a more ancient distinction; the only difficulty in applying such a development in the present case was that these cases had been made after the Revolutionary War, at a point when such decisions should have no bearing on the common law as it existed in the American states. In *Livingston*, Marshall conceded that, while such rulings are not binding on American courts, they are still "entitled to the respect which is due to the opinions of wise men who have maturely studied the subject they decide."[36] In this case, Marshall wrote that the current common law doctrine in Virginia should be read through the lens of the recent British interpretation, given that interpretation's compatibility with long-standing common law principles and the fact that the Virginia legislature had never overturned or rejected that interpretation.[37] It was this introduction of contemporary British rulings to the common law of Virginia—notably without any positive affirmation on the subject from the Virginia legislature—that Jefferson and Tyler took exception to, not the fact that Marshall was referring to common law rights instead of the "rights of men."

Far from opposing the common law tradition as it had grown and developed in Virginia, Jefferson was attempting to defend that local tradition from outside decisions that had not been recognized by Virginia courts or the Virginia legislature. Jefferson maintained that it was decidedly the prerogative of the people composing the "nation of Virginia" to establish, or disestablish, whatever system of laws they thought best suited them. Once they had chosen to govern themselves according to the common law—notably with the caveats that such common law was to be "altered by ourselves occasionally, and adapted to our new situation"[38]—that common law could not thus be altered by any outside force without depriving the people of Virginia of their authority to govern themselves. The settlers in Virginia had chosen to adopt the common law as it existed at the moment of adoption; if, subsequent to that adoption, the common law of England were to change, that change would not take effect in Virginia until it was affirmed by the Virginia legislature or Virginia courts. Nor, as Jefferson emphatically pointed out, was the common law tradition in Virginia in any way altered by the Revolution or the Declaration of Independence from Britain, noting that "because tho' it changed the organs for the future declarations of it's will, yet it did not change it's former declarations that the common law was it's law."[39] Jefferson's absolute insistence throughout both letters remained that the people of Virginia were the only valid authority on determining how much, and what elements, of the British common law tradition were to be introduced in Virginia.

Taken as a whole, then, the letter cannot possibly be read as a blanket rejection of the common law—although, again, Jefferson did also claim his preference for civil, written law over the British common law system—nor can it possibly be read as a denial of the historically indisputable fact that the American colonists did adopt the common law at the moment of their migration to the colonies. On the contrary, Jefferson explicitly affirmed that the people of Virginia were fully competent to choose to be governed by the common law of Britain, and furthermore affirmed that they had chosen to do so, subject to such amendments to that common law that they thought necessary.

What is clear from all of this is that, while Jefferson adamantly opposed a federal common law, he did so not, as Story suggested, out of a general antipathy toward the common law itself, but because, in Jefferson's constitutional theory, the limited scope of the United States—both in its government and in the collective identity of its people as a single nation—made a national adoption of a common law system utterly impossible. Contrary to what Story suggests in his *Commentaries*, Jefferson did not deny that the common law had been adopted by Virginia, but he did adamantly deny that the common law had been adopted—indeed, could be adopted—nationally. Consequently, Jefferson's opposition to extending this same jurisdiction to the federal courts must have come from some difference between the federal and state governments.

COMMON LAW IN THE STATES

Jefferson was not the only opponent of the federal common law to defend the idea that the common law had been uniformly accepted by the states. In fact, all of the Republican voices speaking out against the doctrine were uniform in their recognition that the common law served as the legal foundation of every single state. Tucker, in his 1803 essay on the federal common law question, described the common law adoptions and variations of each colony in turn and then summarized—similarly, at least on this point, to Story—that the common law had been brought over by the first settlers of each colony and had subsequently remained continually in force there, subject to the laws and constitutions of the several colonies-turned-states.[40] Nonetheless, he argued that the use of common law precedent must continue to be exercised—even by the federal courts—solely in accordance with common law as accepted and modified by each state; he insisted, in other words, that the common law in America could exist only "upon the constitutional or legislative authority of each state respectively; as contained in their several bills of rights, constitutions, and legislative declarations" and not by some single national standard.[41] Such a standard was impossible, according to Tucker, since the accepted body of common law precedents was "different in different states, and wholly independent of each other."[42] Like Jefferson, Tucker drew a distinction between the capacity of the state governments and the federal government to adopt the common law, noting that for the federal courts to have a general common law jurisdiction, such a jurisdiction must first be granted to the federal judiciary by the Constitution;[43] since no such general grant of common law jurisdiction can be found, Tucker concluded that the full common law jurisdiction of the state courts must have been among the powers reserved to them in the Tenth Amendment.[44]

Contrary to Story's characterization of the opposition to the federal common law, Tucker's theory did not require federal judges to feign ignorance of the common law. Tucker did allow that, when the Constitution itself grants the federal courts jurisdiction over a case, the common law rules of proceeding may be relied on in the absence of statutory direction, but that the common law could never grant the federal courts jurisdiction in a case that they would otherwise not have been authorized to hear.[45] Consequently, since the Constitution granted the federal courts jurisdiction in cases of equity, admiralty, and maritime jurisdiction, the federal courts may rely on the common law of England, inasmuch as the common law contributed to the basis of those systems of law.[46] Tucker argued, however, that this was far from granting that the common law of England was, in a general sense, the law of the United States, arguing that it stood on the same ground as the law of Russia or Germany in cases involving a contract made in either of those countries; foreign law rules and precedent may thus provide a necessary reference for judges in deciding the particular case, but cannot be argued to be applicable to the whole United States in any sense beyond this, which is what he suggested the advocates of a federal common law were arguing for.[47] Tucker's argument thus drew a sharp distinction between the use of common law precedents by federal judges, who could only rely on the common law in cases where the Constitution itself seemed to assume a common law jurisdiction, and by state judges, who were entitled to full use of the common law as adopted and recognized within their state.

Tucker and Jefferson were not the only Republican opponents of the federal common law to base their opposition on the fear that any federal common law would threaten the common law as adopted, modified, and developed within each of the several states. A few years earlier, James Madison had made a similar argument in his *Report of 1800*, a statement intended to explain the principles that led the Virginia Assembly to pass the Resolutions of 1798. In that report, Madison recognized that the common law of England made up a part of the laws of the several colonies, but emphasized that "it was the separate law of each colony within its respective limits, and was unknown to them, as a law pervading and operating through the whole, as one society."[48] Indeed, Madison noted, "it could not possibly have been otherwise": the common law varied so significantly from colony to colony as to cast doubt on the existence of a single, federal body of common law that all shared.[49] There was, furthermore, no general government over the colonies, and therefore no common judicial branch to carry out the law and no common legislature to adopt it nationally.[50] Consequently, the idea that there was thus a single, uniform set of common law principles shared fully by all colonies before the revolution was demonstrably false.

The idea that there evolved a common law over all of the colonies as a result of the revolution was even more preposterous. Madison summarized the basic legal principle of the American Revolution as the doctrine "that the colonies were co-ordinate members with each other, and with Great Britain, of an empire, united by a common executive sovereign, but not united by any common legislative sovereign."[51] Since the revolution was based around defending the legislative autonomy of each colony, it would be difficult to maintain that the revolution resulted in a single common law adoption "binding on these states as one society."[52] Proceeding onto the Articles of Confederation, Madison argued that there was not even the faintest suggestion "that the parties to it were, with respect to the objects of the common law, to form one community."[53] Madison's language here is interesting: he did not deny the acceptance of the common law by the American colonists; indeed, there is little indication that he would have denied that the Parliament's abridgment of traditional British common law rights lay at the heart of American cries of British tyranny. He carefully clarified, however, that the common law—in any form—was not applicable to all of the American colonists "as one community" or binding on the colonists "as one society." In other words, Madison's language here seems carefully chosen to acknowledge, on the one hand, the acceptance of the common law—or at least some elements of it—by the people of every colony, while denying, on the other hand, that there was a set of common law principles that was shared by the whole American people corporately. When discussing the effect of the Constitution on the question of a federal common law, Madison likewise found that such a grant could not be supported by the text of the Constitution.[54] Like Tucker, Madison allowed for a few exceptions here. First, a recourse to the common law might be warranted for the definition of certain technical phrases[55]—a caveat that most other opponents of the federal common law were willing to make as well. The same Virginia legislature that approved Madison's *Report of 1800* also sent instructions to their senators in Washington instructing them to vocally oppose the doctrine of a federal common law, making an exception for "such particular parts of the common law, as may have a sanction from the constitution, so far as they are necessarily comprehended in the technical phrases which express the powers delegated to the government."[56] Second, Madison allowed that some particular portion or other of the common law might be found to be "necessary and proper" to the carrying out of constitutional functions and thus appropriately adopted by Congress. Beyond these narrow limits, no federal common law adoption was warranted by the Constitution nor by previous history, and there was therefore no evidence for the Federalist contention that the common law formed a unique, national body of law.

This distinction that Jefferson, Tucker, and Madison made between the indisputable adoptions of the common law at the state level and the highly questionable claims of it nationally seem to have been shared by all Republican critics of the federal common law doctrine. As a further example, Madison and Tucker both may have been drawing on some notes written by Edmund Randolph, Attorney General to Washington, who had himself intended to write an essay arguing against the proposition that the common law had been adopted nationally. In these "Notes on the Common Law," Randolph maintained that "some states, perhaps all, but particularly Virginia, had adopted the common law under various modifications," and questioned whether a federal common law jurisdiction would "conform itself to the fluctuations and mutations in the common law of the several States," or whether they would force a single version of the common law on all of them.[57] Thus, Randolph, like his fellow Republicans, readily acknowledged the validity of common law adoptions at the state level, while also joining with the other Jeffersonians in critiquing the idea that there existed a single body of law applying equally to all of them.

CONCLUSION

It is apparent, then, that Republican critics of the federal common law were not opposing the doctrine out of an antipathy toward the common law itself, but out of a desire to protect the separate common law traditions of each particular state. It is also apparent that this disagreement was a part of a larger debate over the role of the states, and of the federal government, in the national system. Advocates of the Compact Theory saw the *real* laws underlying American society not as a national body of law, but as the laws of the several states. There could be no general common law jurisdiction for the federal courts in the same way that there could be no general legislative authority for Congress to draw from: all that the Constitution granted the federal government was a handful of discrete powers: jurisdiction over select categories of cases for the federal courts and legislative authority in select policy areas for Congress. There was no authorization for a "general system of law," as Jefferson described the common law of England, and there was furthermore no *need* for a general system of law, as the legitimate objectives of federal action were few and easily defined; Congress need not pass a law granting the federal courts jurisdiction over the whole breadth of common law crimes, and if they had, it surely would have been unconstitutional as it extended far beyond the constitutional limits of the federal government's scope.

These broader constitutional concerns explain why the Jeffersonians responded so quickly and vigorously to Federalist claims that the common law of England was the law of the United States as a whole. They responded so forcefully because they understood that the claim was premised upon an alternative conception of the union that they considered to be patently false and because they knew that the doctrine of a federal common law, if accepted, would dramatically alter the scope of the federal government's powers. Indeed, they feared that admitting to the existence of a national common law would obliterate the limits that the Constitution placed on the federal government. They even resisted Federalist claims of a modified or curtailed form of the common law—such as Story's claim of a federal common law limited to the scope of the federal government's constitutional grants of power—as they saw such claims as similarly based on a faulty view of the union. Thus, the connection between Story's argument for a federal common law and his Nationalist Theory is even more observable by looking at his critics, whose rejection of Federalist claims of a federal common law was based around their belief in the Compact Theory.

It would appear, then, that arguments on both sides of the debate over the federal common law were contingent upon certain unstated—or, in the case of many of the Republican commentators, stated—assumptions about the nature of the federal union. Analyzing the arguments in light of the assumptions of either the Compact Theory or the Nationalist Theory thus provides a great deal of insight into the debate: on the one hand, it explains why advocates of a common law jurisdiction for the federal courts thought that this common law foundation was so unarguably obvious, as well as why they were so insistent on the absolute necessity of accepting it; on the other hand, it gives some context for why Jeffersonian opponents of that jurisdiction were so horrified by the prospect of it. This historical debate becomes a lot clearer when it is understood that what was really at stake in this debate—at least in the eyes of its participants—was the true nature of the federal union.

NOTES

1. Jefferson to Pinckney.
2. Story, *Commentaries*, Sec. 157, 1:105n4.
3. Ibid.
4. Thomas Jefferson. Thomas Jefferson to John Tyler, June 17, 1812. From *Founders Online*, National Archives, https://founders.archives.gov/documents/Jefferson/03-05-02-0112.
5. Ibid.
6. Story, *Commentaries*, Sec. 157, 1:105n4.
7. Ibid.
8. McClellan, 161.
9. Ibid., 162.
10. Ibid., 164.
11. Ibid.
12. Ibid., 170.
13. Tucker, 326–327.
14. Ibid., 320.
15. Ibid., 323.
16. Ibid., 327.
17. Ibid., 355.
18. See, for instance, Russell Kirk, *John Randolph of Roanoke: A Study in American Politics* (Indianapolis: Liberty Fund Press, 1997), 42–43.
19. John Randolph of Roanoke, "Floor Speech, May 25, 1809." Reprinted in *The Debates and Proceedings in the Congress of the United States, Eleventh Congress, First and Second Sessions* (Washington: Gales and Seaton, 1853), 1:75.
20. Thomas Cooper, *Lectures on the Elements of Political Economy* (Columbia: McMorris & Wilson, 1826), 53–54.
21. John Adams, "A Dissertation on the Canon and Feudal Law, 1765." Available at http://teachingamericanhistory.org/library/document/a-dissertation-on-the-canon-and-feudal-law/.
22. Mogck, 152.
23. Jefferson to E. Randolph.
24. Jefferson to Pinckney.
25. Jefferson to Tyler.
26. Jefferson to E. Randolph.
27. Ibid.
28. Thomas Jefferson. Thomas Jefferson to James Monroe, January 8, 1811. From The Library of Congress, https://www.loc.gov/item/mtjbib020478/.

29. Jefferson to Tyler.
30. Hening, 1: 187. Cited in Jefferson to Tyler.
31. Hening, 2:42. Cited in Jefferson to Tyler.
32. Jefferson to E. Randolph.
33. John Tyler. John Tyler to Thomas Jefferson, May 17, 1812. From *Founders Online*, National Archives, https://founders.archives.gov/documents/Jefferson/03-05-02-0045.
34. Ibid.
35. Jefferson to Tyler.
36. *Livingston v. Jefferson,* 15 Fed. Cas. 660, No. 8,411 (1811), 664.
37. Ibid.
38. Jefferson to Tyler.
39. Jefferson to E. Randolph.
40. Tucker, 363
41. Ibid., 364.
42. Ibid.
43. Ibid., 346.
44. Ibid., 354–355.
45. Ibid., 361.
46. Ibid.
47. Ibid., 362.
48. Madison, "Report of 1800."
49. Ibid.
50. Ibid.
51. Ibid.
52. Ibid.
53. Ibid.
54. Ibid.
55. Ibid.
56. Quoted by Tucker at 370.
57. Randolph, "Edmund Randolph's Notes on the Common Law."

Chapter 5

Interpreting the Federal Common Law Debate

It is apparent from reading the Republican arguments against the idea of a general common law jurisdiction for the federal courts that opponents of the doctrine saw it as a violation of fundamental constitutional principles. The fact that the state governments had all effected a general common law adoption, with modifications and exceptions, and that the federal government was, by its very nature, incapable of doing the same according to Jeffersonians, spoke to a fundamental difference in kind between the state and federal governments. Federalist claims of a federal common law jurisdiction thus threatened to alter the very nature of the union by assigning to the federal judiciary and to Congress powers that it was impossible for them to have if the underlying nature of the republic were to remain unchanged. Consequently, in the 1799 letter to Pinckney, Jefferson warned that recognizing a federal common law jurisdiction would in effect be a "compleat consolidation" of the federal system of divided powers. Meanwhile, proponents of a federal common law jurisdiction obviously did not see it as in tension with the fundamental nature of the union. The debate over the federal common law thus was connected, at least in part, to a debate over the nature of the union and the federal government, to the incommensurable claims of the Nationalist Theory and Compact Theory, in other words.

It remains to be seen, however, whether the debate was also connected to other ongoing debates during this period. In a certain sense, connecting the debate over a federal common law jurisdiction to other pertinent legal issues of the day is not difficult. The drama of the Federalist push for such a jurisdiction played out against the backdrop of numerous wide-ranging and often interlocking debates over fundamental questions like the proper role of government, the meaning and origin of law, and the nature of the federal constitutional union. Much like the legal issues that collectively make up partisan ideologies today, the partisan issues at stake in the early republic often were argued side by side with one another; in many cases, the issues—though often discussed separately—were interconnected. It is thus worth considering the relationship of the federal common law debate to other debates in the period surrounding the nature of federal law and the proper relationship between the legislative and judicial branches of government, both of which generally can be summarized by the question of who, other than Congress, was charged with creating federal law.

The emerging political parties in this period were far from ideologically homogenous—as Story's formal inclusion in the Jeffersonian Republican fold demonstrates. Still, with notable exceptions, it is often possible to draw generalizations about certain political and—to a lesser degree—philosophical positions held in common by most people on the two sides of this debate, and the connection of these positions to the argument over a federal common law will be considered. First, the ambiguous nature of federal law in the young republic deserves consideration, inasmuch as the asserted federal common law jurisdiction was bound to have a profound impact on the scope of federal law. The federal common law question and the question of what constitutes the "Laws of the United States" cannot be easily separated and the latter question thus merits attention.

ASCERTAINING THE SCOPE OF THE "LAWS OF THE UNITED STATES"

Given the overarching uncertainty surrounding the nature of federal law in the young republic, the divergence of opinion surrounding a federal common law jurisdiction is not entirely surprising. The young nation's bodies of statutory and constitutional law were barely out of an embryonic state and their scope was likewise the subject of intense debate. The controversial nature of federal law at this time can be at least partially attributed to the brevity of Article III of the Constitution, which laid out the scope of the new federal judiciary's powers. In extending the federal courts' jurisdiction to "all cases in law and equity arising under this Constitution, the laws of the United States, and treaties made, or which shall be made, under their authority,"[1] the authors of Article III established the federal judiciary with language at the same time sweeping and laconic. To grant the federal courts jurisdiction over cases "arising under" the Constitution seems straight-forward enough, but what exactly was entailed in granting them jurisdiction over cases involving "the laws of the United States"? It was certain that Article I had granted Congress the authority to "make all laws which shall be necessary and proper" for carrying out Congress' enumerated powers.[2] But the question remained whether "the laws of the United States" could encompass more than just the statutes that Congress had passed. On this question, the sparse language of Article III was of little help.

In many ways, the brevity of this description of the federal judicial power had raised more questions about the federal courts than it answered. During the ratification debates, the vaguely defined jurisdictional reach of the federal courts became an easy target for fearful objections from anti-Federalist opponents of constitutional ratification, including the anonymous author Brutus—widely believed to have been New York judge Robert Yates—who argued that the Constitution's extension of federal jurisdiction to "all cases in law and equity" arising under the Constitution and laws of the union would effectively remove the strict constitutional limitations on the powers of Congress and replace them with the uninhibited will of the federal judiciary, thus providing Congress with a way around any constitutional restraints on their power. In his essay Brutus XII, written in February 1788, Yates argued that under the Constitution the federal courts "may establish certain principles, which being received by the legislature, will enlarge the sphere of their power beyond all bounds."[3] He further suggested that the Supreme Court would have the final say in interpreting the Constitution, inevitably basing their decisions on certain assumed "principles," which would themselves become a part of federal law: "These principles, whatever they may be, when they become fixed, by a course of decisions, will be adopted by the legislature, and will be the rule by which they will explain their own powers."[4] Congress would thus end up being bound not by the text of the Constitution but by the much more open-ended scope of what the federal courts would accept.

Consequently, Yates argued that Article III's broad grant of authority to interpret the Constitution—not only in questions of law, dealing with fixed legal construction and terminology, but also of equity, dealing with "explain[ing] the constitution according to the reasoning spirit of it, without being confined to the words or letter"[5]—would result in the Constitution taking on whatever meaning the members of the federal judiciary felt inclined to give it. Based on the encompassing goals listed in the Constitution's Preamble, Yates believed that meaning would likely be very amenable to a broad construction of federal power.[6] Thus, according to Yates, the Constitution's extension of the national courts' jurisdiction to all cases arising under the Constitution and laws of the United States was to grant them powers that were, for all practical purposes, unlimited.

The claim of a federal common law jurisdiction even further exacerbated concerns about the ambiguity of what constituted "federal law." Add to this that the recognition of a federal common law jurisdiction would dramatically increase the scope of what constituted the "laws of the United States." Just as Federalists hoped that the comprehensive body of English common law could fill in the gaps between the sparse statutory enactments of Congress, so did the Republicans fear that recognizing a federal common law jurisdiction would, in a single act, expand the reach of the federal judiciary by extending federal jurisdiction to every area of British law. Consequently, whatever fears of a limitless federal jurisdiction plagued the opponents of constitutional ratification were multiplied by the prospect of a general common law jurisdiction for the federal courts. And on the Federalist side, wholesale adoption of the federal common law seemed to be a panacea against all of the uncomfortable ambiguities that had hitherto surrounded the scope of federal jurisdiction.

This ambiguity over the nature of federal law was intimately related to the ongoing jurisprudential debate over whether common law, as shaped by the judiciary, should take precedence over statutory law. It also was related to political and philosophical tensions between the two parties, inasmuch as Republicans generally desired Congress to be the preeminent branch and Federalists generally saw the courts as a necessary tool for curbing democratic excesses—especially in the wake of the "Revolution of 1800." Consequently, it is worth pointing out that the debate over a federal common law jurisdiction was being carried out at the same time as other disputes over what the role of the common law should be. It is also worth examining how much the debate over a federal common law was a product of a broader separation of powers dispute between the advocates of Congress and the courts.

R. Kent Newmyer depicted the federal common law debate as focused on this distinction in his book Supreme Court Justice Joseph Story: Statesman of the Old Republic, where he stated that Republican opponents of a common law jurisdiction for the federal courts "saw the common-law question as part of the great battle between John Marshall and Thomas Jefferson and between an aristocratic Supreme Court and a democratic Congress."[7] Viewing the debate as a contest between two conceptions of how laws should be made in a republic—with Federalists favoring the common law as shaped by the judiciary and Republicans favoring statutory law—Newmyer portrayed the debate as "the opening battle in the great nineteenth-century war over codification."[8] Thus, according to this interpretation, the debate over a federal common law jurisdiction was at least in part focused on what law was: should law be considered solely as statutes passed by the legislature, or did it include some forms of non-statutory law as well? To assert the former would necessarily tie the judiciary inextricably to the will of the legislature; to assert the latter would allow the judiciary to carve its own course, even in the face of congressional opposition.

It is easy to see this dynamic playing out in the contrasting legal decisions discussed so far. On the one hand, some justices—including most Republicans—thought the courts' primary responsibility in cases was to rely on instructions from the legislature. Justice Johnson in *Hudson and*

Goodwin had declared that, even if a constitutional foundation for a federal common law jurisdiction could be found, it was still decidedly the legislature's prerogative to extend the courts' jurisdiction to their constitutionally permissible limits.[9] Justice Chase, although a Federalist, had expressed a similar position in Worrall, calling it "essential, that congress should define the offences to be tried and apportion the punishment to be inflicted, as they should erect courts to try the criminal, or to pronounce a sentence on conviction."[10] Although Congress could have, in Chase's view, easily chosen to outlaw bribery, the fact that they had failed to, however unwise, still did not grant the courts the power to make up for this neglect by outlawing it themselves.[11]

On the other hand, we can see the more typical Federalist position embodied by Justice Peters' opinion in Worrall: "The power to punish misdemeanors is, originally and strictly a common law power; of which, I think, the United States are constitutionally possessed. It might have been exercised by congress in form of a legislative act; but it may, also, in my opinion, be enforced in a course of judicial proceeding."[12] Thus, according to Peters, the "judicial power" of the federal courts may indeed have an authority that goes beyond the specific authorizations of congressional statute and the narrow grants of jurisdiction in Article III; they might have the authority to take cognizance of a law that is unrecognized, or perhaps even opposed, by the legislature.

Newmyer's depiction of the debate thus seems fair, up to a point. The contrasting claims of proponents and opponents of a common law jurisdiction for the federal courts do seem to generally correspond to differing notions of what the responsibility of the courts is, which are in turn caught up in considerations of the proper relationship between judges and legislatures. Republicans, on the whole, were more sanguine about the prospects of democracy than their Federalist counterparts, and consequently less fearful of the power of popularly elected legislators than the power of unelected judges. Jefferson himself feared that the Constitution had created a judiciary so independent that it could not be effectively held accountable for its actions, and he wrote to Thomas Ritchie in 1820 that "A judiciary independent of a king or executive is a good thing; but independence of the will of the nation is a solecism, at least in a republican government."[13] Certainly, as Newmyer pointed out, the general Republican distrust of courts, fueled by the uniquely partisan nature of Federalist prosecutions under the Sedition Act, can help explain the Republican opposition to a doctrine that could only serve to strengthen the federal judiciary.[14] By providing a non-statutory basis for a set of crimes that could be increased or diminished at the will of the judges without any input from the more politically accountable branches, a federal common law jurisdiction threatened to make the federal judiciary "independen[t] of the will of the nation," as Jefferson had feared.

All of this being acknowledged, this explanation for the origins of Republican opposition to a common law jurisdiction for the federal courts does not seem entirely sufficient, for—similar to the claim that Republicans rejected the federal common law on "natural rights" grounds—it does not explain why the Republicans directed particular criticism at the idea of a federal common law jurisdiction while still supporting—or, at the very least, acknowledging—claims of a common law foundation at the state level. If Republican fears over a federal common law jurisdiction were due solely to worries that it would allow judges to extend their authority past their congressionally conferred jurisdiction, then the same concerns should seemingly apply to the use of the common law at the state level. Yet when Jefferson and Madison separately decried the doctrine of federal common law, they emphasized that they were objecting to the idea, as Madison put it, that the common law "makes a part of the law of these states, in their united and national capacity" (emphasis added).[15] Apparently, while Jefferson and his followers did seem to have some general presumptions in favor of legislative authority over judicial authority, their rejection of a federal common law jurisdiction must have been based upon some more particular objection that did not also include the common law as it existed in the states. Furthermore, the fact that Jefferson and Madison described the doctrine as a "new doctrine,"[16] an "innovation,"[17] and a "novelty"[18] points to the fact that they distinguished the claim of an implied federal common law—which they both unequivocally opposed—with the explicit adoption of common law by the states—which they both readily acknowledged. What made Federalist claims of a national common law jurisdiction so abhorrent to the Jeffersonians was apparently the fact that it was asserted nationally, not the fact that a common law acceptance was claimed at all. The reduction of this debate to a disagreement on the proper relationship of judges to legislators thus is inadequate to provide a full understanding of the Republican opposition to this doctrine.

In fairness, it should also be pointed out that, at least for Jefferson, the question of common law adoption was not wholly separate from his general view of legislative preeminence over the judiciary. At least part of the reason that Jefferson objected to claims of a federal common law jurisdiction was that such a jurisdiction had never been authorized by a "positive adoption" by Congress the way that the state legislatures had formally adopted the common law and authorized their courts to use common law precedent. This dynamic is apparent in a 1799 letter from Jefferson to Edmund Randolph, in which he emphasized that Federalist attempts to establish a federal common law had been made "without the adoption of their legislature."[19] There, of course, Jefferson reiterated the claim that a federal common law jurisdiction was "beyond their [i.e., Congress'] power to adopt," even if they had desired to do so. However, even on particular points of the common law that fell within the constitutional parameters of Congress' authority to legislate—presumably, outlawing the forgery of federal currency or piracy and other crimes on the high seas—the federal courts still could not introduce common law precedent or jurisdiction until so authorized by Congress: "in the cases confided to them, they [presumably, Congress] were free to declare the will of the nation, the law, but till it was declared there could be no law"[20] (emphasis added). Even this general principle Jefferson qualified by stating that any congressional declaration of a common law adoption would be valid "so far only as they were authorized to adopt,"[21] presumably meaning that even in issuing a positive adoption of the common law, Congress could go no further in adopting than the scope of federal powers laid out in the Constitution.

Thus, it can fairly be inferred that Jefferson did disagree with Justice Peters' claim that the common law "might have been exercised by congress in form of a legislative act; but it may, also . . . be enforced in a course of judicial proceeding."[22] Jefferson, on the contrary, held that the formal adoption of the common law had to be made by an affirmative act by Congress before the federal courts could take any cognizance of it. Still, he clarified that Congress was not at liberty to adopt the entirety of the British common law, but only such parts of it as had been "confided to them" by the Constitution. The adoption of "any general system" of law would have transcended the limits of congressional power inasmuch as it would have touched on areas of law that the federal government had no constitutional authority over.[23] Consequently, although Newmyer is correct in pointing out the connection between the federal common law debate and disagreements on the relationship of Congress to the Supreme Court, this explanation fails to adequately explain why opponents of a federal common law jurisdiction still were able to maintain support for the common law traditions within each state.

THE FEDERAL COMMON LAW AND THE NATURE OF THE UNION

The federal common law debate was thus, to some degree, a product of the general ambiguity surrounding the nature of federal law, and was also contemporaneous with a debate over the place of the common law under the Constitution. Nevertheless, any attempt to interpret the debate as entirely focused on the role of the common law as such has been demonstrated to be insufficient, as it fails to explain why it was that Republican opponents of a federal common law jurisdiction nevertheless recognized the adoption of the common law by the several states. The fact that opponents of a federal common law jurisdiction drew this distinction points to some essential difference that they saw between the state and federal governments; similarly, the fact that advocates of a federal common law jurisdiction did not make this distinction—treating the federal government as equally capable of adopting the common law as the states were—points to some essential similarity that they saw between the state and federal governments.

Robert Palmer points to this feature of the debate in his article "The Federal Common Law of Crime,"[24] suggesting that the opposing sides in the federal common law debate relate, ultimately, to perceived similarities or dissimilarities between the two levels of government: "Had the federal and state governments been alike, the federal government would have been a government of inherent authority, capable of acting as required and of receiving or having by nature the common law."[25] If this were the case, the federal government could thus relatively easily be linked to a belief in "the importation of an extensive list of crimes developed in a much more aristocratic society, including seditious libel," a belief that Palmer saw as a "departure from the assumptions on which the federal Constitution was built" as well as a violation of the Tenth Amendment.[26] "On the other hand," noted Palmer, "recognition of the federal government as a government of delegated powers allows exercise of all delegated powers to their fullest extent without contravention of original intent."[27] Such a conception of the federal government, however, might not carry with it the same implicit assumption of an extensive criminal code adoption the way that the alternate conception did.

The question of a federal common law thus hangs on whether the federal government and the states are "alike" in the sense discussed by Palmer. In other words, the question of whether the federal courts are capable of a common law jurisdiction essentially hung on the question of whether the United States was limited in some way that the state governments were not. None could doubt that the people of a nation would more or less automatically possess all the requisite authority to determine a legal system for themselves. Consequently, if the people of the American states had been bound together as a single, sovereign people, either before or at the ratification of the Constitution, then they must also have had the full authority to establish the common law as a national legal code. On the other hand, if the Jeffersonians were right and the union of the states comprised nothing more than a voluntary confederation that had been granted certain enumerated powers, then the federal government was competent to establish a common law foundation only with regard to specific delegated powers of the federal government.

The question then becomes one of who created the American union: the American people in the aggregate or the people of the several states? The answer to this question entirely determines whether or not the federal government was capable of adopting a federal common law. Furthermore, approaching the federal common law question as essentially hinging upon the nature of the American union allows us—unlike the previous explanations—to adequately account for the Republican position on the federal common law: for Republicans maintained not only that the common law had not been adopted nationally, but furthermore that—given the nature of the union—it could not have been adopted nationally, even if Congress had determined to declare it so; all the while, they never questioned the adoption of the common law within their states. Such a position requires the federal government to be essentially different in character from the state governments in its powers and its basis of authority.

The meaning of this contrast between two understandings of the American union is made clearer by contrasting the two views of federal government power that Palmer identifies: the one claiming that the federal government has "inherent authority" and the other that the federal government is a government of "delegated powers." To the Jeffersonians, this distinction lay at the heart of their opposition to a federal common law as incompatible with the nature of the union. Jefferson emphasized the fact that the federal government had been delegated certain powers by the states when they entered the union, and that this delegation of powers constituted an exhaustive list of all of the powers enjoyed by the federal government. Consequently, it was incapable of adopting a comprehensive body of law as Virginia had done. Jefferson's rejection of a federal common law relied explicitly on the fact that the states had chosen to give the federal government certain powers and that it was thereby forbidden from expanding beyond those powers. This underlying principle of Republican constitutional interpretation is reiterated by Tucker when he summarizes that there exists no federal common law jurisdiction, since "no such jurisdiction has been granted; and consequently, that it remains with the states, respectively, in all cases not enumerated."[28] On this point, it is worth distinguishing between the enumerated nature of the federal power and the residuary nature of state power, summed up famously by James Madison's observation in Federalist 45 that "The powers delegated by the proposed Constitution to the federal government are few and defined. Those which are to remain in the State governments are numerous and indefinite."[29] Since, according to Republicans, all of the federal government's powers were explicitly laid out in the Constitution, the federal government was thus incapable of taking a specific action unless directly authorized to do so by a specific constitutional grant of power. Therefore, since the Constitution made no explicit adoption of a federally adopted common law, and since the common law embraced topics beyond the enumerated delegated powers of the federal government, the doctrine was entirely repulsive to the uniquely limited nature of the American federal government.

For Story, on the other hand, acceptance of a general federal common law corresponded to a general assumption that the federal government had been granted its powers not from an agreement between the several states, but rather from a direct grant by the American people as a whole. The United States of America was thus a full-fledged nation and the federal government must necessarily be imbued with all the rights and powers of any other national government. Here it must be acknowledged that Story acquiesced to one of the basic precepts of Jeffersonian constitutional interpretation: he affirmed that the federal government was a government of enumerated powers—that is to say, Story affirmed that all of the federal government's powers are contained in the document either by express grants or "necessary implication."[30] Furthermore, Story also assented to the Jeffersonian understanding of state powers as encompassing everything not touched on by the Constitution, noting in a later case that "it is perfectly clear that the sovereign powers vested in the State governments by their respective Constitutions remained unaltered and unimpaired" by the adoption of the Constitution "except so far as they were granted to the Government of the United States."[31] As evidence of this statement, Story cited the Tenth Amendment.[32] Story thus acknowledged that, in general, there was a difference between the relationship of the U.S. Constitution to the powers of the federal government and those retained by the several states: the former had to be linked to an explicit power grant—or at least necessarily implied—within the text of the federal Constitution and the latter did not. At the same time, the state governments were themselves also governments of enumerated powers: they could not do anything that had not been granted them by the people of their particular state,[33] just as the federal government could not do anything that had not been granted them by the people of the whole union.

There was thus not so much a difference in kind between the state and federal governments as a recognition that both were governments of enumerated powers and both were limited to those powers granted them in their constitutions. This treatment of the federal and state governments as essentially equal in the nature of their powers is what differentiated Story from Jefferson, who saw the federal government as uniquely limited by its very nature in a way that the state governments were not. And it is this aspect of Story's constitutional theory that would allow him to conceive of a federal common law in ways that advocates of the Compact Theory could not. Story's argument for the existence of a uniquely federal common law thus rested, in a variety of ways, on his nationalist reading of American political history.

APPLYING STORY'S NATIONALIST THEORY TO THE FEDERAL COMMON LAW

Story's Nationalist Theory narrative would become the cornerstone of his constitutional theory, as well as of his jurisprudence. Much more than a particular view of American colonial and pre-constitutional history, the Nationalist Theory presented by Story provided a particular lens for interpreting all American political actions, past and present. Through this lens, the states—or rather the people of each particular state—are not so many distinct, solitary actors, but rather a part of a concerted whole. When the American people voted to ratify the Constitution, they undeniably voted within their particular states, but—according to Story and the Nationalist Theory—they did not vote as the people of their particular states. The necessary result of this logic was that if New York voted to ratify and Rhode Island voted not to, then it was not a disagreement between the people of different states, but rather a disagreement among the national American people. Such an interpretation of American legal and political history had significant ramifications for the current powers of the federal government.

On a number of jurisprudential questions, this Nationalist Theory can be seen as central to Story's overarching constitutional theory, as well as to the judicial opinions he authored from the bench. One excellent illustration of this connection is to track the relationship of his Nationalist Theory to one of the jurisprudential positions that would follow Story throughout his career: the quest to recognize a single, federal set of common law precedents in force nationally and available to aid federal judges in deciding cases. Indeed, there are several ways that Story's conception of a federal common law presupposes his claim that the United States government was the direct creation of a national body of people and not the creation of the people of each state.

First of all, Story's general treatment of federal government power—including the jurisdiction of the federal courts—rests on the theory that these powers have been granted to it by the American people who, at the same time, chose to grant certain other powers to the state governments. This conception of federal power more easily lends itself to a recognition of federal implied powers, as well as to a presumption that the federal government has also been endowed with the ability to select the means by which they will pursue each of the broad purposes for which it was created. The federal government, in this theory, has been directly entrusted by the sovereign people of the nation with a number of broad responsibilities and purposes outlined in the Constitution. This leads to a very different presumption of federal power than the one flowing out of the Jeffersonian Compact Theory, where the powers of the federal government are limited to the specific power grants listed in the Constitution. Since the Compact Theory sees every grant of federal power as a grant of power away from the sovereign people of each state, such federal powers must be given explicitly rather than merely implied by the general language or tenor of the document. Consequently, Story's Nationalist Theory leads him to interpret every grant of jurisdiction in Article III as an absolute grant for the federal courts to hear all cases in that category in a manner consistent with the common law system that makes up the foundation of American law.

Second, by treating the United States as a sovereign nation and the American people as a sovereign political community, Story implicitly strengthens the presumption of a comprehensive national body of law. Under the Jeffersonian constitutional framework the federal courts played a very minor role, and the opportunities for the federal government to operate directly on individual citizens were naturally limited; as a result, there was little need for a national body of law, as such a body of law would be both unnecessary—due to its limited contribution to the legal life of the nation—and, moreover, potentially dangerous, as the fundamental role of the federal government under the Compact Theory was to preserve the distinct legal systems of each state. Other than the explicit language of the Constitution and any congressional statutes abiding by a strict interpretation of it, the system of law in the union would be largely left as it was at the moment the thirteen states declared their independence from Britain. By contrast, the Nationalist Theory presumed not only the ultimate sovereignty of the national American people, but also a much more central role for the federal government and the national court system in particular. If America was to be a nation, then it of necessity needed a national body of law; if the federal courts were to be the true judicial branch representing the entire American people, then it is hard to see how they could adequately perform this function while following the disparate legal traditions of the several states.

Most significantly, Story's understanding of pre-constitutional American history as ultimately the product of the actions of the American people as a whole, instead of the peoples of the several states, means that the common law adoptions of the several states must collectively come to represent pieces of a broader national body of common law jurisprudence. Each adoption of the common law by a particular colony is a contribution to the much broader national body of American law. Each modification of the common law by a particular colonial or state legislature is a partial modification of that national body of law. Finally, any differences between the common law as adopted by the different states are treated merely as disagreements or points of confusion within the national body of common law, instead of as differences between the common law as it was practiced within the states.

The result of this is that Story is able to take the near-universal acceptance of the common law within the legal traditions of the states and present it as evidence of a national common law adoption. Put differently, according to Story's theory, the revolution did not leave Americans with thirteen distinct judicial systems, each of which had—with minor differences between them—adopted the common law as the basis of their legal system, but with one great national system of jurisprudence based on the common law. The only court capable of adding to and applying this federal common law was the federal judiciary, as it was the only court system that was competent to address questions of federal law. It was thus up to the federal judiciary and, ultimately, the Supreme Court to simplify the job of the federal lawyer and judge, and to work within a national body of common law precedent that would lead the way for a national body of enlightened jurisprudence and keep the American judicial system moored to its roots in the British common law tradition.

APPLYING THE COMPACT THEORY TO THE FEDERAL COMMON LAW

As with Story, the key to understanding why Jeffersonians were opposed to even the concept of a federal common law—even, as noted, while defending the common law tradition as it was practiced within the several states—lies in their conception of the fundamental nature of the union. Just as support for the doctrine that a general body of common law underlies the federal Constitution was based upon a certain shared theory of the Union, so was opposition to the federal common law based upon a shared opposite understanding of the Constitution. Opponents of a federal common law jurisdiction understood that Federalist arguments for it assumed the basic premise of the Nationalist Theory inasmuch as they viewed the common law as practiced within the several states, when considered collectively, as a national system of American acceptance of the common law that applied equally to all Americans, regardless of state boundary lines. Against this principle, adherents of the Compact Theory uniformly rejected the asserted doctrine of a federal common law as utterly incompatible with what they saw as the true nature of the Union. Republican opposition to the doctrine of a federal common law jurisdiction thus stemmed from their acceptance of the Compact Theory.

On this point, it is worth clarifying again that any characterization of Madison as a Compact theorist has to be provisional. At various points in his career, Madison's understanding of the Constitution seemed to leave him wholly separate from the "states-rights" school that he had seemingly given voice to in his Virginia Resolutions. As historian Kenneth Stampp notes in his article "The Concept of a Perpetual Union," in the wake of the South Carolina nullification controversy Madison devoted much time to arguing against the doctrines of nullification and secession and to defending himself against the charge that he had ever once asserted a similar right.[34] Such defenses were, as Stampp notes, "not altogether convincing,"[35] and Madison's reputation as a constitutional theorist has been marred by the same "discrediting inconsistencies" that he strove so hard to explain away. Nevertheless, it is equally clear that Madison never held to Story's Nationalist understanding of the union either, and in his *Report of 1800*, Madison's views on the nature of the union do not seem remarkably different from Jefferson's. For purposes of understanding his rejection of the federal common law doctrine, Madison can best be understood as an adherent to the Compact Theory.

All of the Republican opponents of the federal common law, Madison included, argued that the federal government, by its very nature, was fundamentally incapable of adopting as comprehensive a body of law as the common law of England, and therefore any attempts to recognize a general common law to be used by the federal courts violated the very essence of the federal compact. More precisely, Republican opponents of a federal common law jurisdiction viewed the inherently limited nature of the American federal government as the key reason why adopting the common law for itself was entirely outside the realm of the federal government's powers. Either explicitly—in the case of Jefferson and Tucker—or implicitly—in the case of Madison and Edmund Randolph—each Republican argument against the doctrine of a federal common law jurisdiction makes a careful distinction between the very different natures of the federal and state governments. On the one hand, all admit that each state was fully competent to create a comprehensive legal system for itself and to amend or entirely replace that system if they should so choose. On the other hand, all assert that the federal government—restrained as it was by the Constitution and by the wills of the states that had created it—was not at liberty to do the same. This was because the Jeffersonians asserted that the federal government did not constitute a nation in the sense that Story had argued it did. If anything, it was—in Jefferson's terms—a nation "for special purposes only."[36] The federal government was thus, unlike the government of Virginia or any other state, inherently limited in its scope; the common law of England, on the other hand, was a "general system"[37] of law inasmuch as it included much more than the Constitution allowed for. Consequently, Jefferson described the idea of "a system of law for the US" as an "audacious, barefaced, and sweeping pretension"[38] and Madison described it as a "pretension" of "novelty" and "extravagance."[39] They considered the federal adoption of the common law to be impossible because the scope of the common law went so radically beyond the limited nature of the American federal government. In other words, while Story spoke in his Commentaries of the American people before the Declaration of Independence as constituting, in some ill-defined sense, a nation, adherents to the Compact Theory steadfastly denied that such a national people existed, except in respect to a small number of policy areas in which the people of each state had chosen to cede control over to the federal government. In all other respects, there existed no national American people to adopt the common law either formally or over time through accepted practice.

Much of the Republican antipathy toward the asserted doctrine stemmed from the fear that a general common law foundation for the federal courts would expand their jurisdiction far beyond what is spelled out in the Constitution. It is true that most of the Republican critics of a federal common law jurisdiction did seem to interpret Federalist claims of such a common law in the most extreme light and thus feared that Federalists were claiming a jurisdiction for the federal courts that was co-extensive with the scope of the common law of England—in other words, making federal jurisdiction virtually unlimited, as it would amount to a "general [jurisdiction] over all cases & persons."[40] Such an expansion of the federal courts' jurisdiction was bound to have effects on the scope of Congress' power as well. Madison noted in his *Report of 1800* that, if there were an implied federal common law jurisdiction for the federal courts, it would either imply an equally broad legislative authorization that extended to all of the same objects—delimiting the scope of congressional power that had been so carefully staked out in the list of legislative powers in Article I, Section 8—or else Congress lacked this broad legislative authority and the common law as available to the federal courts was irrepealable and unalterable by the legislature, which would have led to an even worse result: "the whole code with all its incongruities, barbarisms, and bloody maxims would be inviolably saddled on the good people of the United States."[41] With or without a co-extensive legislative authorization, it was thus hard to grant the full scope of the British common law jurisdiction to the federal courts and still keep the federal government limited: in either the Compact Theory or Nationalist Theory sense of the word.

Federalists were quick to respond to this Republican argument by claiming that the federal common law jurisdiction they were clamoring for was much more limited than Republicans supposed. Most proponents of a federal common law jurisdiction did not argue that the entirety of the British common law had been adopted nationally, but only such parts as related to the powers of the federal government as detailed in the Constitution. Joseph Story's careful argument in Coolidge is in this way typical of many—though not all—Federalist claims of a federal common law. Consequently, it is somewhat plausible that at least some Republican opposition to a federal common law jurisdiction was based on a misconception: Republicans were afraid that Federalists were attempting to expand the jurisdiction of the federal judiciary to encompass the whole of the British common law. For example, in Jefferson's letter to Edmund Randolph, he warned that, if the doctrine of a federal common law were accepted, the federal courts would have "jurisdiction co-extensive with that law, that is to say general over all cases & persons."[42] Arguably, however, no proponent of a federal common law jurisdiction maintained this radical position.

Similarly, John Marshall, in a letter to Tucker, claimed that he had never heard any Federalist make the assertion that both Tucker and Madison were trying to rebut: that the Constitution had, in effect, adopted the common law of England as the common law of America.[43] It may be noted here that Marshall appears to have differed with later decisions by Story, at least with the application of the common law in the federal courts, with Marshall claiming that "the principles of the common law of the state would apply themselves to magistrates of the general as well as to magistrates of the particular [i.e. the state] government."[44] In other words, Marshall suggested that federal judges would be bound by state pronouncements on what portions of the common law had or had not been adopted; Story's opinions, on the other hand, appeared to give judges the authority to choose to ignore state pronouncements on the common law if they felt they differed from some national standard. Given this, it may be well to treat Marshall's assertion in this letter to Tucker that there was no substantial difference between the two sides on the common law question rather cautiously, in consideration of the fact that at least some proponents of a federal common law jurisdiction apparently went beyond Marshall's rather moderate position, as well as the fact that there appears to have been more difference between Marshall's and Tucker's views on the specific case Marshall cites—*United States v. Isaac Williams*—than Marshall either realized or acknowledged.

Still, the harsh Republican response to the assertion of a federal common law jurisdiction was due to more than fears about an unlimited common law jurisdiction: in a variety of ways, it touched on the ways that, according to the Compact Theory, the common law of England could not apply to the federal courts because of the limited nature of the federal government. That these Republican theorists also acknowledged and upheld the use of the common law by the state courts only emphasizes the degree to which they saw the national and state governments as resting on totally different foundations.

In contrasting Republican fears of an unlimited common law jurisdiction against the actual Federalist claims of a federal common law specifically limited to the federal government's constitutional powers, it may seem at first glance that there was actually very little space between what the Compact theorists and Story were advocating. Even Jefferson acknowledged that the federal courts might even rightly be given a limited common law basis for hearing cases, provided that such a limited adoption be effectuated by an act of Congress and extend "so far only as they were authorized to adopt."[45] Still, Jefferson's acceptance of the Compact Theory even prevented him from agreeing to the modified Federalist argument that the federal courts had a federal common law foundation in cases where the Constitution itself gave them jurisdiction. The reason for this was that, according to Story, there already existed a federally adopted common law of somewhat vague parameters, while Jefferson and his fellow Republicans insisted that the common law had never been adopted nationally.

The primary difference between Story and the Compact theorists—on the question of common law adoption as on so many others—stemmed from the fact that, according to the Compact Theory, the Union could be dated back only to a formal agreement between the states. In other words, while Virginia, upon declaring her independence, already had a common law foundation that she left untouched, the United States had no such national common law foundation.[46] Compact theorists treated the common law adoption by the people of each state very differently than Story, Kent, and other proponents of the federal common law who casually spoke of "our ancestors"[47] bringing over such parts of the common law as were suitable to "our situation"[48] and fitted to "our institutions,"[49] implying that all of the colonists were essentially engaged in the same process of bringing over the common law of England and subsequently determining which parts of it were relevant to their collective American situation, rather than bringing over the common law solely as the common law of their particular state and judging its relevance to their own particular situation.

Under Story and Kent's formulation, the acceptance of the common law by the courts of every state heavily implied the adoption of a general, American common law adoption that was shared by the whole American people, as did the presence of common law terminology in the Constitution. For Compact theorists, on the other hand, even if the common law were to exist in identical form in every single state, it still would not imply that a common law had ever been adopted nationally. Given this limited view of American nationhood and the limited scope of the federal government, a wholesale national adoption of the common law was an impossibility, although Congress might instruct the federal courts to abide by the common law in some or all of the particular cases assigned to the federal judiciary by the Constitution. In other words, Story was emphasizing the commonness of the shared common law tradition adopted by the people in each colony, while the Jeffersonians were emphasizing the degree to which the common law traditions in each of the states—as developed and amended by each state's state legislature and judiciary—diverged from the common strain that was the common law of England. Story's view was based on the presumption that the American people acted primarily in their national capacity; the Jeffersonian view was based on the presumption that no such national people existed, and that the people of each state were thus each an independent political community adapting the common law for themselves.

There is a broader way in which these two theories of the Constitution shaped the debate over the federal common law: each theory had ramifications for how the Constitution would be read and interpreted. This aspect of these theories is ironic, inasmuch as proponents of both theories attempted to bolster their argument by appealing to the language of the Constitution; all the while, their own interpretation of that document was significantly impacted by the lens through which they read it. Underlying this difference in constitutional interpretation was a difference in the way each side viewed federal power.

THE COMPACT AND NATIONALIST THEORIES AND CONSTITUTIONAL INTERPRETATION

This divergence in constitutional interpretation is reflected in the question of how the power of the federal government was limited. Both Compact theorists and Nationalist theorists acknowledged that the federal government was limited, but they differed in how it was limited, and whether the state governments were limited in the same sense. Here it seems proper to distinguish between two conflicting ways that the federal government may be said to be one of "limited powers." The first is the sense in which Justice Story used the term. Story held the federal government to be limited in the exact same way that the state governments are limited: both are limited by the will of their respective people, expressed in the granting of specified powers in their respective constitutions. Thus, according to Story, in its basic purpose and construction, the United States Constitution was "in no wise distinguishable from the constitutions of the state governments."[50] Both granted certain powers, both imposed certain restrictions, and both established the division of powers between governmental branches; moreover, the object of both was the benefit of the people and not that of the government.[51] Story summarized this point by stating that the federal Constitution should be given "as favorable" an interpretation as those of the states.[52] From this, it can be reasonably summarized that Story saw the federal Constitution as not significantly different from the state constitutions in the limiting function it performs on the government it establishes. This, combined with the fact that—according to the Nationalist Theory—it was "the people of the United States" who created the federal government, leads to the impression that, under Story's theory, the federal government is indeed limited by the will of the American people, but the American people were free at its inception to give as much or as little power as they desired to the federal government. From this starting point, it was thus not surprising for proponents of the Nationalist Theory to hold that the federal courts should have just as much of a right to make reference to the British common law inheritance as the state courts did; all that was necessary was the suggestion in the text of the Constitution that the American people had intended for the courts to enjoy such a power.

On the other hand, proponents of the Compact Theory described the federal government as limited in a very different sense. According to the Compact Theory, the federal government is essentially dissimilar from the state governments in that it had a different basis for its authority: the latter drew directly on the inherent powers of their sovereign people, while the former's powers consisted solely in specific limitations of that power; consequently, the powers that the federal government was competent to exercise were also different from those open to the states. The difference between the respective powers of the state and federal governments can be seen as basically following the familiar distinction set out by Madison in Federalist 45: "The powers delegated by the proposed Constitution to the federal government are few and defined. Those which are to remain in the State governments are numerous and indefinite."[53] To advocates of the Compact Theory, this was not merely the result of a preference by the American people that the federal government should, for the moment at least, exercise fewer powers than the state governments; it summarized a fundamental difference between the source of each government's legitimate authority. The state governments were sovereign, full-fledged political communities in their own right—Jefferson, as has been noted, made reference in 1799 to the "nation of Virginia."[54] Thus, the states were free to draw upon the authority of their people and to speak on behalf of those people; Virginia, for example, was thus free, within the limits of her state constitution, to declare what the will of the people of Virginia was.[55] On the other hand, the federal government was not created to be a full-fledged sovereign government, but only a partial association or—in Jefferson's telling formulation—"a nation only for special purposes."[56] Every grant of power to the federal government included in the federal Constitution was necessarily a partial surrender of authority and power by the erstwhile-independent sovereign people of each state. Thus, unlike the several state governments, the federal government was created not to be the sovereign governmental voice of the American people—according to the Compact Theory, there was no such thing as the "American people"—but rather to perform a handful of certain, specified tasks, while all other governmental functions continued to reside solely in the people of each state, to be exercised by their respective state governments. Under such a formulation, Story's presumption—that the federal courts should be at least as entitled to the use of British common law precedents as the state courts were—fell apart. The Compact Theory held that the federal government was limited in a way that the state governments were not, and it was the rejection of this peculiarly limited nature of the federal government that made the Federalist assertions of a federal common law so startling to their Jeffersonian opponents.

Even with the recognition that the federal government was one of the enumerated powers, Story's conception of the union nevertheless differed practically from the Jeffersonian understanding in the powers that it allowed for the federal government. Because he viewed the federal union as the creation of the "American people" and not an agreement between separate sovereign political communities, Story still viewed federal power as something that was capable of being expanded beyond the strict limitations of the constitutional text. In other words, Story was able to justify implied grants of power to the federal government in at least three ways that those following the Jeffersonian understanding of the union could not.

First, Story held that as the direct creation of the people of the United States, the federal government was constrained in its powers, not—as Jefferson would have it—by its nature, but only by the apparent will of the American people to give only certain powers to the federal government and leave the rest with the states. If, alternatively, the American people were to subsequently determine that certain state powers would be better exercised by the central government, it was entirely their prerogative to grant those powers to the central government at the expense of the state governments. The people of the United States were even competent to exercise their ultimate sovereign authority and dispense with the ideas of separate state governments altogether.

Story's clearest statement of this belief is given in his opinion in the 1816 case *Martin v. Hunter's Lessee*: "there can be no doubt that it was competent to the people to invest the general government with all the powers which they might deem proper and necessary to extend or restrain these powers according to their own good pleasure, and to give them a paramount and supreme authority."[57] Moreover, Story continued, "the people" were competent also "to prohibit to the States the exercise of any powers which were, in their judgment, incompatible with the objects of the general compact," or to subordinate the powers of the state governments to those of the nation.[58] Story then brought out the central consequence of this view of the Constitution: "The Constitution was not, therefore, necessarily carved out of existing State sovereignties, nor a surrender of powers already existing in State institutions."[59] Thus, according to Story, although the federal government was in principle limited by the Constitution, and although the people had apparently chosen to reserve some powers to the state governments, there was no necessary presumption that this arrangement was inevitable: it simply reflected the momentary will of the sovereign American people. Story's logic in *Martin* flows directly from his conception of the union as the creature of the whole American people.

Consequently, Story was able to justify theoretical expansions of federal power as entirely consistent with the nature of the federal union, inasmuch as the American people, in their sovereign capacity, could give whatever powers to the federal government that they so desired without changing the essence of the American union. The federal government was thus, in itself, competent to wield any power that the people of the union might conceivably entrust it with. Any limitations placed on the authority of the federal government by withholding a certain power from it were thus discretionary, entirely reliant on the will of the American people, and not required by the nature of the union.

Jefferson, by contrast, saw the federal government as different in kind from the governments of the several states. While acknowledging, as Story did, that the federal government was one of the enumerated powers, he nonetheless maintained that the state governments—restricted as they were by the will of the people of each state—were nonetheless competent to receive certain powers and to exercise the popular will in a way that the federal government, by its very nature, was not. One pertinent example of this comes from Jefferson's views on the state of the common law in Virginia.

In writing to Edmund Randolph, Jefferson noted that the "nation of Virginia" was competent to adopt the common law as a comprehensive legal system in accord with the will of the people of Virginia.[60] Furthermore, he wrote that Virginia's national character and its system of common law were not altered by the Revolution, or the Declaration of Independence from Britain, or in the changes to the Virginia government that accompanied the passage of the Virginia Constitution of 1776. Throughout those transformations, Jefferson wrote, the nation of Virginia was not "dissolved" and the "will" of the people of Virginia "remained in full vigour."[61] Consequently, the Revolution and adoption of the new state constitution did nothing to abrogate the previous adoption of the common law by the pre-revolutionary government in Virginia: "on the establishing the new organs, first of a convention, & afterwards a more complicated legislature, the old acts of national will continued in force, until the nation should by its new organs declare it's will changed."[62]

Significantly, however, Jefferson did not see the federal government as endowed with this same set of powers as the state governments had. The federal government was not even a full-fledged "nation" in the way that Virginia was, but—as Jefferson took care to note twice—constituted a nation "only for special purposes."[63] Consequently, the general government was limited to expressing the will of the American people only with regard to the select areas of policy for which it had been created, namely the regulation of international and interstate affairs.[64] This restriction was not one that was set merely by the will of the American nation at a given point in time; rather, the creation of the American nation itself was conditional upon this restriction to certain functions. This indeed was the very reason that Jefferson regarded the notion of a federal adoption of the common law as an utter impossibility: such an adoption by the American people, had it even been attempted, would have "embraced objects on which this association had no right to form or declare a will."[65] The federal government was simply "not the organ for declaring a national will" on any subject matter extending beyond the rather limited purview given to them by the terms of the compact.[66] On matters that did lie within their constitutional jurisdiction, Jefferson conceded that they were "free to declare the will of the nation, the law," but insisted that until it was declared—presumably by Congress—it was not law at all. Thus, even those parts of the common law that most directly touched on the enumerated powers of the federal government—for instance, over maritime law where the federal courts had exclusive jurisdiction—could not be relied on by the federal courts or as a basis for federal prosecution until it was formally adopted by the legislature. "So that the common law," Jefferson summarized, "did not become ipso facto law on the new association, it could only become so by a positive adoption. & so far only as they were authorized to adopt."[67]

Thus, Jefferson argued that the inherent limit on the federal government's powers went well beyond the limitations of having a written constitution. Virginia had a government that was limited by its state constitution, but the government of Virginia was still free to declare what the will of the people of Virginia was. The federal government, by contrast, could only act on behalf of the American people in a very small set of policy areas. This distinction flowed directly from the difference in the relative authority of the two forms of government: Virginia drew its authorization straight from the people and was authorized as the proper organ to express their sovereign will on all matters. The federal government, on the other hand, was created not as the voice of the American people, but as the agent of the people of each state to do only a certain limited number of prescribed tasks.

The second way that Story's Nationalist Theory opened the door for more implied federal powers was that Story's theory allowed for a flexibility of constitutional interpretation in a way that the Jeffersonian understanding of the union did not. If the Constitution is considered to be a direct grant of specified powers to the government by the people of the whole union, inferences can fairly be made in attempting to ascertain the will of the people that would not be justified if the Constitution is seen as a series of power grants away from the sovereign people of each state and to a separate and artificial entity. For Story, the starting point for interpreting the Constitution was an examination of the purposes for creating the federal government; from there, the reader was to interpret the enumerated powers of the government in a way consonant with its full exercise of the general powers conferred on it.

Story explained this process in Book III of his *Commentaries on the Constitution*, noting that the federal Constitution was entitled to "a reasonable interpretation of its language, and its powers, keeping in view the objects and purposes, for which those powers were conferred." Story then went on to clarify that by "reasonable interpretation" he meant that any ambiguities in meaning should be interpreted in the light of "the apparent objects and intent of the constitution" or "that which will give it efficacy and force, as a government, rather than that, which will impair its operations, and reduce it to a state of imbecility."[68] In other words, if the stated objects and purposes of the federal government—notably in the Preamble—have truly been granted to the federal government in general and broad terms, then any ambiguous language surrounding the federal government's enumerated powers should be interpreted with the same degree of latitude to ensure that the federal government is able to adequately meet the rather broad goals for which it was created. Thus, while Story added that this general principle should not be used to stretch the meaning of words "beyond their common and natural sense,"[69] he still argued for a great degree of latitude and flexibility in ascribing certain implied powers to the federal government.

Story had previously demonstrated this principle of interpretation in his opinion in *Martin v. Hunter's Lessee*, where he declared that "where a power [of the federal government] is expressly given in general terms, it is not to be restrained to particular cases unless that construction grow out of the context expressly or by necessary implication."[70] Moreover, Story noted, the Constitution as a whole "unavoidably deals in general language" and does not lay out for the federal government "minute specifications of its powers," the Constitution thus "leav[es] to the legislature from time to time to adopt its own means to effectuate legitimate objects and to mould and model the exercise of its powers as its own wisdom and the public interests, should require."[71] In other words, Story's stated rule of constitutional interpretation was to treat the federal Constitution more as a list of general objectives than as an exhaustive list of all of the specific powers that the federal government was permitted to exercise in order to meet these objectives. Thus, a great degree of latitude is necessary in assigning the federal government the power to perform specific actions or measures.

This latitude of interpretation and resulting openness to inferred powers of the federal government is directly in opposition to the Jeffersonian interpretation of the Constitution. Since the Constitution—according to Jefferson and the Republicans—is not a direct creation of the American people but rather a series of concessions from the people of each state—effectively limiting their own sovereignty—the language of the Constitution must be interpreted much more narrowly than if the powers of the federal government grew organically out of the sovereign authority of the American people. The Republican jurist St. George Tucker demonstrated this effect of the Jeffersonian interpretation of the Constitution in his answer to the Federalist argument that a federal common law jurisdiction was granted, by constitutional implication, in the Constitution: "This is probably the first instance in which it has been supposed that sovereign and independent states can be abridged of their rights, as sovereign states, by implication, only."[72] Tucker thus viewed claims of a federal common law jurisdiction not the way Story did as an exercise of government power, but as an abridgment of power: the difference arising not from a disagreement on the theory of a government of delegated powers, but rather in the question of who had been delegated the powers. For Tucker and Jefferson, the people had delegated powers originally to the state governments and any grants of power to the federal government thus shrunk the capacity of the people of each state to exercise self-government. The fact that this dramatic transfer of power had ostensibly been done by implication was all the more troubling to Tucker: "For, no free nation can be bound by any law but its own will; and where that will is manifested by any written document, as a convention, league, treaty, compact, or agreement, the nation is bound, only according as that will is expressed in the instrument by which it binds itself."[73] It is worth emphasizing again that Tucker viewed any grants of federal power as limiting the power of each state, which would otherwise have the full powers of a "free nation."

Here it is crucial to note Tucker's conception of the U.S. Constitution as the creation of the people of each state. For Tucker, as for Jefferson, any assignment of power to the federal government in the Constitution was not an expression of the will of the sovereign American people—which, both historically and legally speaking, did not exist, every act of the people in American political history having been carried out with the people of each state, or their representatives, voting separately from one another and not as one collective mass—but rather a concession of power away from the sovereign people of each state. Thus, every constitutional grant of power to the federal government is an action to "bind by law" a sovereign nation. This stems directly from Tucker's conception of the states and the federal government as fundamentally dissimilar, due to their differing proximities from the source of all sovereign power and the differing reasons for which they were created. It is entirely reasonable to impose, then, a more exacting reading of federal powers than of the powers of state governments, as the authority for one comes from an artificial contractual agreement and the authority for the other comes organically out of the sovereignty of the people of each state.

To reinforce this point, Tucker quoted a maxim by Bacon: "As exception strengthens the force of a law in cases not excepted; so enumeration weakens it, in cases not enumerated."[74] Tucker then applied this rule to the different situations of the state and federal governments with regard to the Constitution. Since, for Tucker, grants of power to the federal government constitute individualized exceptions from the general mass of power previously held by the state governments, their claim to powers not explicitly given is made stronger by the list of exceptions.[75] Conversely, the very act of enumerating all of the federal government's powers in the Constitution serves to weaken the federal government's claim to any powers not enumerated.[76] Thus, the different natures of the federal and state governments lend to them different degrees of latitude in constitutional interpretation.

On this point, it is worth noting again that Story explicitly disagreed with Tucker that the state and federal governments fundamentally differ in the source of their authority or in the role that they play in the American system. Story described the U.S. Constitution in his *Commentaries* as identical in its essence, and in its powers, to the state constitutions: in viewing the Constitution as "a frame, or fundamental law of government, established by the PEOPLE of the United States, according to their own free pleasure and sovereign will," he emphasized that "in this respect it is in no wise distinguishable from the constitutions of the state governments."[77] Each of the state constitutions had been established for similar purposes and upon similar authority, and both conferred powers and imposed authorities as the people saw necessary for the public good.[78] Story summarized this point by stating that, the two forms of government being thus the same in their essence, "the constitution of the United States is to receive as favorable a construction, as those of the states."[79] Thus, Story's theory, by positing both the state and federal constitutions as being the direct creations of the sovereign people of their respective spheres, allows for greater flexibility in interpretation than the constitutional theory espoused by Jefferson and Tucker, which treats the federal government as essentially different in its foundation from the governments of the several states.

Third, Story's constitutional theory naturally led to the assumption that the federal government—as a sovereign government in its own right and the official organ of the sovereign American people—could be considered to have certain inherent powers simply by virtue of its status as a sovereign nation. Put differently, there are certain attributes shared by all sovereign nations that, if the Story interpretation of the American union is correct, we should expect the federal government to have. Here it should be acknowledged that Story himself seems to have approached the doctrine of inherent powers with caution, declining to lay out the exact limits of such powers.

The fact that such inherent attributes of sovereignty are not listed in the Constitution naturally leads to an ambiguity surrounding which, if any, of these attributes the federal government is endowed with. This ambiguity is multiplied in the American system, where the federal government shares sovereignty with the states. Judge Story was not only sensitive to this ambiguity, but was also very skilled at framing his arguments in the most unobjectionable, inoffensive light; he was thus characteristically cautious when attributing inherent powers to the United States, although such powers should have flowed quite naturally from his understanding of the federal government as the direct creation of the sovereign American people. Story seemed to equivocate on the central question of whether the United States government enjoyed the undivided sovereignty of any other nation or whether some of the inherent sovereignty of the American people had been bestowed by the people exclusively on the state governments; Story was reluctant to publicly affirm the former position, and it is altogether unclear whether this reluctance was the result of a cautious framing of the issue due to the demands of political necessity or from a genuine belief that the federal government shared some of the normal attributes of sovereignty with the states, and was thus not exclusively sovereign. Consistent with his belief spelled out in *Martin v. Hunter's Lessee* that the federal and state governments were both created by the people and endowed with specified portions of the people's sovereignty,[80] Story may have held that there were limits to the inherent sovereignty of the United States government with the caveat that the sovereignty of the United States, like the United States Constitution, should receive "as favorable a construction, as those of the states," which is to say a liberal construction, as discussed previously.

Whether or not Story thus believed the sovereignty of the United States government had been limited by the American people, Story did believe that the federal government should have the inherent attributes of sovereignty, at least as far as the Constitution conferred powers on the federal government. Consequently, Story held that the federal government did enjoy certain inherent powers, simply by nature of the authority that had been granted to it by the American people. Such an inherent power he referred to in his *Commentaries on the Constitution* as a "resulting power," noting that such powers arose "from the aggregate powers of the national government."[81] In other words, because the federal government was endowed with a certain degree of sovereign national authority—even if it did not hold other portions of sovereign authority that the people had chosen to give to the states—it was thus entitled to some inherent powers resulting from the powers it had been given, even if they were not necessarily ancillary to an enumerated power: for instance, in holding that the federal government would possess exclusive jurisdiction over foreign territories conquered in war, Story argued that this would "rather be a result from the whole mass of the powers of the national government, and from the nature of political society, than a consequence or incident of the powers specially enumerated."[82] Similarly, while the Constitution did not enumerate the federal government's power to bring a lawsuit, this was another "natural incident, resulting from the sovereignty and character of the national government."[83]

Although these inherent powers are distinct from the expressly given federal powers listed in the Constitution, they nonetheless are linked to the federal government's ability to fully exercise those powers, even if not "incident to" any of them, thus making such inherent powers distinct from other "implied powers." When writing of the inherent power of the United States to enter into contracts, he noted that this is "an incident to their general right of sovereignty, so far as it is appropriate to any of the ends of the government, and within the constitutional range of its powers."[84] Thus, Story's conception of the inherent powers enjoyed by the United States government on account of its national "sovereignty and character" gives insight into the Federalist desideratum of a common law jurisdiction for crimes against the United States.

Story, as was noted in chapter 2, fully supported such a jurisdiction and held that Congress undeniably had the authority to pass a statute that would confer a common law jurisdiction on the courts for all offenses against the sovereignty of the United States. To this end, he wrote to Nathaniel Williams, asking him to "Pray induce Congress to give the Judicial Courts of the United States power to punish all crimes and offences against the Government, as at common law."[85] Story held that this inherent power to prosecute offenses against it—with or without statutory foundation—was an inherent power of the federal government not only in their constitutionally conferred jurisdiction over admiralty and maritime cases, but further extended to "all other places where it exercises a legitimate authority."[86] Consequently, Story's conception of a federal common law was intimately connected to his conception of the United States government as a sovereign national power, entitled to certain inherent powers by the "mass of powers" given to it by the American people.

For Jefferson and the Republicans, such a conception of inherent sovereign powers fundamentally mischaracterized the nature of the American union. The United States may have been created as a nation for "special purposes" as Jefferson wrote, but such a qualified national identity did not give the federal government any claim to the inherent attributes of sovereignty, as those attributes all remained with the separate state governments, even in spite of their self-limiting grants of power to the federal government. Tucker explained the Republican conception of residual state sovereignty by arguing that the Tenth Amendment was "nothing more than an express recognition of the law of nations," quoting as authority the position of the Swiss philosopher Emer de Vattel "that several sovereign, and independent states may unite themselves together by a perpetual confederacy, without each in particular ceasing to be a perfect state."[87] In such a federal republic, according to Vattel, "the deliberations in common will offer no violence to the sovereignty of each member, though they may in certain respects put some constraint on the exercise of it, in virtue of voluntary engagements.'"[88] Consequently, Tucker conceived of no inherent powers due to the federal government since it, unlike the states, is not imbued with the same attributes of sovereignty that any other national government would be. The very fact that the federal government is a government of delegated, enumerated powers with all of its powers listed out in the document points to the non-existence of any non-enumerated powers.

Put differently, according to Tucker, the federal government does not even have the same potential or capacity for sovereignty that the state governments have; had the states chosen to delegate more powers to the central government, they would still have done so as sovereign states entering into, in Vattel's words, a "voluntary engagement" and thus never have lost an ounce of the sovereignty that they had held under the Articles of Confederation. Consequently, Tucker disagreed with Story that the federal government is entitled to some inherent attributes of sovereignty by nature of the powers delegated to it by the Constitution. This is because Tucker saw the federal government's powers not as grants of power from the sovereign American people—which, as has already been noted, would put it on par with the states—but as stemming from its creation as an artificial, non-sovereign agent of the sovereign people of each state, represented through their sovereign organs in the state governments. Since the people of each state constitute a sovereign and independent political community and the people of the United States are not such a community, any powers inherent in belonging to the community of nations would continue to reside with the governments of the states and not the federal government.

CONCLUSION

The Compact and Nationalist Theories thus created, in effect, not so much two very different interpretations of the same Constitution as two different constitutions altogether, each with a very different purpose and a very different source of authority. Ultimately, these two constitutions were necessitated by two wholly incompatible views of the union. The debate over the federal common law thus played out against a series of interwoven debates: over the permissible sources of federal law, over the proper role for courts in the constitutional system, and over the nature of the union itself. In many ways, it is likely that the singular importance placed on the federal common law question by participants on both sides of the debate was the result of its contribution to many of these larger questions: certainly the Jeffersonian opponents of the federal common law objected to it because they saw in it a threat to the underlying nature of the union; for Story and other proponents of the federal common law, the prospect of a federal common law not only helped judges prosecute offenses in the absence of congressional statute, but also promised to elevate the role of federal courts—and federal law—over the state courts in terms of setting judicial policy.

Story's eventual establishment of a federal common law in civil cases in *Swift v. Tyson* in 1842 promised to do just this, by providing an avenue for the federal courts to develop a system of law that would be applied nationally. This purely federal common law could then transcend all of the fluctuations between the common law as it was practiced in the several states and establish instead a single overarching line of common law jurisprudence that would not only provide a consistency to federal case law but would also provide a single standard for state courts to model their own systems upon. It was Story's presumption that, at least in the area of commercial law, the growing interconnectedness of the American economy and a global tendency of commercial law systems to naturally converge would compel the state courts gradually to grow closer to one single standard of their own accord: his federal common law established in Swift offered them the opportunity to do so. Story believed, with Cicero, that there was a law above laws and that the federal law he had helped establish—if aligned with certain enduring and timeless universal principles—might accomplish gradually and peacefully what the Republicans had once feared might happen by sudden force: the assimilation of American law into a single coherent system. Story's grand ambitions, however, would never be realized.

NOTES

1. U.S. Constitution, Article III, Section 2.
2. U.S. Constitution, Artilce I, Section 8.
3. Robert Yates, "Brutus XII," February 7, 1788, reprinted in Ralph Ketcham, ed., *The Anti-Federalist Papers and the Constitutional Convention Debates* (New York: Penguin Publishing Group, 2003), 299–300.
4. Ibid.
5. "Brutus XI," 295.
6. "Brutus XII," 300.
7. Newmyer, 102.
8. Ibid.
9. *Hudson and Goodwin*, 33.
10. *Worrall*, in Tucker, 365.
11. Ibid., 366.
12. Ibid., 367.
13. Thomas Jefferson. Thomas Jefferson to Thomas Ritchie, December 25, 1820. From *The Writings of Thomas Jefferson*, ed. Andrew A. Lipscomb and Albert Ellery Bergh (Washington, DC: The Thomas Jefferson Memorial Association, 1903).
14. Newmyer, 102.
15. Ibid.
16. Jefferson to E. Randolph.
17. Madison, "Report of 1800."

18. Ibid.
19. Jefferson to E. Randolph.
20. Ibid.
21. Ibid.
22. *Worrall*, in Tucker, 367.
23. Jefferson to E. Randolph.
24. Palmer, 267–323.
25. Ibid., 286.
26. Ibid.
27. Ibid.
28. Tucker, 354.
29. James Madison, "Federalist No. 45," in *The Federalist* (New York: Barnes & Noble Publishing, 2006), 259.
30. *Martin*, 326.
31. Ibid., 325
32. Ibid.
33. Ibid.
34. Stampp, 30–31.
35. Ibid., 30.
36. Jefferson to E. Randolph.
37. Ibid.
38. Ibid.
39. Madison, "Report of 1800."
40. Jefferson to E. Randolph.
41. Madison, "Report of 1800."
42. Jefferson to E. Randolph.
43. John Marshall to St. George Tucker, November 27, 1800, Reprinted as Appendix A in Jay, 1326.
44. Ibid.
45. Jefferson to E. Randolph.
46. Ibid.
47. Story, *Commentaries*, Sec. 156, 1:105.
48. *Patterson*, 241.
49. Kent, Part II, Lecture XVI, 322.
50. Story, *Commentaries*, Sec. 186, 1:138.
51. Ibid.
52. Ibid., Sec. 186, 139.
53. Madison, "Federalist 45," 259.
54. Jefferson to E. Randolph.
55. Ibid.
56. Ibid.
57. *Martin,* 324–325.
58. Ibid., 325.
59. Ibid., 324–325.
60. Jefferson to E. Randolph.

61. Ibid.
62. Ibid.
63. Ibid.
64. Ibid.
65. Ibid.
66. Ibid.
67. Ibid.
68. Story, *Commentaries*, Sec. 419, 1:310.
69. Ibid.
70. *Martin,* 326.
71. Ibid., 326–327.
72. Tucker, 355.
73. Ibid.
74. Bacon, *Of the Advancement of Learning* (1605), quoted at Tucker, 346.
75. Tucker, 346.
76. Ibid.
77. Story, *Commentaries*, Sec. 409, 1:302.
78. Ibid.
79. Ibid., Sec. 416, 1:306.
80. *Martin*, 325.
81. Story, *Commentaries,* Sec. 1256, 2:142.
82. Ibid., Sec. 1256, 2:142.
83. Ibid., Sec. 1256, 2:143.
84. Ibid., Sec. 1256, 2:143.
85. Joseph Story. Joseph Story to Nathaniel Williams, October 8, 1812. Reprinted in *Life and Letters*, I:243.
86. Story, *Life and Letters*, I:297.
87. Tucker, 345.
88. Ibid.

Chapter 6

The "Swift Doctrine": 1842–1938

In *Swift v. Tyson*, Story had achieved the culmination of a career-long pursuit of a federal common law basis for the federal courts. In stark contrast to the contentious response to claims of a federal jurisdiction for crimes under common law in the 1790's, Story's eventual establishment of a federal common law seems not to have caused much of a stir in its own time; nor is there even any indication that Story himself considered it to be a major accomplishment.[1] While it may be fair to hypothesize, judging by his prior writings on commercial law and his career-long quest for a federal common law jurisdiction, Story had high hopes for the far-reaching implications of this achievement, but the impact that Swift would have on future jurisprudence was at this point by no means certain. And indeed, judging by the notoriety it eventually received, as well as the number of cases it impacted, Swift did prove to be one of Story's most influential contributions to Supreme Court doctrine, even if it did not achieve the lofty results that Story had hoped a federal common law jurisdiction would bring. Nor, however, did it have the effect of totally dismantling the distinctions between the common law jurisprudences of the different states, as Jefferson and his followers had feared.

Most immediately, the establishment of a federal common law instantly put all federal judges in a much better position to decide civil cases: future questions of federal law would be decided according to a single national common law jurisprudence, developed over time by the greatest legal minds in the union, instead of being left "to the mere arbitrary pleasure of the judges, to an uncontrollable and undefined discretion," as Story had warned in *Coolidge*.[2] And indeed, from the creation of a federal common law over the principles of a "general commercial law" established in *Swift* until the eventual demise of that body of law in the 1938 case *Erie Railroad Co. v. Tompkins*, federal judges did develop a much broader body of federal common law—in the era of federal political and economic enlargement following the Civil War—than the one called for by the strict language of *Swift v. Tyson*.[3] Story had hoped that this body of jurisprudence would lead to a national legal uniformity, but such aspirations were ultimately left unmet.

A "UNIVERSAL EMPIRE OF JURIDICAL REASON"

In part, Story's desire for a degree of national uniformity in the law was imminently practical: reducing the number of discrepancies between the common law practices of the different states would only simplify the then-difficult job of both the federal judge and the lawyer presenting cases. But Story's pursuit of a federal common law had a higher purpose in mind as well: the establishment of a single, national common law in civil cases promised to foster a greater degree of national homogeneity in American law than had previously been possible. More broadly, the development of a national body of common law—albeit only in civil cases—promised to lift the sights of American jurists and lawyers toward a more universal body of law.

This surprising element of Story's judicial thought best can be seen by looking at his 1835 essay *A Discourse on the Past History, Present State, and Future Prospects of the Law*—published seven years prior to his opinion in *Swift*—in which Story laid out his highest aspirations for the federal law, as well as his fears that such aspirations may never be met. There, Story made a surprisingly frank assessment of the differences in common law practices from state to state: "while the States retain their independent sovereignties, as they must continue to do under our federative system," wrote Story, "it is hopeless to expect that any greater uniformity will exist in the future than in the past."[4] Later in the essay, Story again predicted that "American jurisprudence can never acquire a homogenous character."[5] Indeed, Story even acknowledged that this lack of standardization might not be a bad thing: he surprisingly allowed that a greater uniformity in applying the common law might not even be conducive to the great ends of "domestic happiness and political convenience," notwithstanding its simplification of the difficult role of the lawyer or judge.[6]

Even with this frank confession, however, it is apparent throughout the article that Story saw adherence to a uniform system of jurisprudence as a good in itself, largely because it promised to shift the focus of American legal practitioners away from the particularized and regional concerns of state law and instead usher in a new era of law based upon universal maxims and principles. Story had long believed that there existed a universal natural law which underlay the common law. Such a belief was not a unique or novel development: Blackstone, among others, had written on the relationship between the two. Still, this grand ambition of Story's deserves special attention, as it hints at a driving purpose behind Story's pursuit of a federal common law.

At least in this 1835 essay, Story's primary inspirations for this elevated goal of universal jurisprudence seem to have been Cicero and Lord Mansfield. Speaking of Mansfield's contributions to the field of maritime law, Story declared that his influence went far beyond the British legal system: "The maxims of maritime jurisprudence which he engrafted into the stock of the common law, are not the exclusive property of a single age or nation," Story declared, "but the common property of all times and all countries."[7] These maxims—"built upon the most comprehensive principles, and the most enlightened experience of mankind"—were to be "of universal application" as opposed to a more local application: "not the law of a particular country, but the general law of nations."[8] Story traced this grand ambition of a universal law back to Cicero, whose passage from *De Re Publica* Mansfield had also cited: *"Non erit alia lex Romae, alia Athenis; alia nunc, alia posthac; set, et apud omnes gentes et omni tempore, una eademque lex obtinebit."*[9] ("There will not be one law at Rome, another at Athens; one now, another henceforth; but the same one law will prevail among all nations and in all times.") It was this belief in a fundamental universal law that appealed to Story, particularly in the area of commercial law. While he had equivocated on whether a general confluence of the common law practices of the many states was possible, or even desirable, he confidently held that in the case of commercial law, a worldwide uniformity was both probable and also unexceptionally desirable in every way.[10] This timeless, universal body of commercial law—described by Story as a "universal empire of juridical reason"— would wipe away "the oppressive schemes of holy alliances in a general conspiracy against the rights of mankind" and allow for "the establishment of such a beautiful system of juridical ethics" upon which judges in every nation could base their decisions.[11]

While acknowledging the probably irreconcilable differences between the common law practices of the many states, Story thus still believed that a global confluence of legal systems—at least in questions of commercial law—was inevitable. Thus, the impossibility of a truly national jurisprudence, while discouraging, was not insurmountable. It was up to the jurist and to the lawyer to place national jurisprudence upon the firm foundations of the "universal empire of juridical reason" depicted by Mansfield and Cicero. He includes in the essay an exhortation to his fellow members of the legal profession to reach further than the mere application of state law "lest, by being split up into distinct provincial bars, the profession become devoted to mere state jurisprudence" and thus "abandon those more enlightened and extensive researches which form the accomplished scholar, and elevate the refined jurist; which ennoble the patriot, and shed a never dying lustre round the statesman."[12] Story held out hope that this tendency toward differentiation between state legal systems might be partially mitigated by the "salutary influence" of the federal courts' carrying out of their full "constitutional jurisdiction."[13]

The general character of the federal courts, as well as the types of questions that they dealt with, promised to draw the attention of the most able lawyers in all of the states.[14] The federal courts then, as opposed to the state court systems, had the opportunity to draw from the best legal minds that the states had to offer, ultimately leading to a new class of professional jurists who could combine mastery of the particularities of local law with an attentiveness to the grand universal principles and timeless truths of "general jurisprudence."[15] Here, Story's general disdain for state court judges can clearly be seen. McClellan suggests that this prejudice was probably due as much to a low opinion of the poor legal training they were likely to have received as to their greater susceptibility to popular pressures[16]—particularly in the midst of the storm of Jacksonian democracy that was brewing everywhere around Story in 1835.

This universal vision seems thus to have been a driving motivator in Story's pursuit of the federal common law in civil cases established in *Swift v. Tyson*. More directly, Story's goal in *Swift* was to give birth to a national body of commercial law that might clear a way between the various competing common law rules in the state court systems and instead foster a national union of commercial codes that would encourage national economic growth.[17] In an era when the state governments—including the state court systems—endangered the rights of moneyed elites and threatened to replace the juridical wisdom of the great English common law commentators with the demands of an increasingly democratized populace, establishing a uniform body of commercial law promised to link American law instead to the timeless principles that Mansfield and Cicero had sought after; it is in this sense that McClellan interprets Story's victory in *Swift* as part of Story's much larger philosophical project of mooring modern democratic man against the storms of modernity by giving him a permanent link to the timeless insights of the ancients.[18]

In truth, however, *Swift* failed to accomplish any of these goals: it of course failed to establish the glorious "universal empire of juridical reason" dreamt of by Mansfield and Cicero, but it also failed to lead the way for a generally agreed-upon standard in civil cases. To achieve the latter, it would have required the state court systems to eventually coalesce around the new body of commercial law being propounded by the federal courts. Such a convergence would have been voluntary, based on shared economic incentive, instead of legally mandated. The end result, however, would have been the same: a harmonization of commercial codes into a single system that would encourage national economic development.[19] Such a harmonization, however, never materialized.

JEFFERSONIAN FEARS AND THE "*SWIFT* DOCTRINE"

At the same time as Story's hopes for a gradual convergence of commercial law never materialized, it can similarly be argued that much of the Jeffersonian alarm surrounding the recognition of a federal common law did not come about from Story's precedent in *Swift*. Republican opponents of the doctrine of a federal common law had feared the doctrine for many reasons. Most fundamentally, as has been the purpose of this book to argue, they recognized that it implied an origin and character of the union that was fundamentally flawed: they resisted it because to recognize its existence would have been to go against their entire constitutional theory. But there were many practical fears that they had too. By 1842, it seems, such fears no longer held the imagination of states' rights advocates, who had by then shifted their attention to fighting other battles and largely allowed Story's pronouncement of a federal common law to go by without controversy.[20]

In a certain sense, the precedent established by Story was much more limited than the one that Jeffersonians had so long feared—and this may go a fair way to explaining the lack of outcry over *Swift* when compared with the earlier Republican furor over a federal common law. Chief among the fears of Republican critics of the federal common law had been that recognizing a national common law adoption underlying federal law would have meant that some form of the British common law—even, as it were, modified to fit the American national experience as Story postulated—was thus a part of the "laws of the United States." This would, of course, have granted the federal courts virtually unlimited appellate jurisdiction, as Article III had given federal courts such jurisdiction over all cases "arising under this Constitution, [or] the laws of the United States."[21] In addition to extending the reach of the federal judiciary, it would have also logically meant that the whole British common law would have become the "supreme law of the land" under the Supremacy Clause of Article VI, thus potentially invalidating any changes that the courts or legislatures of any of the states had made to the inherited common law. Once the existence of a federally adopted common law was admitted, opponents argued that every adoption of common law within the states that varied from that uniform standard would have been just as unconstitutional as a state law or constitution that conflicted with a constitutional act of Congress.

And yet, as has been noted, *Swift v. Tyson* did not obliterate any common law rulings at the state level; it merely created a national set of common law principles to exist alongside it. *Swift* merely held that federal courts were free to develop a federal common law but did not prohibit New York judges, or any judges, from abiding by the common law rulings of their own particular state. Story had indeed hoped that the states would eventually coalesce around the uniform body of commercial law being propounded by the federal courts, but such a convalescence would have been voluntary and not coerced.

The result—two sets of common law rules existing alongside one another within each state—might have surprised the Jeffersonians for its failure to apply what they saw as the rather obvious implications of the Supremacy Clause, but it flows rather predictably out of the text of Story's opinion in *Swift*. As was his tactic in many of the opinions he had written, Story went out of his way to frame his argument in *Swift v. Tyson* in as unobjectionable a light as possible: the federal common law he propounded applied only to "the general principles and doctrines of commercial jurisprudence"[22] and did not extend his decision to embrace "application to state laws strictly local."[23] The opinion in *Swift* can be read even more narrowly: as focused on the application of a federal set of common law principles "to the construction of ordinary contracts or other written instruments, and especially to questions of general commercial law."[24] Moreover, *Swift* dealt solely with diversity of citizenship cases where, it could plausibly be argued, it would be unfair to one party to apply the law of the other's state; the very reasoning of Article III in allowing for federal jurisdiction in diversity cases seemed to point to Story's conclusion in *Swift*. For these reasons, Newmyer argues that Story's original opinion in *Swift* was far from the sweeping power grab that the Court would treat it as in *Erie*; the overreach was actually due to future justices stretching Story's opinion beyond its original meaning: "Had later judges attended more carefully to the limits Story imposed in *Swift*, they might not have leaped so boldly from bills of exchange to torts and beyond."[25] As Story's precedent was expanded and, moreover, as it mixed with the judicial politics of the Progressive Era, opposition to the doctrine would slowly begin to ossify; in 1842, the proponents of the Compact Theory were focused on different issues.

Story thus showed no interest in overriding the common law practices of each state, only in exploring the parameters of a federal common law that embraced all of them. Of course, it was still true—according to Jeffersonian principles—that such a federal common law had never existed, but with the willingness of Story to allow the two distinct sets of common law rulings to peacefully coexist within the borders of each state, the dangers of embracing a federal common law jurisdiction as Story had done became much more muted. Over time, Story's distinction between state laws of "general" versus "strictly local" applicability would eventually erode, and it was only then that opposition to the "*Swift* doctrine" began to gain steam.[26]

From a different perspective, of course, opponents of a federal common law could argue that every case decided under the federal common law—at least in those cases where it differed from the common law standard of each state—was itself an unconstitutional deprivation of the rights of each state and that the citizens of a state should not be bound by the rules of the British common law until the agents of their state government had explicitly chosen to adopt such rules. But the argument over how the general principles of contract enforcement—at least while Story's principle was confined to such ground—apparently failed to excite the passions of Southern lawmakers and jurists the way that non-statutory criminal indictments at common law had during the Washington and Adams administrations. At least in *Swift*, Story had based his opinion on the language of section 34 of the Judiciary Act of 1789, and thus it was not solely a matter of the common law being imposed on the states. Ostensibly, the federal courts had the authority to grant federal judges a limited cognizance of common law rules and procedures in diversity of citizenship cases; the only question was whether they had actually done so. Such a question was a much narrower one than the one that much of the debate over a general federal common law *jurisdiction* had been based upon, and this no doubt also helped to reign in some of the farther-reaching effects of the federal common law that frightened Republicans but never ultimately came to fruition.

THE JUDICIAL POLITICS OF THE "*SWIFT* DOCTRINE"

Despite Story's prediction of a global convergence of commercial legal codes, the court systems of each state proved stubbornly resistant to such a standardizing influence. All that Story's creation of a federal body of common law precedents did was create an alternative body of American common law that coexisted alongside the various state systems of law. Having set out to simplify American law, Story's opinion in *Swift* had done just the opposite: he had created within every jurisdiction an alternate body of commercial law that frequently clashed with the given commercial law particular to each state. The consequent divergence between state and federal commercial laws would of course lead to different legal outcomes, depending on whether the case was heard by a federal or a civil court. This led to the emergence of a practice referred to in legal circles as "forum shopping," with litigants frequently choosing between state and federal court systems depending on which promised to give them the most favorable outcome.

The result was not only legal confusion but also a growing tension between state judges who were attempting to develop and apply their state's particular body of commercial law and the federal courts that provided parties with an alternative forum for hearing the case, provided that they could establish federal jurisdiction in the case. The main losers of the new federal common law were the state governments, who no longer had exclusive control over various areas of the law that had originally been left to them by the Constitution; similarly, among those benefiting the most from Story's decision in *Swift* were large interstate corporations that did business in multiple states and were thus eligible to claim diversity-of-citizenship jurisdiction and skirt the economic regulations set by the state governments.[27] Similarly, United States Attorney General Robert H. Jackson—himself later an Associate Justice on the Supreme Court—argued that multi-state corporations were "the chief beneficiaries of the doctrine of *Swift v. Tyson*" and noting that "Such a corporation could claim that it was a citizen only of the state of its incorporation, and so when sued elsewhere, where they did business, they could remove cases freely to the federal courts on the ground of diversity of citizenship."[28] The federal common law created by Story thus created a loophole for large corporations, apparently allowing them to bypass the law of their state in cases where the federal courts were willing to offer a ruling more sympathetic to their interests.

What made the doctrine in *Swift* all the more contentious was the common perception—whether warranted or not—that the federal courts were frequently engaged in excessive judicial activism, striking down progressive economic regulations by the states whenever such regulations violated the judges' more *laissez-faire* notions of property rights. This perception drew on several infamous Supreme Court decisions such as *Lochner v. New York*,[29] where the Court overturned a state economic regulation on the grounds that it violated the "liberty to contract" that federal judges saw as embedded in the Fourteenth Amendment's Due Process Clause. It may be noted that this conventional perception of the federal judiciary in this period has lately been criticized by later historians who have pointed out that the federal judiciary was, on the whole, much less stringent in dealing with protective economic regulations than has previously been assumed.[30] Nevertheless, the popular image of the federal court in the Progressive Era as composed largely of reactionary, anti-progressive judicial legislators has been difficult to shake, particularly when read against the backdrop of numerous progressive voices in this period calling out the federal judiciary for its perceived opposition to protective economic regulations. Amid this judicial environment—with federal judges perceived as freely applying the loose principles of *Lochner* to overturn progressive regulations at the state level—many reform-minded jurists, such as Oliver Wendell Holmes Jr. and Louis Brandeis attacked the federal judiciary for violating the principles of federalism.

Moreover, critics of the federal court charged that the federal common law established by Story in *Swift* was itself—along with the development of the "substantive due process" doctrine in *Lochner*—a useful tool for federal judges to protect corporations. Many progressives argued that the use of the federal common law by the courts often preserved parts of the common law that, while favorable to businesses, had arguably outgrown their usefulness in an increasingly industrialized society.[31] For example, federal courts still enforced the fellow-servant rule,[32] removing the liability of employers for injuries that resulted from the negligence of a fellow employee.[33] The widespread perception was that the federal courts were invariably "prorailroad, procorporation, and procapitalist"[34] and that they were consequently an impediment to the democratic reform measures that were constantly bubbling up at the state level.

This perceived federal opposition to reform was made even more pronounced by the fact that the federal common law allowed judges to ignore the common law accepted in the state courts. In an era where most of the state courts, like the state legislatures, were generally sympathetic to reform efforts, corporations were able to evade progressive state judiciaries by claiming diversity jurisdiction. Many states passed statutes modifying outdated common law rules, such as the fellow-servant rule, and in such states, the state courts would willingly abide by their legislature's wishes. Anti-Progressive federal judges such as David Josiah Brewer, on the other hand, could strike down these legislative alterations of the common law, leaving only the federal common law to take their place.[35] On the whole, historian Melvin Urofsky notes, "rather than as bastions of reaction, most state courts could be fairly characterized as upholder of the best common-law tradition, attempting to meet the new social and economic conditions of the country."[36] While state judiciaries may not have been totally immune from criticism that they overly favored corporate interests and impeded protective economic regulations, one can see how federal judges, working within the framework Story laid out in *Swift*, were particularly subject to criticism.

By the New Deal era, the political ramifications of *Swift* remained largely the same as they had been during the Progressive Era: economic conservatives in the federal judiciary were still portrayed as a bulwark against progressive economic regulations at the state level. It is thus not surprising that when *Swift* was finally overturned in *Erie Railroad Co. v. Tompkins* in 1938, the two dissenting justices in the case were Pierce Butler and James Clark McReynolds: remnants of the *laissez faire* "Four Horsemen" bloc on the Court that had overturned much of Roosevelt's New Deal legislation until the retirements of justices George Sutherland and Willis Van Devanter in 1937.

In a dissenting opinion joined by McReynolds, Butler accused the majority in *Erie* of judicial activism and going out of its way to invalidate *Swift*, given that the petitioner to the Court did not bring up the issue of the federal common law's constitutionality in their petition for a *writ of certiorari* and that the case could easily be decided without invalidating the Court's precedent in *Swift*. Butler noted that the Court had "often emphasized its reluctance to consider constitutional questions, and that legislation will not be held invalid as repugnant to the fundamental law if the case may be decided upon any other ground."[37] In this particular case, there was no indication that considering the broader question of a federal common law was necessary to deciding the case. Moreover, Butler questioned the majority's willingness to target Story's questionable interpretation of section 34 of the Judiciary Act of 1789, which underlies his pronouncement that federal judges need not abide by the common law traditions of the several states: that interpretation had lasted such a length of time that it should not be summarily dismissed without even so much an argument from the attorneys.[38]

Butler's dissent may have been focused on procedural complaints, rather than debating Brandeis' interpretation of Section 34 on its own merits. But whatever the authors of the Judiciary Act intended to say—whether they intended for federal courts to be bound by the common law pronouncements of state court judges or not—there is an element of Butler's critique that strikes at a broader point: it was unnecessary for the majority to wipe away almost a century of federal common law jurisprudence in answering the case. Since counsel on both sides did not argue based on the constitutionality of the *Swift* precedent, it may fairly be said that Brandeis went well out of his way to strike a fatal blow against the federal common law. What was it in the doctrine that led Brandeis to oppose it?

THE "DECLARATORY" VIEW AND ITS CHALLENGERS

In answering this question, some legal commentators have directed attention to a contemporary shift in the way that law was conceptualized and taught in law schools, discussed at length in the introduction. The federal common law, it is sometimes argued, was but one casualty of an ongoing war of legal theory, due to the increasing prominence of the early proponents of Legal Realism—which held law to be the product of numerous social, political, and economic forces of which it could never be fully independent. Contrary to this view would be the traditional understanding of the common law, espoused by Story and his contemporaries, which relied on the "declaratory" theory of law: the view that law was composed of general principles that existed independent of individual legislative enactments or judicial opinions.[39] Under such a conception, it was the job of the jurist to "discover" law (rather than create it) and then to apply it to the particular circumstances. To the Legal Realists, Story's federal common law, divorced as it was from the political practice of the states and reminiscent as it was of the natural law theorizing of Blackstone and Cicero, was all-too-conspicuous a target.

Interestingly, at least one modern critic of the Court's decision in *Erie* has argued against the decision largely on these grounds. In his article *Finding Law*,[40] Stephen E. Sachs begins the article by bringing out the old distinction between finding and making law: "This Article defends the view that unwritten law can be found, rather than made" and quickly acknowledging that "this view is not in vogue."[41] In arguing that the Court erred in overruling *Swift* in *Erie*, it becomes clear that his main objection to *Erie* goes much further than that case, indeed much further than the federal common law established by Story in *Swift*; Sachs objects to what he sees as the premise underlying *Erie*: that, in principle, there can be no such independently existing body of unwritten law that was not created by someone (either a legislature or a court) and thus eligible to be *found*, rather than made. On the contrary, Sachs offers examples of bodies of social norms (what Austin would have called "improper laws," as opposed to laws of a political superior to inferiors[42]): fashion, etiquette, and language all can be said to have an independent existence—Miss Manners columns are ostensibly more focused on "finding" than "making" rules of etiquette, just as English teachers and dictionary editors are more focused on "finding" than "making" the rules of the English language.[43]

Sachs also points out that Holmes' Austinian positivistic premises—the "strongest pillar" upholding the "*Erie* doctrine"[44]—are now rejected among nearly all legal philosophers,[45] and that that flawed legal theory that judges can only make and not find law is essential to the logic of the decision. Since Holmes assumed that all judges—state as well as federal—*made* law, then he assumed that state courts had also been given power to make law under their state constitutions, an assumption that Sachs sees as deeply suspect, especially when considering that many state constitutions predated the positivist revolution that led to Holmes' view of state judges making law.[46] Without that, Sachs argues that it is not obvious that the federal courts are obligated to follow state courts' interpretation of unwritten law for the state, due to the fact that if a body of unwritten law (the common law, for instance) were said to have an independent existence outside of a state judiciary and that judiciary were tasked only with finding or declaring that body of law and not with making it, then the state judiciary could then be wrong about that body of law, and the federal courts would be under no obligation to follow the state courts' erroneous findings.[47] And Sachs notes that in applying Holmes' assumptions about the common law being judge-made to the federal courts, *Erie*'s effects are even more striking. On the same day the Court decided *Erie*, they also decided the case *Hinderlinder v. La Plata River & Cherry Creek Ditch Co.*,[48] which they deemed to hinger on the meaning of a "federal common law" in certain categories of cases. By transforming the federal courts' pursuit of a general common law into a unique body of "federal common law"—common law created by the federal courts, under Holmes' logic—*Erie* led the way for the federal courts to develop their own body of common law, separate from the "actual common law rules" the federal courts could be tasked with finding, if the common law was thought of as something that could be found and not made.[49]

On this note, it may be worthwhile to contrast the Jeffersonian critique of the federal common law doctrine with later Realist critics of *Swift* who found voice in the writings of Holmes and Brandeis. As has been said, at the time of the debates that this study has focused on—from the Federalist prosecutions for common law crimes to the Court's decisions in *Hudson and Goodwin* and then *Swift*—the declaratory theory was predominant, and there seems no reason to believe that Jefferson thought of the common law as something that judges made, rather than found. The same can be said of Madison, Tucker, Marshall, and indeed all of the other eighteenth-century legal minds who expressed disbelief in a general federal common law jurisdiction. Critics of the federal common law may, and presumably did, assume that state jurists found and did not make the common law in their states; the common law may have been amended by the state legislature or have been further developed as it was interpreted and applied by the state courts, but it was not up to state judges to declare or make it.

A slight difficulty comes when looking at the insistence by Jefferson and Madison that the common law must be positively adopted before it could be considered by the courts; in particular, it was argued that before the federal courts could make use of the common law—even in cases where they had jurisdiction—that it had to have been adopted by Congress. For instance, in the 1812 letter to John Tyler cited by Story to demonstrate Jefferson's antipathy to the common law and discussed in chapter 4, Jefferson held that the common law had not been adopted in Virginia until it was formally adopted by the people of Virginia through their government.[50] Similarly, in his 1802 memorandum *Observations on the Common Law and Hardin's Case*, Jefferson held that Republican critics of the federal common law doctrine "declared heretical" the idea "that Congress can pass any law not authorized by the Constitution, and that the [federal] judges can act on any law not authorized by Congress, or by the Constitution in very direct terms."[51] But this view, whether correct or incorrect, is far from the idea that the common law itself was a creation of the judges applying it or of denying the possibility of an unwritten law having an independent existence. In focusing their arguments on the need for proponents of the federal common law to demonstrate its adoption through statute or through the Constitution itself, they may have held different assumptions than Story did about the common law automatically being the birthright of all Americans, but they were far from denying, with Brandeis and Holmes, the possibility of judges "finding" law.

UNDERSTANDING *ERIE RAILROAD CO. V. TOMPKINS*

There were also at least two other sources of criticism that contributed to the rejection of the *Swift* doctrine. Edward A. Purcell Jr., in an insightful book on Brandeis' decision in *Erie*, identifies "three distinct but partially overlapping sources" of opposition to the federal common law: progressive political actors, defenders of state sovereignty, and those who decried the declaratory legal theory as outmoded.[52] All three can be seen reflected in Brandeis' opinion: one in Brandeis' own original contributions to anti-*Swift* literature, and two in the thought of prior justices that Brandeis quoted and relied on. In overturning *Swift* and the long line of cases applying its underlying principle—the competence of the federal courts to develop an independent common law for questions of general commercial law—Brandeis relied heavily upon dissenting opinions by two former justices: Associate Justice Stephen Field's 1893 dissent in *Baltimore & Ohio Railroad Co. v. Baugh*[53] and the recently deceased Oliver Wendell Holmes' dissents in *Kuhn v. Fairmont Coal Co.*[54] and *Black & White Taxicab Co. v. Brown & Yellow Taxicab Co.*[55] Field's dissent, arguably the first attack on the *Swift* doctrine, was occasioned by one of the federal common law's most dramatic expansions, as the opinion of the Court in *Baugh*—authored, coincidentally, by Field's nephew, Justice Brewer—expanded Story's limited ruling into the area of tort law, allowing federal judges to rely on it in the politically charged area of industrial injuries.[56]

Field's reasons for opposing the federal common law were strikingly reminiscent of the Jeffersonian critiques almost a century before, arguing that the lack of protest by Congress and the states on the question of a federal common law did nothing to make it more constitutional: "Such silence can neither augment the powers of the general government nor impair those of the states." Not only could the tacit consent of Congress and the state governments "not change the constitution," but it could not alter the fundamental nature of the union as would be required in order to "convert the national government from one of delegated and limited powers, or dwarf the states into subservient dependencies."[57] In contrast to the subservient role that recognizing a federal common law reduced the states to, Field noted that the Constitution "recognizes and preserves the autonomy and independence of the States—independence in their legislative and independence in their judicial departments," and argued that federal judicial supervision of either one, except where warranted by the Constitution, was "an invasion of the authority of the State and, to that extent, a denial of its independence."[58] Field's argument against the federal common law thus echoed perfectly the Jeffersonian opposition to the doctrine as incompatible with the limited nature of the federal government; Field even cited Tucker's essay against the federal common law in defense of treating the common law as distinct within each state and not some "general law floating about all the states, not belonging to any of them, and of which the federal judges are the especial possessors and guardians," free to apply it whenever the judicial decisions of the state courts conflicted with their own preferences.[59]

Brandeis' published opinion in *Erie* cited Field's dissent approvingly, and like Field, Brandeis too would often reflect the same sensitivity for protecting the role of states in setting their own policy. Yet, in the early drafts of his opinion, Brandeis ignored Field's attack on the federal common law doctrine in *Baugh*, relying instead solely on Holmes' dissents. Holmes had been Brandeis' friend and frequent collaborator on the court, and it seems likely that Brandeis' opinion in *Erie* was, at least in part, an homage to the recently deceased Holmes.[60] Holmes himself had been a frequent critic of the *Swift* precedent, albeit for a slightly different reason: for Holmes, *Swift* was emblematic of the older "declaratory" theory of law,[61] which was inconsistent with the demands of legal positivists like Holmes, who saw the law not as an independently existing entity to be discovered but as the "command of a sovereign," to use the definitions of Jeremy Bentham and John Austin.[62] Similarly, Holmes famously declared in a 1917 dissent that "[t]he common law is not a brooding omnipresence in the sky, but the articulate voice of some sovereign . . . that can be identified."[63] This adherence to the central thesis of legal positivism was one of the cornerstones of progressive jurisprudence. It also lay at the core of Holmes' critique of the federal common law.

In his dissent in *Black & White Cab v. Brown & Yellow Cab*, Holmes held that the Court, in relying on *Swift*, based their decision on a "subtle fallacy."[64] That fallacy was based on a misconception of what was meant by the phrase "the common law": discussions of the common law generally tended to assume, as Story did, that "*the* common law" was signified a single unified body of law in both England and America —"one august corpus," in Holmes' words—that was to be presumed as obligatory in each of the states until changed by the legislature.[65] The fundamental problem, according to Holmes, was that no such body of law existed: "law in the sense in which courts speak of it today does not exist without some definite authority behind it."[66] Thus, the common law as it existed in each state was not a reflection of a larger body of law but was the law of that particular state, backed by the authority of that state's authority—in the case of common law precedents, of that state's judges—regardless of how the common law of England or of any other state might differ.[67] This "subtle fallacy" of treating the common law as a single body of law independent of any particular manifestation of it was thus not a purely academic question but rather had brought about "an unconstitutional assumption of powers" by the federal courts[68] in taking away from the state judiciaries the authority to determine what the law of their state should be.

Brandeis' opinion in *Erie* thus relied on a number of previous dissents, but also contributed a new critique of the federal common law. As Purcell bears out in *Brandeis and the Progressive Constitution*, unlike Field and Holmes, Brandeis criticized *Swift* for its consequences: "Experience in applying the doctrine of *Swift v. Tyson* had revealed its defects, political and social," while "the benefits expected to flow from the rule did not accrue."[69] Story's intention had been to create a system in which all American court systems would coalesce around a single body of uniform law, but such uniformity was blocked, Brandeis noted, by the "persistence of state courts in their own opinions on questions of common law."[70] Moreover, the line that Story had attempted to draw between questions of a general nature and those purely local turned out also to be a difficult distinction for the courts to maintain.[71] At the same time, the existence of multiple available forums with different predicted legal outcomes provided a benefit to noncitizens of the state who had the ability to choose whether the case would be heard in state or federal court; consequently, Brandeis charged that the *Swift* doctrine "rendered impossible equal protection of the law."[72] The irony was, of course, that *Swift* had been designed to allow for uniformity of law; in practice, it had ensured an unequal application of the law, depending on whether the case was heard in state or federal court.[73] After almost a century of legal practice, the *Swift* doctrine had led to "injustice and confusion," leading some to question the utility of diversity of citizenship jurisdiction altogether.[74] Setting aside the states-rights critique of Field and the legal positivism of Holmes, the practical results of *Swift* spoke as much against it as any other critique. And although Brandeis insisted that the Court was overturning the doctrine based on its unconstitutionality and not its adverse social and political consequences, it is hard to divorce the Court's opinion in *Erie* from the growing sentiment that it was adversely affecting judicial politics and American legal culture.

CONCLUSION

Having provoked criticism from these multiple strands of legal thought, Story's establishment of a recognized federal common law jurisdiction thus proved not to be permanent, and the federal common law that he had such high aspirations for eventually was ultimately discarded. Far from destroying the legal distinctions between the states or delimiting the jurisdiction of the federal courts, as Jefferson and Tucker had feared, the federal common law jurisdiction achieved by Story in *Swift* did little more than to create a temporary allowance for multi-state corporations to evade economic regulations. By the time of the doctrine's death in 1938, writes McClellan, "there were many who did not mourn its passing."[75]

To the extent that Story had hoped that the federal common law he established would protect property rights from regulation by the state legislatures and encourage interstate commercial development, he likely would have approved of the way the doctrine was used throughout the Progressive Era. Nevertheless, Brandeis' opinion in *Erie* turned Story's establishment of a federal common law from a powerful tool to protect property interests to a historical curiosity: *Erie,* like *Swift*, is now known primarily as a mainstay of Civil Procedure courses for first-year law students. At any rate, even before the *Swift* precedent was finally rejected by the Court, Story's grand ambitions had already fallen through as the states refused to coalesce around a single legal standard and American commercial law thus never became the "universal empire of juridical reason" that Story had hoped it would. Nevertheless, much of what Story intended to accomplish through his ruling—such as the development of a truly national body of law—has been accomplished, even in spite of the demise of the "*Swift* Doctrine." And Brandeis' opinion in *Erie* has done little to take away from Story's overall influence on American constitutional doctrine.

NOTES

1. Newmyer, 336.
2. *Coolidge*, 620.
3. Newmyer, 335.
4. Story, *Past History,* 21.
5. Ibid., 35.
6. Ibid., 21.
7. Ibid., 11.
8. Ibid.
9. Ibid.
10. Ibid., 23.
11. Ibid., 24.
12. Ibid., 35.
13. Ibid.
14. Ibid., 36.
15. Ibid.
16. McClellan, 261.
17. Ibid.
18. Ibid., 183.
19. Ibid., 179.

20. Newmyer, 336.
21. United States Constitution, Article III, Section 2.
22. *Swift*, 2.
23. Ibid., 1.
24. Ibid., 19.
25. Newmyer, 342
26. Ibid., 335–336
27. Ibid., 335.
28. Robert H. Jackson, *The Struggle for Judicial Supremacy* (New York: Alfred A. Knopf, Inc., 1941), 279. Quoted in McClellan, 183n80.
29. *Lochner v. New York*, 198 U.S. 45 (1905).
30. Melvin I. Urofsky, "Myth and Reality: The Supreme Court and Protective Legislation in the Progressive Era." *Yearbook of the Supreme Court Historical Society* (Washington, 1983), 53–72.
31. Craig Green, "Can Erie Survive as Federal Common Law?" *William & Mary Law Review* 54, issue 3 (February 2013), 813–844, 820.
32. Ibid.
33. Melvin I. Urofsky, "State Courts and Protective Legislation during the Progressive Era: A Reevaluation." *The Journal of American History* 72, no. 1 (June, 1985), 63–91.
34. Green, 820.
35. Edward A. Purcell, Jr., *Brandeis and the Progressive Constitution: Erie, the Judicial Power, and the Politics of the Federal Courts in Twentieth-Century America* (New Haven: Yale University Press, 2000), 52.
36. Ibid., 91.
37. *Erie Railroad*, 88.
38. Ibid.
39. Purcell, 51.
40. Stephen E. Sachs, "Finding Law." *California Law Review* 107 (2019), 527–582.
41. Ibid., 529.
42. Austin, vii.
43. Sachs, 531.
44. Ibid., 532.
45. Ibid., 554, 571.
46. Ibid., 574.
47. Ibid., 574–575.
48. *Hinderlinder v. La Plata River & Cherry Creek Ditch Co.*, 304 U.S. 92, 110.
49. Ibid., 571, 577–578.
50. Jefferson to Tyler.
51. Jefferson, "Observations on the Common Law and Hardin's Case."
52. Purcell, 66–67.
53. *Baltimore & Ohio Railroad Co. v. Baugh*, 149 U.S. 368, 390 (1893).
54. *Kuhn v. Fairmont Coal Co.*, 215, U.S. 349, 370 (1910).
55. *Black & White Taxicab Co. v. Brown & Yellow Taxicab Co.*, 276 U.S. 518 (1928).

56. Purcell, 52.
57. *Baugh*, 399.
58. Ibid., 401.
59. Ibid., 399.
60. Purcell, 139–140.
61. Ibid., 66.
62. Ibid., 67.
63. *Southern Pacific Co. v. Jensen*, 244 U.S. 205, 222.
64. *Black & White*, 532.
65. Ibid., 533.
66. Ibid.
67. Ibid., 533–534.
68. Ibid., 533.
69. *Erie Railroad*, 74.
70. Ibid.
71. Ibid.
72. Ibid., 75.
73. Ibid.
74. Ibid., 77.
75. McClellan, 184.

Conclusion

Contemporary Relevance of Story's Nationalist Theory

Story's long-sought-after affirmation of a single, federal line of common law precedent in *Swift v. Tyson* thus ended up being only a temporary victory. To the extent that Story had hoped that the federal common law he established would protect property rights from regulation by the state legislatures and encourage interstate commercial development, he likely would have approved of corporations using the federal common law he created to skirt Progressive Era economic regulations. Nevertheless, *Erie Railroad* wiped away this option, and at any rate, American commercial law arguably never became the "universal empire of juridical reason" that Story had hoped it would. As one man standing against the rising tide of Jacksonian democracy, Story could do little to change the course of American political development. Yet it would be a grave mistake to write off this episode in American legal history as an irrelevant historical anecdote. Much of what Story intended to accomplish through his ruling—such as the development of a truly national body of law—has been accomplished, even in spite of the demise of the "*Swift* Doctrine."

To study the constitutional legacy of Joseph Story is to deal with an incredible irony: as a jurist, Story's ability to achieve his goals were significantly hampered by the fact that he was a man out of step with his times; yet since his death, future constitutional developments have tended to move in directions that he might not necessarily have foreseen, nor even fully approved of, but which are still unquestionably reliant on Story's constitutional theory. The twentieth-century jurist Roscoe Pound described this effect in discussing Story's effect on the legal codification debate: "What Story the judge could not do, Story the text writer largely accomplished."[1] In similar fashion, Story's Nationalist Theory view that the United States government is the creation of a single, sovereign body of American people has come to be widely accepted within the community of constitutional scholars, but this acceptance doubtless owes more to Story's legal treatises—most notably *Commentaries on the Constitution*—than on his landmark judicial opinion in *Martin v. Hunter's Lessee* that dealt with the same topic. Arguably, then, the Nationalist Theory that Story articulated in his constitutional writings thus has exerted a considerably higher degree of influence over subsequent legal history than the precedents set by Story's legal opinions, and it was through these constitutional and legal treatises that Story's influence can be seen as continuing to grow. Even this sustained influence, however, has not resulted in a uniform acceptance of Story's nationalism. On the contrary, although twenty-first-century constitutional realities are perhaps closer to Story's vision than that of Jefferson or Tucker, there are many ways in which the original tension between Compact Theory and Nationalist Theory continues to shape American constitutional debate.

U.S. TERM LIMITS V. THORNTON

A good example of the continuing relevance of Story's Nationalist Theory—as well as of Story himself—is the 1995 Supreme Court case *U.S. Term Limits v. Thornton.*[2] The case dealt with the constitutionality of an amendment to the Arkansas Constitution that placed term limits on members of the United States Congress from that state. The court's decision was issued at a moment when questions of judicial federalism were particularly charged for the Court, as the conservative majority on the Rehnquist Court had just weeks earlier overturned the Gun-Free School Zones Act as an overextension of Congress' regulatory power under the Commerce Clause[3]—the first attempt by the Court to place limits on that power since the New Deal.

Questions of federalism, indeed, played a central role in the *Thornton* case as well, and the same two contrasting theories of the Constitution that led to disagreement over the asserted federal common law can here be clearly seen driving a disagreement over the constitutionality of state-imposed term limits for members of Congress. Taking up the mantle of Story and other defenders of the Nationalist Theory, Associate Justice John Paul Stevens—writing for a majority on the Court—declared that the Arkansas amendment ran afoul of the "fundamental principle of our representative democracy," that "the people should choose whom they please to govern them."[4] Relying on the Court's earlier ruling in *Powell v. McCormick,* Stevens argued that the problem with the amendment lay in the fact that it was an attempt by the people of Arkansas—who had ratified the amendment through a direct vote in the 1992 general election—to place restrictions on the election of Members of Congress, who represented not just them, but the people of the nation as a whole. As Stevens explained, "allowing individual States to adopt their own qualifications for congressional service would be inconsistent with the Framers' vision of a uniform National Legislature representing the people of the United States."[5] In other words, Stevens wrote that any attempt by the people of Arkansas to regulate the election of congressmen, even from their own state, improperly put themselves in between "the people of the United States" as a national whole and that national people's representatives in Congress. Justice Anthony Kennedy summarized this view in a concurring opinion in the case, claiming that the Constitution creates "a relationship between the people of the Nation and their National Government, with which the states may not interfere."[6] Since Congress, in Stevens' estimation, represented the whole American people, the Constitution placed the right to choose Members of Congress solely in the hands of that people and any act by the people of any particular state to place restrictions on that choice was an affront to the sovereignty of "the people."

Stevens acknowledged that, as a general rule, the states reserved all powers not delegated by the Constitution to the federal government. Still, he argued that—even though the Constitution did not grant Congress the authority to regulate the election of Members of Congress either—this power could not be considered a reserved power of the states, since it was not a power that the states had *before* the ratification of the Constitution, Congress obviously not existing then.[7] Implicit in this argument is the assertion that the United States Congress, under the Constitution, is fundamentally a different entity from the Congress that existed under the Articles of Confederation; the states did place their own limitations on the election of representatives to the Confederation Congress but to treat that power as analogous to what Arkansas had done was to conflate two very different types of congresses. As Stevens put it, assuming that the power that states had to regulate their choice of representatives under the Articles of Confederation was somehow retained under the United States Constitution "overlooks the revolutionary character" of the United States Constitution.[8] That "revolutionary character" referred to the dramatic break that the Constitution made from the confederal nature of the Articles. To demonstrate this radical break, Stevens quoted from the 1964 Supreme Court case *Wesberry v. Sanders* which contrasted the general system under the articles where "the States retained most of their sovereignty, like independent nations bound together only by treaties"[9] with the eventual product of the Constitutional Convention: "a plan not merely to amend the Articles of Confederation but to create an entirely new National Government with a National Executive, National Judiciary, and a National Legislature."[10] Stevens argued that this "revolutionary" shift dramatically changed the relationship of the American people to the central government: "In adopting that plan, the Framers envisioned a uniform national system, rejecting the notion that the Nation was a collection of States, and instead creating a direct link between the National Government and the people of the United States."[11] In other words, Stevens argued that the "revolutionary" nature of the United

States Constitution was due to the fact that Constitution, unlike the Articles of Confederation, created a government for a national American people. Since, apparently, this national people either did not exist at the time of the Articles or did exist but was somehow not comprehended by the articles, the ratification of the United States Constitution created a truly national legislature in a way that was completely new. Consequently, the power to regulate the election of this new national legislature could not possibly fall into that category of powers that the states retained to themselves under the Constitution, since it was one that they had never possessed before the Constitution's ratification. Thus, Stevens' acceptance of the Nationalist Theory contention that the United States Constitution was the creation of the national American people—even if he also hinted at a disagreement with Story and Dane's claim that this American people preexisted the Constitution—allowed for a restriction of the "reserved powers" of the states and prevented them from exercising any influence over the working of the federal government.

It is apparent, then, that Stevens' argument that the Arkansas amendment is unconstitutional is premised heavily upon Story's Nationalist Theory. The centrality of the Nationalist Theory to the majority's reasoning in *Thornton* is underscored by the outright rejection of that theory by Clarence Thomas in his dissenting opinion. Thomas' dissent goes straight to what he sees as the heart of the majority's misunderstanding of the Constitution: the implicit belief by Stevens and Kennedy that the Constitution was the creation of a national body of people. Arguing that the majority of the Court "fundamentally misunderstands the notion of 'reserved powers,'" Thomas opted to begin his dissent with a set of "first principles."[12] In particular, Thomas identified "one overriding principle" on which the entire constitutional system rested: "All power stems from the consent of the people."[13] This pronouncement is reminiscent of Chief Justice Marshall's similar pronouncement in *McCulloch v. Maryland*; Marshall had gone on to imply that this principle undercut the argument that the union was acceded to by the state governments. Thomas, however, suggested that this assumption by Marshall—and indeed by a majority of the Court in the present case—stemmed from a lack of precision in what *people* was being discussed: "To phrase the principle in this way, however, is to be imprecise about something important to the notion of "reserved" powers."[14] Unlike Marshall, however, Thomas clarified that *the people* that the powers of the federal government stemmed from were not, as Marshall had assumed, the people of the whole union but the people of each particular state: "The ultimate source of the Constitution's authority is the consent of the people of each individual State, not the consent of the undifferentiated people of the Nation as a whole."[15] Thomas thus attempted to undercut what he sees as the basic assumption underneath the majority's reasoning: that the Congress is the creation of the whole American people and is designed to be their representative. On the contrary, Thomas insisted that the Constitution was created not by some national body, but as an agreement between the people of each state. Put differently, Thomas' description of the Constitution is compatible with the Jeffersonian view which treated the Constitution as a *compact* between the people of each state, with Thomas pointing to a "fundamental principle that all governmental powers stem from the people of the States."[16] Thomas emphasized this point by pointing to the procedure for ratification outlined in Article VII, which declared that, following the Constitution's ratification by popular conventions in nine states, "the Constitution went into effect only 'between the States so ratifying the same';[17] it did not bind the people of North Carolina until they had accepted it."[18] If the Constitution were the creation of the whole American people as the majority in this case insisted, then it would stand to reason that any portion of that people could be bound by the decision of the others to ratify the Constitution—particularly if Story's claim of a pre-constitutional American people was accepted.

Furthermore, the description by Stevens and proponents of the Nationalist Theory that the Constitution created a purely *national* government with which the people of each state were forbidden from interfering would seem to require that American people vote or act on a national scale; and yet, as Thomas took care to emphasize, "the Constitution does not call for Members of Congress to be elected by the undifferentiated national citizenry; indeed, it does not recognize any mechanism at all (such as a national referendum) for action by the undifferentiated people of the Nation as a whole."[19] Thus, while Thomas agreed with the majority that there was meant to be some "direct link"[20] between the Members of the House of Representatives and the people, Thomas nevertheless insisted that this link must be understood to be a link between the representatives from a particular state and the people of that same state.[21] Thomas went as far as to note that a majority of his fellow justices—with their Nationalist Theory presumptions about the Constitution—would "surely fit more comfortably within a system of nationwide elections"[22] and theorized that the system that the Constitution creates must seem baffling to them. "The United States obviously is a Nation," wrote Thomas, and it "obviously has citizens," but it nowhere creates a mechanism by which the American people can act together as a concerted whole.[23] Thomas concluded that the constitution is decidedly *not* the creation of the people of the United States as an undifferentiated mass, but rather of the people of each separate state.[24]

It is striking that, nearly a century and a half after Story's death, the conflict created by his argument that the Union was the creation of the American people can still be seen driving constitutional debates. The influence of the theory laid out in Story's *Commentaries* can easily be seen in Stevens' opinion, and the rejection of that theory provides a natural starting point for Thomas. Even more striking for examining Story's continued influence is the fact that neither side was willing to allow the shade of Joseph Story to hide in the background of this argument: in the contrasting opinions in *Thornton*, a debate over the nature of the Union shifts seamlessly into a debate over the authority of Judge Story. Among other early historical sources, such as Alexander Hamilton in Federalist 60, Stevens quoted[25] Story's claim in his *Commentaries on the Constitution* that each member of Congress is "an officer of the union, deriving his powers and qualifications from the constitution, and neither created by, dependent upon, nor controllable by, the states."[26] Moreover, Stevens appears to have gotten the basic thrust of his argument from Story, including his argument that regulation of federal officers falls outside of the "reserved powers" of the states, since in Story's words, "No State can say that it has reserved what it never possessed."[27] Stevens' argument is thus deeply indebted to Story's understanding of the Constitution in more ways than one, and his citation of Story's *Commentaries* is very telling.

Likewise, Justice Thomas also referenced Story in his dissent. Although he made attempts to demonstrate the compatibility of his less-Nationalist understanding of the Union with some of the sources cited by Stevens—arguing, for example, that Hamilton's words in Federalist 60 must be understood against the backdrop of state restrictions on the franchise[28]—he found it necessary to address the incompatibility of his position with the authority of Story head-on, calling Justice Story a "brilliant and accomplished man" whose views could not be lightly dismissed.[29] "On the other hand," wrote Thomas, "he was not a member of the Founding generation, and his Commentaries on the Constitution were written a half century after the framing. Rather than representing the original understanding of the Constitution, they represent only his own understanding."[30] Thomas went further, suggesting that the nationalist bias evident in Story's *Commentaries* made them a less-reliable guide for understanding the Constitution: "In a range of cases concerning the federal/state relation, moreover, this Court has deemed positions taken in Story's *Commentaries* to be more nationalist than the constitution warrants."[31] Thomas' explicit, if also somewhat deferential, rejection of Story's authority on constitutional questions—at least as regards issues of state-federal relations—is striking. It seems that Thomas—while clearly desiring to demonstrate that his own understanding of the Union was compatible with that of the Framers—saw his own understanding of the Union as utterly incommensurable with Story's. It is very telling, and entirely appropriate, that, in any debate over the nature of the Union, Story's authority would be brought into question. It also speaks to Story's central role in the development of the Nationalist Theory that a debate over the "national" nature of Congress should hinge on the reliability of Story's views on state–federal relations.

CONTEMPORARY RELEVANCE OF STORY'S NATIONALIST THEORY: OTHER APPLICATIONS

The fact that the fundamental question of the true nature of the Union—"Whether a Compact," as Story had framed the question in his *Commentaries*—should be brought up on a debate over the constitutionality of state-imposed term limits may seem surprising at first. But upon further reflection it should be clear that the question is tied to a host of interrelated contemporary and historical constitutional debates. Indeed, the acceptance of either the Compact Theory or the Nationalist Theory as the proper lens through which the Constitution and the Union are to be viewed is bound to have an endless number of far-reaching political and legal implications. It would be difficult to find any question of constitutional interpretation that would not be affected by accepting one constitutional theory over the other.

Many of the foregoing chapters have attempted to demonstrate the numerous ways that the assumptions required by either constitutional theory are intimately tied to the legal positions for and against the federal common law. As the opinions in *Thornton* demonstrate, however, the original tension that divided the delegates of large states and small states against each other in the Continental Congress still is capable of creating constitutional disagreement. To further demonstrate the relevance of this debate to contemporary constitutional issues, three other issues will be briefly discussed here: the question of whether the government of the United States enjoys certain "inherent powers" in addition to the powers explicitly or implicitly granted by the Constitution, the perennial push—renewed in the aftermath of the 2016 election—to eliminate the electoral college and replace it with a more direct system of presidential selection, and finally the lately reemerging doctrine of state nullification.

First, the acceptance of either the Compact Theory or the Nationalist Theory has significant import for the question of whether the United States government enjoys certain "inherent powers," which can generally be described as powers that it enjoys solely on account of its very nature as a government. "Inherent powers" are different from what are commonly referred to as "implied powers" inasmuch as the latter must necessarily be given by implication somewhere in the text of the federal Constitution, whereas the former are said to be held by the federal government as a result of its inclusion in the community of sovereign nations. Here, immediately, the objection to such powers from the Compact Theory becomes clear: by denying that the United States government is a full-fledged sovereign nation, the Compact Theory asserts that the United States still might not be endowed with some powers enjoyed by all fully sovereign nations. Furthermore, since all powers of the federal government are restrictions on, or concessions from, the original sovereignty of the people of each state, there is a built-in presumption against the existence of unstated "inherent powers," as any powers that are not explicitly granted by the Constitution are presumed, as a fundamental rule of legal construction, to still lie with the sovereign people of each state.

Indeed, if anything, it would be the state governments that would be implied to hold such inherent powers, to the extent that—under the Compact Theory—the state governments are more fundamentally sovereign, as they are the direct representatives of their respective peoples and are thus properly considered to be the true members of the community of sovereign nations—albeit bound by the terms of their mutual compact to not engage in diplomacy with other foreign nations. Justice Thomas summarizes the Compact Theory understanding of the federal government's powers when he writes in *Thornton* that "the people of the several States are the only true source of power," and therefore "the Federal Government enjoys no authority beyond what the Constitution confers: The Federal Government's powers are limited and enumerated."[32] Here, it might be added that Justice Thomas holds, with Jefferson and other Compact theorists, that the federal government is limited in a way that the state governments are not: the state governments are considered to hold all of the residual powers inherent to governments that have not been granted to the federal government, whereas all of the federal government's powers come exclusively from the terms of the federal compact as laid out in the Constitution—not from a direct grant from a national people as the Nationalist Theory asserts.

By contrast, from the perspective of the Nationalist Theory, a certain degree of "inherent powers" is to be expected. In his *Commentaries on the Constitution*, Story himself described a similar set of federal powers as "a result from the whole mass of the powers of the national government, and from the nature of political society."[33] Such "resulting powers" are, as Story indicates, difficult to separate from "implied powers," which Story termed "incidental powers," but Story noted that certain powers "resulting from the sovereignty and character of the national government" may be discovered as "incident[al] to their general right of sovereignty, so far as it is appropriate to any of the ends of the government, and within the constitutional range of powers."[34] This line of reasoning—crucial to Story's earlier advocacy of a federal criminal common law jurisdiction for crimes against the United States—contains key differences from the view of federal powers allowed by the Compact Theory. First, Story spoke of the "general right of sovereignty" enjoyed by the United States government, while under the Compact Theory, such a right would have to rest solely on the text of the constitution itself, instead of existing by implication as it does in Story's account. Second, if the United States government was the direct creation of the national American people, then it could safely be presumed that all of the sovereign governmental powers they enjoyed—or at least a substantial number of the most important ones—would likely have been given to the government that represented the whole American people; the Compact Theory obviously shared no such presumption. Third, in this passage, Story referred to the United States as a "political society." The implication throughout this passage—supported, indeed, by the rest of Story's discussion of the scope of federal power throughout the *Commentaries*—is that the United States is entitled to certain "inherent powers" because, by looking at the "whole mass of powers" it is granted under the Constitution, the United States government's status as a member of the community of sovereign states could not be doubted. The competing demands of the Nationalist and Compact Theories thus point in completely different directions on the question of whether the federal government enjoys "inherent powers."

Another contemporary issue where the impact of the irreconcilable claims of the Compact Theory and Nationalist Theory can be felt is in proposals to eliminate the Electoral College and replace it with a national popular vote for President. In the wake of the 2016 presidential victory of Donald J. Trump, a handful of petitions began to collect signatures on websites such as MoveOn.org—where one petition[35] had garnered over 618,000 signatures as of January 2017—Daily Kos—where a petition to the governments of all 50 states had gathered over 784,000 votes by the same time[36]—and Change.org, where a separate petition[37] had collected over 68,000 signatures. The rationale behind such petitions, and presumably many other such proposals, was that the Electoral College allowed for the election of a president who did not win the votes of a majority—or at least a plurality—of the American people, considered of course in the national aggregate. As the Change.org petition suggests, the Electoral College makes the presidential selection process "a contest of winning states instead of people" which "warps" the process and endangers "the values our country was built on."[38] In a similar manner, the MoveOn.org petition suggests that the basic democratic principle of "One person one vote" should be used to "determine the one leader who is supposed to answer to all the people of the country."[39] Such petitions presuppose the basic premise of the Nationalist Theory: that the federal government is the government of the American people as a national whole, and that this people ought to thus exercise as direct a control as possible over the national government. Thus, the petitions cited above only make sense within a Nationalist Theory framework.

It should be noted that, even accepting the Nationalist Theory, an argument could be made for the maintenance of the Electoral College. If indeed the president is designed to be the sole elected representative of the whole American people, then the Electoral College may still be a helpful way of implementing checks on the democratic will of that people. Thus, Story cited the argument of Hamilton in *Federalist 68* that the point of the Electoral College was to ensure that the selection was made by individuals who knew the character and qualities of the candidates for president, as well as to limit the possibility of popular outcry against the outcome of the elections.[40] At the same time, Story disagreed with Chancellor Kent that the Electoral College was necessary in order to prevent the annihilation of state sovereignty that would inherently come with popular election.[41]

On the other hand, while accepting the Nationalist Theory may not necessarily predispose one to support the direct election of president, any proposals to replace the Electoral College with a national popular vote are so inherently caught up in the Nationalist Theory as to make no sense apart from it. It would be difficult for an advocate of the Compact Theory to argue that the president should be selected by popular vote, and on the contrary, the Compact Theory would cite the selection of the president on the basis of which *states* the president wins as yet another piece of evidence that the Constitution did not intend to create a national system of government whereby the people of the whole nation could exercise their will. Since, according to the Compact Theory, the president is not a national representative of the whole American people, but rather is entrusted by the sovereign people of each state with certain specified powers granted to him by them, it makes perfect sense that the president would be selected on the basis of the support *by* the people of separate states.

Lastly, the distinction between the Nationalist Theory and the Compact Theory can clearly be seen by looking at relatively recent state claims of the power of *nullification* or of the right of the state governments to declare a federal law to be unconstitutional. The doctrine of state nullification can be traced at least as far back as the Kentucky and Virginia Resolutions—written by Jefferson and Madison, respectively—and received its fullest exposition by John C. Calhoun, who in his 1828 *South Carolina Exposition and Protest*, declared that under the Constitution, the states reserved the right to judge the limits of federal powers for themselves. Although the doctrine appears to have little support among mainstream constitutional and legal scholars, during the Obama administration it received renewed attention in the political arena, as many states asserted the doctrine as a response to what they saw as federal overreach on a variety of issues. One of the issues that seemed to be of particular importance to these twenty-first-century nullifiers was the protection of gun rights: a 2013 article on *ProPublica.org* focused on Kansas' "Second Amendment Protection Act"[42] noted that at least 37 other states had passed similar acts.[43] The Kansas legislature notably did not shy away from the dramatic implications of the right they were asserting, declaring any federal law or regulation in violation of the Second Amendment of the United States Constitution to be "null, void and unenforceable in the state of Kansas"[44] and making it a felony for any "official, agent or employee" of the federal government to enforce any such law.[45] The Kansas bill explicitly used the language of the Compact Theory, repeatedly declaring the "state and people of Kansas" to be a party to the "compact" at the time of their agreement to join the union.[46] Following the passage of the Kansas law, United States attorney general Eric Holder wrote a letter[47] to Kansas governor Sam Brownback informing him that the state law violated the Supremacy Clause. Brownback responded with a letter stating that he was committed to "defending the sovereignty of the State of Kansas as guaranteed in the Ninth and Tenth Amendments to the United States Constitution"[48] and that "the people of Kansas have clearly expressed their sovereign will."[49] The controversy faded away as the Republican-controlled Congress turned a deaf ear to the Obama Administration's call for new federal gun regulations. But the interchange between Attorney General Holder and Governor Brownback pointed to a deep disagreement over the nature of the constitution that—as the widespread popularity of laws such as the "Second Amendment Protection Act" demonstrates—remains largely unresolved.

The reliance of the doctrine of state nullification on the Compact Theory is easily demonstrated, as is the Nationalist Theory's inherent rejection of the doctrine. At stake is the question of which "people" retain ultimate sovereignty under the Constitution: the people of each separate state, or the people of the United States as a national, undifferentiated whole. Attempts by states to interpose themselves between their citizens and the federal government are inevitably based upon the claim that the people of each state retained their essential sovereignty when joining the union and that the authority to interpret the federal "compact" for themselves continues to lie with the people of each separate state as the sovereign body that authorized the union. As one example, Calhoun based the right of state nullification on the residual sovereignty of the states: "The right of judging [constitutionality], in such cases, is an essential attribute of sovereignty, of which the States cannot be divested without losing their sovereignty itself, and being reduced to a subordinate corporate condition."[50] Thus, according to Calhoun, any denial of the right of state nullification ultimately stems from a misunderstanding of the basic nature of the American union by treating the states not as sovereign political units in their own right but as artificial corporations created by the federal government.

On the other hand, if the states—or more precisely, the people of the states—were not themselves parties to a compact creating the union, but the federal government were on the contrary created by the American people as a national whole, the argument for state nullification of federal laws quickly falls apart. If the Constitution was created by the national American people, the people of any state would have no authority on their own to interfere with federal operations, being nothing more than a constituent part of that national sovereign body. Moreover, the logic of the Nationalist Theory would seem to dictate that efforts at state nullification should be seen as actions undertaken by the *governments* of the states, and not actions of *people* of the states, albeit acting through their normal elected representative bodies. This is, indeed, how advocates of the Nationalist Theory describe state nullification efforts. For example, in a speech before the Senate, Daniel Webster argued that no state government had the authority to stand between "the People"—meaning, presumably, the people of the entire nation—and the federal government.[51] This is based on the Nationalist Theory assumption that the only "people" existing at the moment of national creation was the national one; the American people may have subsequently chosen to create state governments to share power with the federal government, but that did not turn the people of each state into a separate political community capable of independent action. Any actions purportedly taken on behalf of the people of a particular state are thus interpreted by the Nationalist Theory as unconstitutional attempts by the state governments to interject themselves in the politics of the national American people.

CONCLUSION

Such contemporary constitutional debates are only a small sampling of the many debates to be born out of the fundamental lack of consensus on the nature of the Union. From the debates in the Continental Congress regarding representation in the Articles of Confederation through calls for the elimination of the Electoral College following the 2016 election, the federal union has always been plagued by a lack of certainty over its true nature: Is it the creation of a single American people, or was it formed—and does it continue to exercise authority—by the separate permission of the people of each state? Such questions now may feel more academic than they did in the 1790s—American political culture is undeniably much more nationalized than it once was, and even Justice Thomas admitted that "the United States obviously is a Nation,"[52] making a concession that his fellow believer in state sovereignty Thomas Jefferson may have felt the need to qualify. At the same time, the fractured nature of contemporary constitutional discourse—as evidenced by the dueling letters of Holder and Brownback—seems to be built as much on a disagreement over the history of American sovereignty as it does the text of the Constitution. The contrasting opinions of Justices Thomas and Stevens in *Thornton* were thus not an anomaly, but a rare moment of constitutional clarity, as both sides of a constitutional debate saw the origins of their disagreement in contrasting historical narratives of the American founding. The first step toward moving past such debates, if it is possible, is to understand the degree to which contemporary constitutional argumentation is based upon rival understandings of the origins of the Constitution—even of the nature of the union itself.

This book has attempted to demonstrate the extent to which an understanding of this fundamental debate—of the contrast between the competing claims of the Compact Theory and the Nationalist Theory—is necessary in order to understand the debate over the existence of the federal common law. Still, it would be an oversimplification to argue that the federal common law debate was nothing more than a proxy debate for an underlying issue or that both sides were intentionally using the common law jurisdiction of the federal courts as a code-word for their broader constitutional aspirations and fears. To be sure, the federal common law debate dealt with a variety of other issues and concerns that were valuable and interesting in their own right. Still, to the twenty-first -century reader, the debate over the federal common law can feel curiously familiar—both its contentious nature and the unshakeable sense that the two sides were merely arguing past, and not with each other seem all too similar to contemporary constitutional debates. It is possible that both of these features are due to the fact that this debate, like so many debates over constitutional interpretation today, cannot be truly understood without a thorough re-examination of the rival constitutional theories that underlay the federal union at its inception.

This ongoing debate continues to ensure Story's continued importance as a constitutional thinker, and the ingrained nationalism that at times seemed so out of sync with his immediate political climate has instead made his contributions to American constitutional theory timeless. And it is this aspect of Story's thought that has contributed most to his ongoing significance for understanding American constitutionalism: for although Story's legal treatises and commentaries have had a formative influence on a variety of fields of American law—most notably his work on "conflict of laws"—and his jurisprudence has shaped Supreme Court doctrine in a wide range of issues, it is his contributions as a constitutional theorist that he has made the most lasting and memorable impact. Other than *The Federalist*, it is hard to imagine any other work of constitutional theory that has had the long-term impact that Story's *Commentaries on the Constitution* has enjoyed.

The undisputed importance of Story's constitutional theory has not left it immune from criticism; instead, it has made Story's legacy a lightning rod for critics of the Nationalist Theory. In every generation there have been critics of Story's theory who have charged that he over-stated the case for American nationalism: starting in 1840 with Abel Upshur's *Brief Enquiry into the Nature and Character of Our Federal Government*, picked up again in 1870 with Alexander Stephens' *Constitutional View of the War between the States*, and continuing ever since, with historians and lawyers all pointing to the same weaknesses in Story's historical analysis. Some have merely urged that the theory be taken with a grain of salt; others argue that the errors in Story's historical analysis make the entire work suspect. One of his harshest critics, the 1920's progressive historian Vernon Louis Parrington, saw the work as marking "the triumph of the lawyer over the historian and political philosopher,"[53] noting that while Story's legal acumen may have made his arguments credible to a legal audience, "to the historian his exposition is often weak, his data inadequate, and his conclusions not infrequently contrary to fact."[54] Parrington was willing to concede Story's mastery of the law and to restrict his criticism to grounds he felt himself more competent to judge him on, but such a firm separation between the historical and legal examination of the Constitution as Parrington draws is not without a major weakness of its own: Story, whatever flaws or overstatements he may have made in his historical analysis, understood the absolute importance of setting the historical record straight before any of his finer principles of legal interpretation could be settled upon. Story's application of legal principles and maxims to the interpretation of the Constitution was wholly inseparable from his historical interpretation of the founding: one could not be true without the other. Story recognized this, as did his opponents such as Tucker and Madison; the question of how the constitution should be interpreted and who was sovereign under it could not be easily separated from the question of which "people" it was that had created it.

For all of his scholarliness, Story was not an impartial commentator in the various political and legal battles fought over the nature of the union, but rather a vigorous contender for American nationalism. Consequently, any assessment of Story's long-term success as a constitutional interpreter must be rather mixed. On the one hand, the opposing theory to Story's has been rendered less respectable through both the military defeat of the proponents of "southern particularism"—to use Parrington's term[55]—on the battlefields of the Civil War and the historical association of the Compact Theory with a defense of slavery and segregation. Undeniably, the Compact Theory enjoys considerably less acceptance than it once did. At the same time, the perceived disreputability of his opponents has done little to cover over the historical problems posed by Story's own constitutional theory. Moreover, since the publication of Story's *Commentaries*, there has appeared no work to replace it as the fullest and strongest articulation of the Nationalist Theory; the question of American nationalism is thus inexorably caught up in the question of the reliability of Story as both a historian and a constitutional theorist. "Story the text writer" may indeed have "largely accomplished" what "Story the judge" could not, as Roscoe Pound noted, but even he could not fully push the Compact Theory out of the American constitutional imagination.

NOTES

1. Roscoe Pound, *The Formative Era of American Law* (Gloucester, MA: Peter Smith, 1960), 154.
2. *U.S. Term Limits v. Thornton*, 514 U.S. 779 (1995).
3. *United States v. Lopez*, 514 U.S. 549 (1995).
4. *Thornton*, 783, quoting the Court's opinion in *Powell v. McCormack*, 395 U.S. 486, 547 (1969).
5. *Thornton*, 783.
6. Ibid., 845.
7. Ibid., 803.
8. Ibid.
9. *Wesberry v. Sanders*, 376 U.S. 1, 9 (1964).
10. Ibid., 10.
11. *Thornton*, 803.
12. Ibid., 846.
13. Ibid.
14. Ibid.
15. Ibid.
16. Ibid., 851.
17. Constitution of the United States, Article VII.
18. *Thornton*, 846.
19. Ibid., 858.
20. Ibid., 803.
21. Ibid., 859.
22. Ibid., 860.
23. Ibid., 859.
24. Ibid., 847.
25. Ibid., 799.
26. Story, *Commentaries on the Constitution*, Sec. 627, 1:446.
27. Ibid.
28. *Thornton*, 885.
29. Ibid., 856.
30. Ibid.
31. Ibid.
32. Ibid., 847.
33. Story, *Commentaries on the Constitution*, Sec. 1256, 2:142.
34. Ibid., Sec. 1256, 143.
35. "Abolish the Electoral College." MoveOn.org, http://petitions.moveon.org/sign/abolish-the-electoral-6.
36. "Sign the Petition: Elect the President by National Popular Vote." Daily Kos, https://www.dailykos.com/campaigns/petitions/sign-the-petition-abolish-the-electoral-college.
37. "U.S. Senate- Abolish the Electoral College." Change.org, https://www.change.org/p/u-s-senate-abolish-the-electoral-college.

38. Ibid.
39. MoveOn.org petition.
40. Story, *Commentaries on the Constitution*, Sec. 1457, 2:295.
41. Ibid., Sec. 1457, 296.
42. Second Amendment Protection Act. Kansas Senate Bill 102, Session of 2013–2014, http://www.kslegislature.org/li_2014/b2013_14/measures/documents/sb102_enrolled.pdf.
43. Lois Beckett, "Nullification: How States are Making it a Felony to Enforce Federal Gun Laws." ProPublica, May 2, 2013, https://www.propublica.org/article/nullification-how-states-are-making-it-a-felony-to-enforce-federal-gun-laws.
44. "Second Amendment Protection Act," Sec. 6 (a).
45. Ibid., Sec. 7.
46. Ibid., Sec. 2 (a–d).
47. Eric Holder to Sam Brownback, April 26, 2013. Published online by ProPublica and available at https://www.propublica.org/documents/item/695506-attorney-general-holder-letter-to-kans-gov.
48. Sam Brownback to Eric Holder, May 2, 2013. Published online by the Tenth Amendment Center and available at http://blog.tenthamendmentcenter.com/2013/05/sam-brownback-brushes-off-eric-holders-opinions-on-2nd-amendment-protection-act/.
49. Ibid.
50. John C. Calhoun, "South Carolina Exposition and Protest" (1828). Reprinted in *Union and Liberty: The Political Philosophy of John C. Calhoun*, ed. Ross M. Lence (Indianapolis: Liberty Fund, 1992), 311–365.
51. Daniel Webster, "Second Reply to Hayne." Floor Speech in the United States Senate, January 26–27, 1830. Available through *The Webster-Hayne Debate on the Nature of the Constitution: Selected Documents*, ed. Herman Belz on the Online Library of Law and Liberty, by Liberty Fund, available online at http://oll.libertyfund.org/titles/1557#Webster_0099_277.
52. *Thornton*, 859.
53. Parrington, 303.
54. Ibid., 302.
55. Ibid.

References

Adams, John. *A Dissertation on the Canon and Feudal Law*, 1765.

Addison, Alexander. "A Charge to the Grand Juries of the County Courts of the Fifth Circuit, of the State of Pennsylvania." Philadelphia, January 1799. Reprinted in Mark de Wolfe Howe, *Readings in American Legal History*. Cambridge: Harvard University Press, 1949. 349–353.

Aristotle. *The Politics*, trans. T.A. Sinclair. London: Penguin Books, 1992.

Austin, John. *The Province of Jurisprudence Determined.* London: John Murray, 1832.

Baltimore & Ohio Railroad Co. v. Baugh, 149 U.S. 368 (1893).

Bauer, Elizabeth Kelley. *Commentaries on the Constitution 1790-1860.* New York: Columbia University Press, 1952.

Bayard, James. Floor Speech, February 20, 1802. Recorded in *Annals of Congress, House of Representatives, 7th Congress, First Session.* Washington: Gales and Seaton, 1801.

Beckett, Lois. "Nullification: How States are Making it a Felony to Enforce Federal Gun Laws." ProPublica, May 2, 2013. https://www.propublica.org/article/nullification-how-states-are-making-it-a-felony-to-enforce-federal-gun-laws.

Black & White Cab v. Black & Yellow Cab, 276 U.S. 518 (1928).

Blumberg, Phillip I. *Repressive Jurisprudence in the Early American Republic: The First Amendment and the Legacy of English Law.* Cambridge: Cambridge University Press, 2010.

Brownback, Sam. "Sam Brownback to Eric Holder, May 2, 2013." Published online by the Tenth Amendment Center and available at http://blog.tenthamendmentcenter.com/2013/05/sam-brownback-brushes-off-eric-holders-opinions-on-2nd-amendment-protection-act/.

Burke, Edmund. *Reflections on the Revolution in France.* London: Penguin Books, 2004.

Calder v. Bull, 3 U.S. 386 (1798).

Calhoun, John C. *A Discourse on the Constitution and Government of the United States*, reprinted in *Union and Liberty: the Political Philosophy of John C. Calhoun*, ed. Ross M. Lence. Indianapolis: Liberty Fund, 1992. 79–284.

Calhoun, John C. "South Carolina Exposition and Protest," (1828) reprinted in *Union and Liberty: The Political Philosophy of John C. Calhoun*, ed. Ross M. Lence. Indianapolis: Liberty Fund, 1992. 311–365.

Carpenter v. Providence Insurance Co., 16 Peters 495 (1842).

Change.org petition: "U.S. Senate—Abolish the Electoral College," April 6, 2016. https://www.change.org/p/u-s-senate-abolish-the-electoral-college.

Chisolm v. Georgia, 2 U.S. 419 (1793).

Chroust, Anton-Hermann. *The Rise of the Legal Profession in America*. Norman: University of Oklahoma Press, 1971.

Clinton, Robert Lowry. *God and Man in the Law: The Foundations of Anglo-American Constitutionalism.* Lawrence: University Press of Kansas, 1997.

Commonwealth v. Schaffer, 4 Dallas App. xxv (1797).

Constitution of Delaware, 1776. Available online through the National Humanities Institute.

Constitution of Massachusetts, 1780. Available online through the National Humanities Institute.

Cooper, Thomas. *Lectures on the Elements of Political Economy*. Columbia: McMorris & Wilson, 1826.

Daily Kos petition: "Sign the Petition: Elect the President by National Popular Vote." https://www.dailykos.com/campaigns/petition/sign-the-petition-abolish-the-electoral-college.

Dane, Nathan. *A General Abridgment and Digest of American Law*, Vol. VI. Boston: Cummings, Hilliard, & co., 1824.

Dane, Nathan. *A General Abridgment and Digest of American Law*, Vol. IX. Boston: Hilliard, Gray, Little, and Wilkins, 1829.

Du Ponceau, Peter Stephen. "A Dissertation on the Nature and Extent of the Jurisdiction of the Courts of the United States." Valedictory address at the Law Academy of Philadelphia, April 22, 1824.

Erie Railroad Co. v. Tompkins, 304 U.S. 64 (1938).

Farber, Daniel. "The Constitution's Forgotten Cover Letter: An Essay on the new Federalism and the Original Understanding." *Michigan Law Review* 94, issue 3 (1995), 615–650.

Farrand, Max, ed. *Records of the Federal Convention of 1787*. New Haven: Yale University Press, 1911.

Ford, Paul Leicester, ed.. *Pamphlets on the Constitution of the United States, Published during its Discussion by the People, 1787–1788*. Union: The Law Book Exchange, Ltd., 2000.

Ford, Worthington et al., ed. *Journals of the Continental Congress, 1774–1789*. Washington, DC: Government Printing Office, 1904–1937.

Goebel, Julius. *History of the Supreme Court of the United States, Antecedents and Beginnings*. New York and London: Cambridge University Press, 1971.

Granger, Gideon. Gideon Granger to Thomas Jefferson, February 22, 1814. From *Founders Online*, National Archives.

Green, Craig. "Can Erie Survive as Federal Common Law?" *William & Mary Law Review* 54, issue 3 (February, 2013), 813–844.

Hamilton, Alexander, James Madison, and John Jay. *The Federalist*. New York: Barnes & Noble Publishing, 2006.

Henfield's Case, 11 Fed. Cas. 1099, No. 6,360 (1793).

Hinderlinder v. La Plata River & Cherry Creek Ditch Co., 304 U.S. 92 (1938).

Hobbes. *Leviathan*, Ch. XXVI. London: Penguin Classics, 2017.

Holder, Eric. Eric Holder to Sam Brownback, April 26, 2013. Letter. Published online by ProPublica and available at https://www.propublica.org/documents/item/695506-attorney-general-holder-letter-to-kans-gov.

Holmes, Oliver Wendell. "The Path of the Law." *Harvard Law Review* 10, no. 8 (March, 1897), 457–478.

Hovenkamp, Herbert. *Enterprise and American Law, 1836–1937*. Cambridge: Harvard University Press, 1991.

Howe, Mark deWolfe. *Readings in American Legal History*. Cambridge: Harvard University Press, 1949.

"Instructions to Virginia Senators," passed by the General Assembly of Virginia on January 11, 1800 and reprinted in Tucker, *Views of the Constitution of the United States, with Selected Writings*, ed. Clyde N. Wilson. Indianapolis: Liberty Fund, 1999, 369.

Iredell, James. "Marcus," *Answers to Mr. Mason's Objections to the New Constitution, Recommended by the Late Convention*. 1788. Reprinted in *Pamphlets on the Constitution of the United States, Published during its Discussion by the People, 1787–1788*, ed. Paul Leicester Ford. Union: The Law Book Exchange, Ltd., 2000. 333–370.

Iredell, James. *The Life and Correspondence of James Iredell*, ed. Griffith J. McRee. New York: D. Appleton and Company, 1949.

Jackson, Robert H. *The Struggle for Judicial Supremacy*. New York: Alfred A. Knopf, Inc., 1941.

Jay, John. *The Correspondence and Public Papers of John Jay*, ed. Henry P. Johnston. New York: G.P. Putnam's Sons, 1890–1893.

Jay, Stewart. "Origins of the Federal Common Law: Part Two." *University of Pennsylvania Law Review* 133, no. 6 (July, 1985), 1231–1333.

Jefferson, Thomas. *Declaration of Independence*, 1776.

Jefferson, Thomas. "Observations on the Common Law and Hardin's Case, 11 November 1802." From *Founders Online*, National Archives.

Jefferson, Thomas. Thomas Jefferson to Albert Gallatin, September 27, 1810. From *Founders Online*, National Archives.

Jefferson, Thomas. Thomas Jefferson to Charles Pinckney, October 29, 1799. From *Founders Online*, National Archives.

Jefferson, Thomas. Thomas Jefferson to Edmund Randolph, August 18, 1799. From *Founders Online*, National Archives.

Jefferson, Thomas. Thomas Jefferson to James Monroe, January 8, 1811. From Library of Congress.

Jefferson, Thomas. Thomas Jefferson to John M. Goodenow, June 13, 1822. From *Founders Online*, National Archives.
Jefferson, Thomas. Thomas Jefferson to John Tyler, June 17, 1812. From *Founders Online*, National Archives.
Jefferson, Thomas. Thomas Jefferson to Thomas Lomax, March 12, 1799. From *Founders Online*, National Archives.
Jefferson, Thomas. Thomas Jefferson to Thomas Ritchie, December 25, 1820. From *The Writings of Thomas Jefferson*, ed. Andrew A. Lipscomb and Albert Ellery Bergh. Washington, DC: The Thomas Jefferson Memorial Association, 1903.
Jefferson, Thomas. Thomas Jefferson to William H. Crawford, June 20, 1816. From *Founders Online*, National Archives.
Judiciary Act of 1789. 1 Stat. 73 (1789).
Kent, James, *Commentaries on American Law*, 2nd ed. New York: O. Halstead, 1832.
Kirk, Russell. *John Randolph of Roanoke: A Study in American Politics*. Indianapolis: Liberty Fund Press, 1997.
Kuhn v. Fairmont Coal Co., 215, U.S. 349, 370 (1910).
Lee, Henry. *Plain Truth: Addressed to the People of Virginia*. Petersburg: Richmond, 1799.
Leiter, Brian. "American Legal Realism," Ch. 3 in *The Blackwell Guide to the Philosophy of Law and Legal Theory*, ed. Martin P. Golding and William A. Edmundson. Malden: Blackwell, 2005.
Levy, Leonard W. *Jefferson and Civil Liberties: The Darker Side*. New York: The New York Times Book Company, 1963.
Lincoln, Abraham. "Special Session Message to Congress, July 4, 1861." Address to Congress. From *Modern History Sourcebook, Abraham Lincoln (1809-1865)*, Fordham University.
Livingston v. Jefferson, 15 Fed. Cas. 660, No. 8,411; 1 Brockenbrough 211 (1811).
Madison, James. *Notes of Debates in the Federal Convention of 1787*. New York: W.W. Norton & Co., 1987.
Madison, James. "The Report of 1800," January 7, 1800. From *Founders Online*, National Archives.
Maier, Pauline. *American Scripture*. New York: Vintage Books, 1997.
Maier, Pauline. *Ratification: the People Debate the Constitution, 1787-1788*. New York: Simon & Schuster, 2010.
Marshall, John. John Marshall to st. George Tucker, November 27, 1800, Reprinted as Appendix A in Stewart Jay, "Origins of the Federal Common Law: Part Two." *University of Pennsylvania Law Review* 133, no. 6 (July, 1985), 1231–1333, 1326.
Martin v. Hunter's Lessee, 14 U.S. 304 (1816).
Mason, George. George Mason to George Washington, October 7, 1787. Reprinted in *Pamphlets on the Constitution of the United States, Published during its Discussion by the People, 1787–1788*, ed. Paul Leicester Ford. Union: The Law Book Exchange, Ltd., 2000. 329–332.
McClellan, James. *Joseph Story and the American Constitution*. Norman: University of Oklahoma Press, 1990.
McCulloch v. Maryland, 17 U.S. (4 Wheat.) 316 (1819).

Mogck, Derek L. "Connecticut Federalists in President Jefferson's (Republican) Court: United States v. Hudson and Goodwin." *Connecticut History* 41, no. 2 (September 2002), 144–172

MoveOn.org petition: "Abolish the Electoral College." http://petitions.moveon.org/sign/abolish-the-electoral-6.

Newmyer, R. Kent. *Supreme Court Justice Joseph Story, Statesman of the Old Republic*. Chapel Hill: University of North Carolina Press, 1985.

O'Scannlain, Diarmuid F. "Rediscovering the Common Law." *Notre Dame Law Review* 79, issue 2 (February, 2004), 755–763.

Palmer, Robert C. "The Federal Common Law of Crime." William & Mary University, *Faculty Publications*, Paper 900 (1986): 267–323.

Parrington, Vernon Louis. *Main Currents in American Thought*. New York: Harcourt Brace And Co., 1927.

Patterson v. Winn, 30 U.S. 233; 5 Peters 233 (1831).

Pendleton, Edmund. *The Danger Not Over*. Published in the *Richmond Enquirer*, October, 1801. Accessed online from the Mises Institute.

"Pennsylvania Minority," "The Address and Reasons of Dissent of the Minority of the Convention of Pennsylvania to their Constituents," December 12, 1787.

Peters, Richard. Richard Peters to Nathaniel Williams, May 27, 1813. Quoted in James McClellan, *Joseph Story and the American Constitution*. Norman: University of Oklahoma Press, 1990.

Peters, Richard. Richard Peters to Timothy Pickering, December 5, 1807. Pickering Papers, Massachusetts Historical Society 28:99. Quoted in Kathryn Preyer, "Jurisdiction to Punish: Authority, Federalism and the Common Law of Crimes in the Early Republic." *Law and History Review* 4, no. 2 (Autumn, 1986): 223–265, 242.

Pickering, Timothy. Timothy Pickering to George Cabot, January 29, 1804. Reprinted in *The Founder's Constitution*, ed. Philip B. Kurland and Ralph Lerner. Chicago: University of Chicago Press, 1987. 1:235–236.

Pound, Roscoe. *The Formative Era of American Law*. Gloucester: Peter Smith, 1960.

Powell v. McCormack, 395 U.S. 486 (1969).

Presser, Stephen B. "The Supra-Constitution, the Courts, and the Federal Common Law of Crimes: Some Comments on Palmer and Preyer." *Law and History Review* 4, no. 2 (Autumn, 1986), 325–335.

Preyer, Kathryn. "Jurisdiction to Punish: Authority, Federalism and the Common Law of Crimes in the Early Republic." *Law and History Review* 4, no. 2 (Autumn, 1986): 223–265.

Purcell Jr., Edward A. *Brandeis and the Progressive Constitution: Erie, the Judicial Power, and the Politics of the Federal Courts in Twentieth-Century America*. New Haven: Yale University Press, 2000.

Quigley, Micah S. "Article III Lawmaking." *George Mason Law Review* 30, issue 1 (April, 2022), 279–348.

Ragsdale, Bruce A. *The Sedition Act Trials*. Washington: The Federal Judicial Center, 2005.

Ramsey, David. *The History of the American Revolution*, ed. Lester H. Cohen. Indianapolis: Liberty Fund, 1990.

Randolph, Edmund. Edmund Randolph's Notes on the Common Law, [ca. September] 1799. From *Founders Online*, National Archives.

Randolph, John. Floor Speech, February 20, 1802. Recorded in *The Annals of Congress, House of Representatives, 7th Congress, First Session*. Washington: Gales and Seaton, 1801.

Randolph, John. Floor Speech, May 25, 1809. Recorded in *The Debates and Proceedings in the Congress of the United States, Eleventh Congress, First and Second Sessions*. Washington: Gales and Seaton, 1853.

Rawle, William. *A View of the Constitution of the United States of America*, 2nd ed. Philadelphia: Philip H. Nicklin, 1829.

Rowe, Gary D. "Jeffersonian Ascendancy and the Abolition of federal Common Law Crimes." *The Yale Law Journal* 101, no. 4 (January 1992), 919–948

Sachs, Stephen E. "Finding Law." *California Law Review* 107 (2019), 527–582.

Second Amendment Protection Act. Kansas Senate Bill 102, Session of 2013–2014.

Sewall, Samuel. Samuel Sewall to Joseph Story, February 12, 1799. Quoted in James McClellan, *Joseph Story and the American Constitution*. Norman: University of Oklahoma Press, 1990. 163.

Southern Pacific Co. v. Jensen, 244 U.S. 205 (1917).

Stampp, Kenneth. "The Concept of a Perpetual Union." *The Journal of American History* 65, no. 1 (June, 1978), 5–33.

Stephens, Alexander. *A Constitutional View of the Late War between the States*. Philadelphia: National Publishing Company, 1868.

Stoner, James R. *Common Law and Liberal Theory*. Lawrence: University Press of Kansas, 1992.

Stoner, James R. *Common Law Liberty: Rethinking American Constitutionalism*. Lawrence: University Press of Kansas, 2003.

Story, Joseph. *A Discourse on the Past History, Present State, and Future Prospects of the Law*. Edinburgh: Thomas Clark, 1835. Digitized by the University of Michigan.

Story, Joseph. "An Oration," Speech delivered in Salem, MA on July 4, 1804.

Story, Joseph. *Commentaries on the Constitution of the United States*. 4th ed. Boston: Little, Brown, and Company, 1873.

Story, Joseph. *Digests of the Common Law*. Reprinted in *The Miscellaneous Writings of Joseph Story*, ed. William W. Story. Boston: Charles C. Little & James Brown, 1852. 379–407.

Story, Joseph. Joseph Story to Nathaniel Williams, October 8, 1812. Reprinted in *Life and Letters of Joseph Story*, ed. William W. Story. London: John Chapman, 1851. I:243.

Story, Joseph. *Life and Letters of Joseph Story*, ed. William W. Story. London: John Chapman, 1851.

Story, Joseph. Manuscript on "Ā Bill further to Extend the Judicial System of the United States," ostensibly sent to Charles Pinckney. 1816. Reprinted in *Life and Letters of Joseph Story*, ed. William W. Story. London: John Chapman, 1851. I:293–303.

Story, Joseph. *The Miscellaneous Writings of Joseph Story*, ed. William W. Story. Boston: Charles C. Little & James Brown, 1852.

Stumpf, Samuel Enoch. "Austin's Theory of the Separation of Law and Morals." *Vanderbilt Law Review* 14, issue 1 (December 1960), 117–149.
Swift v. Tyson, 41 U.S. 1 (1842).
Town of Pawlet v. Clark, 13 U.S. 292; 9 Cranch. (1815).
Tucker, Henry St. George. *Lectures on Government*. Charlottesville, 1844.
Tucker, Nathaniel Beverly. *Lectures on the Science of Government*. Philadelphia: James Alexander, 1845.
Tucker, St. George. *Views of the Constitution of the United States, with Selected Writings*, ed. Clyde N. Wilson. Indianapolis: Liberty Fund, 1999.
Tushnet, Mark. "Swift v. Tyson *Exhumed.*" *The Yale Law Journal* 79, no. 2 (1969): 284–310.
Tyler, John. John Tyler to Thomas Jefferson, May 17, 1812. From *Founders Online*, National Archives.
United States v. Burr, 25 Fed. Cas. 55, No. 14,693 (1807).
United States v. Clark, 25 Fed. Cas. 441, No. 14,804; 1 Gall. 497 (1813).
United States v. Coolidge, 24 Fed. Cas. 619, No. 14,857; 1 Gall. 488 (1813).
United States v. Coolidge, 14 U.S. 415 (1816).
United States v. Hoar, 26 Fed. Cas. 329 (1821).
United States v. Hudson and Goodwin, 11 U.S. 32 (1812).
United States v. Lopez, 514 U.S. 549 (1995).
United States v. Ravara, 27 Fed. Cas. 713, Nos. 16,122-16,122a (1794).
United States v. Smith, 27 Fed. Cas. 1147, No. 16,323 (1797).
United States v. Worrall, 28 Fed. Cas. 744, No. 16,766 (1798).
United States v. Wonson, 28 Fed. Cas. 745 (C.C. Mass. 1812), No. 16,750; 1 Gall. 5 (1812).
Upshur, Abel Parker. *A Brief Enquiry into the Nature and Character of our Federal Government: Being a Review of Judge Story's Commentaries on the Constitution.* Reprinting. Philadelphia: John Campbell, Publisher, 1863.
Urofksy, Melvin I. "Myth and Reality: The Supreme Court and Protective Legislation in the Progressive Era." *Yearbook: Supreme Court Historical Society* (1983), 53–72.
Urofksy, Melvin I. "State Courts and Protective Legislation during the Progressive Era: A Reevaluation." *The Journal of American History* 72, no. 1 (June, 1985), 63–91.
U.S. Term Limits v. Thornton, 514 U.S. 779 (1995).
Van Ness v. Pacard, 27 U.S. 137; 2 Peters 137 (1829).
Van Reimsdyk v. Kane, 28 Fed. Cas. 1062, No. 16,871 (1812).
Washington, George. "Letter of the President of the Federal Convention, Dated September 17, 1787, to the President of Congress, Transmitting the Constitution." Available through The Avalon Project: Documents in Law, History, and Diplomacy of Yale Law School.
Webster, Daniel. "An Address Delivered Before the Washington Benevolent Society." Speech at Portsmouth, July 4, 1812. Digitized by the University of Missouri-Columbia.
Webster, Daniel. "Second Reply to Hayne." Floor Speech in the United States Senate, January 26–27, 1830. Available through *The Webster-Hayne Debate on the Nature*

of the Constitution: Selected Documents, ed. Herman Belz on the Online Library of Law and Liberty, by Liberty Fund.

Webster, Daniel. "The Constitution Not a Compact Between Sovereign States." Floor Speech in the United States Senate, February 16, 1833. *Register of Debates in Congress, Senate, 22nd Congress, 2nd Session.* Washington: Gales and Seaton, 1833. 553–587.

Wesberry v. Sanders, 376 U.S. 1 (1964).

Wharton, Francis, ed. *State Trials of the United States during the Administrations of Washington and Adams*. Philadelphia: Carey and Hart, 1849.

Williams v. Suffolk Insurance Co. 3 Sumner 270; Fed. Cas. 1406, No. 17,739 (1838).

Williams' Case, 29 Fed. Cas. 1330, No. 17,708 (1799).

Wilson, James. "State House Yard Speech, October 6, 1787." Reprinted in *Collected Works of James Wilson*, ed. Kermit L. Hall and Mark David Hall. Indianapolis: Liberty Fund, 2007. 1:171–177.

Wood, Gordon. *The Creation of the American Republic*. Chapel Hill: University of North Carolina Press, 1998.

Yates, Robert, "Brutus," *Brutus XI–XII*. Reprinted in Ralph Ketcham, ed. *The Anti-Federalist Papers and the Constitutional Convention Debates*. New York: Penguin Publishing Group, 2003.

Index

About the Author

Benjamin Clark is a senior lecturer at Georgia College and State University in Milledgeville, Georgia, where he teaches courses in political theory and American government. He holds a PhD in political theory from the Catholic University of America.

www.ingramcontent.com/pod-product-compliance
Lightning Source LLC
Chambersburg PA
CBHW051256200926
51612CB00002B/64
* 9 7 8 1 6 6 6 9 6 5 8 4 1 *